Astrology
for Writers

About the Author

Corrine Kenner specializes in bringing metaphysical subjects down to earth.

She has written sixteen books, including *Tarot and Astrology, Tarot for Writers,* and *Tarot Journaling.* Some of her books have been translated for a worldwide audience; they're available in French, Italian, Japanese, Polish, Portuguese, Romanian, and Russian.

A former newspaper reporter and magazine editor, Kenner has also edited five anthologies and several astrological publications, including Llewellyn's *Astrological Calendar, Daily Planetary Guide,* and *Sun Sign Book.*

Kenner has been a keynote speaker at national and international tarot conferences, and she has taught tarot, astrology, and creative writing in England, Canada, and across the United States.

Kenner was raised on a farm in North Dakota. She has lived in Brazil and Los Angeles, where she earned a degree in philosophy from California State University, Long Beach. She currently lives in Minneapolis, Minnesota, with her husband, a software developer. They have four daughters.

You can find her website at www.corrinekenner.com.

Astrology for Writers

Spark Your Creativity Using the Zodiac

CORRINE KENNER

Llewellyn Publications
Woodbury, Minnesota

FIRST EDITION
First Printing, 2013

Cover art: Typewriter: iStockphoto.com/Diane Diederich
       Venus, Mars, and Mercury: iStockphoto.com/parameter
       Full moon: iStockphoto.com/Magnilion
       Page curl: iStockphoto.com/khalus
Cover design by Kevin R. Brown
Editing by Andrea Neff
Interior art by the Llewellyn Art Department

Llewellyn Publications is a registered trademark of Llewellyn Worldwide Ltd.

Library of Congress Cataloging-in-Publication Data (Pending)
ISBN: 978-0-7387-3333-3

Llewellyn Worldwide Ltd. does not participate in, endorse, or have any authority or responsibility concerning private business transactions between our authors and the public.
    All mail addressed to the author is forwarded but the publisher cannot, unless specifically instructed by the author, give out an address or phone number.
    Any Internet references contained in this work are current at publication time, but the publisher cannot guarantee that a specific location will continue to be maintained. Please refer to the publisher's website for links to authors' websites and other sources.

Llewellyn Publications
A Division of Llewellyn Worldwide Ltd.
2143 Wooddale Drive
Woodbury, MN 55125-2989
www.llewellyn.com

Printed in the United States of America

Also by Corrine Kenner

Tarot and Astrology

Wizards Tarot

Susan and the Mermaid

Tarot for Writers

Simple Fortunetelling with Tarot Cards

Crystals for Beginners

Tarot Journaling

Tall Dark Stranger: Tarot for Love and Romance

The Epicurean Tarot

Strange But True

The stars we are given. The constellations we make.
That is to say, stars exist in the cosmos,
but constellations are the imaginary lines
we draw between them, the readings we give the sky,
the stories we tell.

—Rebecca Solnit, *Storming the Gates of Paradise*

Contents

Introduction

A Match Made in Heaven

More than 3,000 years ago, the visible planets—the wandering stars—corresponded to the gods and goddesses of ancient myth. The constellations illustrated their stories of heroic battles and adventures, as well as their rising and falling fortunes.

The ancient Greeks used myth as we use science today, to explain the creation of the universe and to help describe man's place in the cosmos. While modern physicists now can explain many of the physical principles that underlie the working of the universe, it is storytellers who continue to put science into context and help us understand our spiritual place in the universe.

Today, we can still be inspired by the figures we see in the sky. Everything old is new again, and the ancient myths can serve as models for contemporary stories. The stars are still there, too. They're beckoning you now, waiting to be used as a cosmic model for the creative journey.

Drama on a Cosmic Scale

The night sky has inspired storytellers since the dawn of time. For thousands of years, people have gathered around a fire, looked up at the heavens, and spun stories on the strands of starlight. Today, the imagery and symbolism of astrology can inspire your writing, too.

In fact, every constellation in the sky is associated with a corresponding myth or legend. Those stories have become part of our collective memory, and they make up a shared language of myth and metaphor that illustrate the human condition.

Writers and astrologers have a lot in common. They're both students of human behavior, with a fascination for discovering hidden motivations, secret fears, and boundless dreams. They're natural observers who have a knack for tuning in to conflicting emotions, subconscious behavior, and mystery.

The language of astrology is the language of drama—of conflict and resolution, courage and compassion, and life-changing growth and development. A lot of astrologers even describe the zodiac as a cosmic drama, and they point out that the planets move through the signs of the zodiac like players on a celestial stage.

Whether or not you use astrology for inspiration, every story shares the same elements: characters, plot, setting, and theme. You might be surprised, however, at how quickly astrology can help you create and develop those components, and weave them seamlessly together.

The Science of Astrology

Astrologers were our first astronomers, and they've been plotting the movement of the planets since the beginning of recorded history. Originally, the priests and philosophers who studied the skies were searching for signs and omens from above, which they could relay to their leaders and kings.

Contrary to popular belief, however, astrologers don't think the planets control our behavior. You'll be hard-pressed to find any astrologer who believes that the stars create our destiny. In fact, astrologers have a saying: "The stars impel. They do not compel."

William Shakespeare put it even better when he wrote, "It is not in the stars to hold our destiny but in ourselves."

In fact, astrologers have noted that the movements of the planets mirror events on Earth—primarily because the planets move in predictable cycles, and people are creatures of habit. Astrology isn't superstition. It's the study of patterns, both in nature and human nature. And while astrology can sometimes be used to predict the future, it also puts the past and present into context.

Of course, it's also true that no one is entirely predictable. That's the secret weapon in every writer's arsenal. Writers and astrologers alike can see the contradictions, quirks, and foibles that add drama to every life.

At its heart, astrology is a symbolic language. Astrology offered us our first model of the human psyche, which makes it a form of primeval psychology. Today, astrology offers us a context that can help us see our place in the larger universe.

Astrology offers a timeless framework for viewing—and understanding—the human condition. Writers and artists who can tap into the cycles of astrology have a magic window into the world of human experience.

Why Use Astrology?

Why should writers use astrology? Because it works.

When you're staring at a blank page of paper, face to face with writer's block, astrology gives you a starting point for the process of creation. Astrology is an open invitation to the gods of time and the sky to enter your life, have a seat at your table, and share their stories through you. In the act of using astrology to create, your creativity will be unleashed.

What's more, you'll be working in familiar territory. You probably know your own Sun sign, as well as the astrological signs of several friends and family members. You know the planets from sixth-grade science—and you're probably familiar with the mythic gods and goddesses for whom they're named.

The study of astrology, like the study of storytelling, can be a lifelong fascination and pursuit. While this book can't teach you everything there is to know about astrology, it will give you enough tools to use astrology confidently, accurately, and well.

Overview

In this guide, we'll look at the planets as people and characters, the signs of the zodiac for storylines and plot, and the houses of the horoscope as settings.

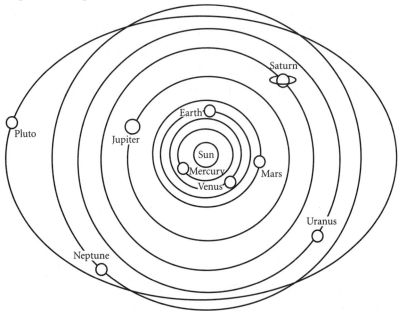

The cast of any story revolves around the lead character, just as the planets orbit around the Sun.

Here's what you'll find in the three main sections of this book.

1. The Planetary Players. The planets are the guiding lights of the night sky and the actors in the drama of the cosmic stage. They make perfect models for the characters in a world of your creation. We can examine their motivations and goals, as well as their hopes and fears. We can let them reveal themselves through dialogue. We'll determine which characters are the center of the action, and which characters make up the supporting cast.

2. The Signs of the Zodiac. Just as the planets revolve around the Sun, your characters will move through the signs of the zodiac. In the process, their stories will unfold. We'll follow the plot, and discover what obstacles and conflicts keep them from reaching their goals.

We'll also study the ways that the symbolism of the same twelve signs can be the foundation of story structure, theme, and symbolism.

3. The Houses of the Horoscope. The twelve houses of the horoscope provide a backdrop and setting for the drama of human experience.

There's no shortage of material when you use astrology as a brainstorming tool. Between the ten planets, twelve signs, and twelve houses of the horoscope, you'll discover 1,440 creative combinations. Throw in a few extras, like asteroids, fixed stars, and constellations, and you'll have as many writing possibilities as there are stars in the sky.

How to Use This Guide

This guide is designed to stimulate your imagination by introducing you to the classic connections between astrology and storytelling. We'll cover the core concepts of astrology—the planets, signs, and houses—and discover how they correspond to the elements of fiction.

Creative Guidance

Throughout this guide, you'll find a wide range of creative ideas to help you add astrology to your writing practice, including writing prompts, writing suggestions, and encouragement for you to make your own cosmic connections.

The ideas are designed to spark your creativity. Feel free to adjust or adapt them however you like. You can even mix and match them. After all, astrology itself is based on a few basic concepts that can be rearranged in countless combinations.

You can use this book as a source of ideas and inspiration or as a creative writing companion. Think of it as a tool kit to help you create characters, develop dialogue, and plot scenes and stories from beginning to end.

In some ways, you might think of this book as a reference guide or an astrology primer. I say that with some hesitation, though, because you don't have to become a serious student of the art in order to benefit from its wisdom. In fact, you don't need to have any knowledge of astrology at all in order to use the techniques in this book. I've tried to explain the principles in plain English, so you can experiment with its tools and techniques however you like—and gain the confidence you need to incorporate it into your work.

In fact, by the end of this book, you should feel comfortable picking and choosing the elements of astrology to create your own unique twist on character, story, and setting.

Creative Guidance

If you like, you can compare the information in this guide to the signs and symbols in your own birth chart. You can calculate a free natal chart online at www.astro.com, buy beginner's astrology software from a site like www.halloran.com, or order an astrology chart, complete with a detailed explanation, from the publisher of this book. Visit www.llewellyn.com for details. Later, as you start to write, you can also cast fictional horoscopes for your creations.

PART I

The Planets

We'll begin our study of astrology for writers by looking at the planets—the major players in the drama of the night sky. In this section, you'll learn how to develop fictional personalities based on planetary characteristics. You can assign one planet to each member of the cast, or mix and match them, just like real life.

Meet the
Planetary Players

The Wandering Stars

For thousands of years, astronomers and astrologers could see only the visible bodies: the Sun, Moon, Mercury, Venus, Mars, Jupiter, and Saturn.

They referred to the seven ancient planets as "wandering stars," because the orbs seemed to travel through the night sky at will—separate and removed from the backdrop of fixed stars.

In practical terms, however, the planets were also thought of as gods, casting their light across the heavens. Whether they took human form or wandered across the celestial vault, their movements could have profound significance for people on Earth.

Today, we're rational, scientific beings—but nothing can dim the magic and mystery of the stars. You might not worship the planets, but you can still think of them as guiding lights—yours to enjoy in a universe of your own creation.

You'll find an entire cosmic lineup waiting for you on the next page.

The Planetary Pantheon

The planetary bodies were all named in honor of the gods—most of whom were known by several names themselves. In this book, we use their astrological monikers. For clarity and reference, though, you'll find both their Greek and Roman names listed in the following chart.

Greek Name	Roman Name	Description
Aphrodite	Venus	Goddess of love and beauty; born of the blood of the sky god Ouranos and the foam of the sea
Apollo	Apollo	God of light, sun, truth, prophecy, healing, divination, and the arts; son of Zeus and Leto the swan; twin brother of Artemis
Ares	Mars	God of war; son of Zeus and Hera
Artemis	Diana	Virgin goddess of wilderness, the hunt, and the new moon; guardian of childbirth; twin sister of Apollo
Athena	Minerva	Warrior goddess of wisdom and justice; daughter of Zeus
Chiron	Chiron	A centaur; the wounded healer and teacher of the gods
Cronos	Saturn	Titan father of the Olympian gods and goddesses; husband to Rhea; like Father Time, he devoured his own children Demeter, Hades, Hera, Hestia, and Poseidon. Rhea tricked him into sparing Zeus, who freed his brothers and sisters.
Demeter	Ceres	Goddess of fertility and harvest; her mourning for her lost daughter Persephone made the earth barren for a third of each year
Gaia	Tellus	Mother Earth
Hades	Pluto	God of the underworld and ruler of the dead; son of Cronos and Rhea
Hecate	Trivia	Ruler of the night and goddess of the dark moon; patron of magic and enchantment; guardian of crossroads and the passages of birth and death; daughter of the Titans
Hera	Juno	Goddess of marriage; wife of Zeus; daughter of Cronos and Rhea

Greek Name	Roman Name	Description
Hermes	Mercury	Messenger of the gods; son of Zeus and the nymph Maia
Kore/ Persephone	Proserpina	The maiden goddess, kidnapped by Hades, who became queen of the underworld; daughter of Demeter
Poseidon	Neptune	God of the sea; son of Cronos and Rhea
Hades	Pluto	God of the underworld
Rhea	Cybele	Goddess of the sky; wife of Cronos; mother to the Olympians Demeter, Hades, Hera, Hestia, Poseidon, and Zeus
Selene	Luna	Goddess of the full moon
Uranus	Ouranos	God of the sky
Hestia	Vesta	Goddess of the hearth; keeper of the sacred flame
Zeus	Jupiter	King of the gods and ruler of Mount Olympus; son of Uranus and Gaia

Creative Guidance

While Western astrologers rely on Greek and Roman myths, everyone loves the stars. If you have a special interest in other cultures or other branches of astrology—such as Chinese, Vedic, or Native American traditions—you can easily adapt the techniques in this guide to suit your work.

The Sun:
The Star of the Show

The Hero of the Story

Whether I shall turn out to be the hero of my own life, or whether that station will be held by anybody else, these pages must show.
—Charles Dickens, *David Copperfield*

The Center of the Action

The lead player in the drama of the heavens is the Sun. It's the brightest light in the sky, and it's the most prominent star on the celestial stage. All the planets revolve around the Sun: it's the center of the solar system and the center of the action.

The Sun is the source of light and heat on Earth. It's the starting point for our earthly existence and a focal point for any story.

In literary terms, that means the Sun embodies all the qualities of a protagonist—the hero of the story.

Because the Sun is the centerpiece of our cosmic story, the Sun symbolizes the one character who can't be cut from the script. After all, if the protagonist dies, the story ends, and the fictional universe collapses in on itself like a black hole.

Of course, the star of your story might not be as bright as the Sun. He might be a tragic hero, an unwilling hero, or an antihero. It doesn't matter. He's still the star of the show, and an astrological assessment can reveal surprising new depths and dimension to his role.

Mythic Models: The Gods of Light

Storytellers have been casting the Sun as the hero of their stories since the dawn of recorded history. In ancient times, the Sun was something of a superhero, with epic qualities that led to Greek and Roman myths and legends.

In Homer's time, the Sun was Helios, who rode through the sky in a chariot by day and a golden bowl by night. From that vantage point, Helios could see and hear everything on Earth—and he could contribute to other myths and legends, too. He told Ceres about the abduction of her daughter, and he told Venus's husband that his wife was notoriously unfaithful. (We'll explore their stories later in this book.)

As centuries passed, Helios became known as Apollo, the Greek and Roman god of music, healing, truth, and light. Apollo was the oracular god who cast light on the future. He also killed the Python, the monster of darkness that made the oracle at Delphi inaccessible.

The Sun, which sets every night and rises every morning, is a timeless symbol of death and rebirth. In ancient times, the Sun was worshipped like a god—and some characteristics of ancient gods even found their way into biblical descriptions of Jesus Christ. Like a Sun god, a Sun-inspired character may have supernatural gifts and talents—including the power to rise from the dead.

Interactions with the Sun can also serve as cautionary tales. Think of Phaethon, the son of Helios, who wanted to drive his father's chariot of the Sun. The vehicle was too much for him; he couldn't control the solar horses, and he scorched the earth when he flew too low. To save the world, Jupiter had to strike Phaethon down with a lightning bolt.

Another legend describes what happened when ordinary mortals flew too close to the Sun. When Daedalus was imprisoned with his son Icarus in King Minos's labyrinth, he fashioned wings of wax so they could fly to freedom. Daedalus warned Icarus not to fly too close to the Sun, but the young man ignored his father's warnings. Instead, he soared to heights no man had ever experienced. The Sun's rays were merciless—and when his wings melted, Icarus plunged to his death in the sea. The moral was clear: no man was meant to venture too close to God.

The Astrology of the Sun ☉

The glyph for the Sun looks like the light at the center of the solar system.

The Sun is an important focal point in an astrological chart, whether it belongs to a real person or a fictional character. The Sun represents the center of every individual's universe: himself.

The Sun symbolizes your characters' core sense of identity and conscious awareness. It offers a dramatic vision of their confidence and self-esteem, as well as their willpower, purpose, and drive. It reveals their greatest strengths—and their corresponding weaknesses. The Sun is a symbol of virility, vitality, and energy.

The Sun also represents consciousness and enlightenment. It's a depiction of your characters' inner light, and it describes the ways in which they shine.

In a storyline, the Sun symbolizes your characters' destiny, drives, and desires. The Sun sheds light on their sense of purpose, as well as their life's path. The Sun also illuminates the way in which each person will express the divine light of God, and how they'll assert their moral right to rule their own kingdoms.

Because the Sun is so visible in the sky, its placement in an astrological chart can highlight areas of fame, public recognition, and acclaim. The Sun shows where your characters will shine, and where they'll expend the most energy in pursuit of their goals. The Sun will also show you how and where they want to be recognized for their accomplishments.

In short, the Sun reveals every character's truest self. The Sun is each person's birthright.

Creative Guidance

Most people associate astrology with Sun signs, because the Sun moves through all twelve zodiac signs during the course of a year. Its position on any given day determines every person's Sun sign. While no two individuals will channel the light and heat of the Sun in exactly the same way, people who share a Sun sign often share a similar worldview. That's one reason that Sun sign astrology has become the mainstay of newspaper horo-scopes: it's a simplified way to summarize the essential nature of people who were born in the same sign.

Archetypal Roles

Another easy way to develop characters is to think of them as arche-types—prototypes and models of personality, and cosmic stereotypes that transcend the limits of time and place. Archetypal characters regularly appear in our dreams, myths, and stories. They're also the figurative heroes of fable and legend. In fact, many societies and cultures throughout history have shared similar stories and made use of the same symbols.

In traditional astrology, the Sun is a symbol of rulers and kings.

In modern astrology, the Sun often signifies a father figure—although the patriarchy is usually reserved for Saturn, the authoritarian and disciplinarian. In a woman's chart, the Sun can also represent a husband.

- The Sun can be a golden child, like Hercules, or a *puer aeternus* (eternal boy), like Peter Pan.
- The Sun can symbolize God or a divine child, a Christlike newborn, or a messiah.
- The Sun is connected with creativity, which makes it the mark of an artist; health, which makes it the mark of a healer; and divination, suggesting a seer or a prophet.
- The Sun's golden rays might remind you of Midas, who turned everything he touched into gold. As a writer, you know that's not necessarily a good thing. What's more, not everything that glitters is gold.

A Quick Guide to Character Creation with the Sun

Astrology is a form of character analysis. For writers, astrology can also be a tool for character creation and character-driven stories. Keep these facts in mind.

Sign Rulership: The Sun rules Leo, the sign of creativity and self-expression.

Signature Creature: Leo is represented by a lion, the king of the beasts. Characters who are based on the Sun will be lionesque: bold, brash, regal, privileged, and proud.

House Rulership: The Sun rules the fifth house of a horoscope chart, where astrologers look for information about recreation, procreation, and creativity. Any character based on the Sun will embody an element of playfulness and fun. They'll be attractive, hot, and loaded with sexual magnetism, too.

Physical Associations: The Sun rules the heart and the spine. Both find expression in everyday language when we describe people with courage and heart, or willpower and backbone.

Geographical Associations: The Sun is associated with hot, dry places.

Element: The Sun corresponds to the element of fire. It's blazing hot, mesmerizing, uncontrollable, dangerous, and compelling. That energy could be expressed as a raging inferno or a slow, controlled burn. At times, it could be banked in embers, waiting to be reawakened.

Masculine/Feminine: The Sun's energy is masculine and direct. Even female characters who embody the energy of the Sun will be dramatic, forthright, fully conscious, and self-aware—or they'll discover those qualities in themselves in their travels through the landscape of the stars.

Metal: Gold is malleable enough to craft into ornaments and jewelry, intrinsically valuable, and artistically pleasing.

The Sun's Strengths and Weaknesses

The Sun, at the height of its powers, is strong, confident, truthful, direct, brave, visionary, optimistic, radiant, charitable, and humane. While no one can look directly at the Sun without going blind, the Sun illuminates the darkest shadows and reveals the truth of any situation. It's a powerful disinfectant.

When the Sun's energy is blocked, thwarted, or misdirected, though, it can be dangerous. It can be vain, arrogant, self-centered, egocentric, egotistical, and narcissistic. It can burn, and it can even be blinded by its own brilliance.

Creative Guidance

Most of us are taught to think of each new day as starting at sunrise. Each new story begins at dawn and moves into clearer focus as the Sun rises. At high noon, everything is illuminated. As the day lengthens, the shadows do as well, until at sunset the Sun moves into the netherworld, and then slips out of view entirely.

The cyclical nature of the Sun's movement symbolizes a story arc, as the plot unfolds and new developments are brought to light. It also symbolizes the hero's journey, in which the hero is forced to travel between two worlds—the ordinary and the supernatural—to discover a sense of balance and wholeness, and to integrate two halves.

Think about the Sun's movement as a tool for outlining plot, and guide your character through the story like the Sun travels through the sky—from its dawn at sunrise, to the pinnacle of high noon, its death at sunset, and its travel through darkness before being born again.

The Sun's Goals and Motivations

You could create a character based entirely on the archetypal qualities of the Sun. However, if you're trying to build a character piece by piece, based on all the planets in his or her birth chart, you'll want to consider the Sun's position in the signs of the zodiac. You'll learn more about the signs in the next section—but for now, here's a handy reference guide.

With the Sun in ...	Your character's primary mission in life will focus on ...
Aries	Leadership and initiation
Taurus	Stability, security, and comfort
Gemini	Communication and learning
Cancer	Home and family
Leo	Celebrity status, recognition, and admiration

With the Sun in ...	Your character's primary mission in life will focus on ...
Virgo	Work, service, and responsibility
Libra	Popularity, charm, grace, and style
Scorpio	Understanding the deepest, darkest mysteries of life
Sagittarius	Exploration, travel, and wide-ranging experience
Capricorn	Worldly success and accomplishment
Aquarius	Innovation and visionary thinking
Pisces	Spiritual existence

Twenty Questions

1. Write a quick character sketch based on the characteristics of the Sun. Because the Sun is the central figure in any drama, write about a protagonist who embodies the mythical, astrological, or literary archetypes you associate with the star of the show.

2. Write a first-person passage in which you assume the mantle of the Sun. What do you see during the course of a day? Where do your travels take you?

3. Go a step further. Write as if you've already seen everything under the Sun ... until one day you see something you've never seen before.

4. What happens when your character goes outside?

5. What happens when your character is in the public eye?

6. What fears must your character overcome in order to take center stage?

7. Write about the one thing that the Sun—like God—cannot have.

8. Write about the Sun's birth and death.

9. The Sun is used to being the center of attention, the most visible light in the sky. What does the Sun do when no one is looking?

10. Make a list of adjectives that describe the Sun—and which could describe your character in the process. Start with "hot, fiery, and radiant."

11. What literary characters do you think best embody the characteristics of the Sun?

12. *Explore the source of your character's energy. What fuels him?*

13. *How does he shine?*

14. *What is his reason for being?*

15. *What is most obvious about him?*

16. *What blinds your character?*

17. *What happens when your character's passions are extinguished? Hidden? Shrouded in darkness?*

18. *What time does your character rise for the day? When does he set? Where does your character travel in the course of a day?*

19. *Who are the people who surround your character?*

20. *How is your character's health?*

The Rest of the Show

A great story brings fictional characters to life, just as astrology brings real life into focus. The protagonist, of course, is the hero of the story. Most stories also include a constellation of characters that surround the protagonist, including friends, foes, co-workers, and casual acquaintances. They're usually categorized like this:

Antagonists. Conflict is the heart of drama, which means that every hero has an opponent who wants to block his happiness and progress. Even though the antagonist isn't the star of the story, he should be an equal match. A great antagonist is just as interesting as the protagonist, with just as much astrological depth and dimension. He might even outmatch the hero.

Friends and Foils. Because everyone needs a friend, most literary characters have foils—sidekicks who illustrate the hero's strengths and weaknesses. They might complement the hero, or serve as a striking contrast. They can contradict the hero, or complete him.

Supporting Characters. Figures who pop up throughout the course of a story—without taking leading roles themselves—are supporting characters. They usually have their own backstories, crises, and concerns; you can develop astrological profiles for them, too.

Stock Characters. Almost every story includes stock characters, such as bartenders, taxi drivers, and mail carriers. They're usually nameless, but they step in as needed to keep the story moving. You can base your stock characters on simplified planets or signs.

Astrology has countless characters to inspire you, whether you're looking for heroes, villains, or supporting players. You can choose from a celestial lineup of planetary personalities, as well as asteroid gods and goddesses. You can clothe them in the costumes of the signs, and imbue them with the full range of humanity's strengths and weaknesses.

Every person is a universe unto himself. As Walt Whitman wrote, "I am large, I contain multitudes."

Creative Guidance

Traditionally, astrologers have referred to planets and signs as masculine or feminine. In real life, of course, every individual embodies traits we could categorize as masculine or feminine. In literature, it's amusing and inventive to experiment with traditional gender roles. While this guide describes the planets and signs by their traditional pronouns, you're encouraged to mix and match their characteristics for maximum effect.

Heroes and Villains

While a protagonist is usually the hero of the story, heroes and villains can't exist one without the other. Each one is an inverse reflection and counterpart.

Generally speaking, heroes should be likeable. They might be quirky, but they should always be charming and charismatic. Like Boy Scouts, real heroes are loyal, brave, trustworthy, and true. They're modest and kindhearted. They adhere to a moral code—which may be perfect or imperfect, but is dependable and consistent. They rise to a challenge, and inspire others with their bravery and daring. They keep their promises and they play fair. That doesn't mean they won't break the rules and make mistakes. They will. That's part of what keeps them interesting.

What's more, most of their good qualities should come without a struggle—or without a price. In fact, their motivations should always be based on a fair amount of self-interest. While you don't need to incorporate a tragic flaw that will doom your heroes, they should have a dark side that they struggle to contain, control, or overcome.

Heroes should be attractive, physically and spiritually. They should be smart. They can be inexperienced—at least when the story starts—but they should be quick learners once they've enrolled in the school of hard knocks. They should be calm, cool, and collected in the face of a crisis.

And there will be a crisis—often in the form of a villain.

Villains are dark. They're unreliable and egotistical. They're untrustworthy. They break promises—and hearts—without care or concern for others. Their morals shift on loose sand. They lie, cheat, and steal. Sometimes they kill. They're selfish, and they don't show—or feel—remorse. They think their actions are justified.

Villains usually have some physical flaw that reflects their character defects and deficiency. Even so, they see themselves in the best light imaginable. They think they're handsome, charming, and smart. They can't laugh at themselves—and they certainly can't stand to be laughed at. They think they're better than everyone else—which could suggest a powerful sense of insecurity—or insanity—deep beneath the surface. They're bullies. Sometimes, they're psychopaths. They tend to panic under pressure. Ultimately, they're cowards.

Creative Guidance

Follow this checklist, and all of your characters will come to life. Do your heroes and villains measure up?

- *Heroes and protagonists have drives and desires—passions that burn as hot as the Sun.*
- *Villains and antagonists are always an even match for the heroes. They, too, have goals and motivations—and they see their counterparts as thwarting their mission.*
- *Every character's hopes and dreams should be both internal and external. No one lives in a vacuum. A personal goal should have a measurable target in the outside world.*
- *In fiction, no character's path should be smooth. If there's no rain on the parade, there should at least be clouds in the sky.*
- *Heroes and villains aren't caricatures. They're complex and multidimensional. Like everyone with a birth chart, they're fully rounded individuals.*
- *Even heroes are deeply flawed—perhaps irredeemably so.*
- *Their charm and talent might make up for their flaws—or camouflage them.*

- *Both heroes and villains are logical, and their reasoning is clear to the reader.*
- *Given the option, most characters would never choose to learn and grow, because every lesson comes at a cost. In fact, most characters, like most people, resist change; they have to be forced into it. Even when they're unhappy in their daily lives, most people know what to expect each day—and fear of the unknown is usually enough to keep anyone frozen in place.*
- *Your heroes might find that destiny is thrust upon them by forces that are outside their control. Eventually, however, every protagonist must take an active hand in determining his own fate.*
- *In the process, your heroes' greatest weaknesses can be transformed into their greatest strengths—and your villains' pride will be their undoing.*

Perspective and Point of View

Astrology can help you see life through your characters' eyes. As the author, you get to decide what—and how much—you'll reveal to your readers.

You can assume the omniscient form of the Sun, and report the story as it plays out under your watchful eye.

You can step into your character's shoes, and give a first-person account.

You can also write strictly as a mortal observer, in the third person.

Whatever point of view you choose, don't reveal too much. As the writer, you're omniscient, but you're not a court reporter. Leave some details to your readers' imagination.

Creative Guidance

Use straightforward astrological metaphor in your work: He shone like the sun. She glowed like the moon. He was as slippery as quicksilver. Try the technique with every planet in the solar system.

The Moon

Queen of the Night

She walked with measured steps, draped in striped and fringed cloths, treading the earth proudly, with a slight jingle and flash of barbarous ornaments. She carried her head high; her hair was done in the shape of a helmet; she had brass leggings to the knee, brass wire gauntlets to the elbow, a crimson spot on her tawny cheek, innumerable necklaces of glass beads on her neck; bizarre things, charms, gifts of witch-men, that hung about her, glittered and trembled at every step.

—Joseph Conrad, *Heart of Darkness*

The Constant Companion

The Moon is a constant companion to the Sun. She shares his joys and sorrows—and in the cosmic drama of the sky, she represents a partner, friend, and confidant.

She could be a wife, a mother, or any variation on the female theme, like a sister, a soul mate, or simply the girl next door. In any light—and any context—the Moon is decidedly feminine.

The Moon doesn't generate light and heat of her own. Instead, the Moon reflects the light of the Sun, changing and adapting each day as she orbits around the earth. The Moon's position is constantly changing, as she waxes from new to full and back again. And while the Moon fades from view once a month, her influence never disappears.

The Moon reveals herself in bits and pieces—and in the process, she serves as a reflection, a sounding board, and a measure of your hero's growth and progress over time.

Mythic Models: The Lady of the Night

The Sun and the Moon are linked in a cosmic dance, perpetually following each other's footsteps through the sky. Some cultures consider the two luminaries brother and sister, while others refer to them as husband and wife. In either case, they are a primordial couple, and their heavenly partnership symbolizes the constant give and take between light and dark, action and reaction, masculine and feminine, radiance and reflection, and the conscious and subconscious mind.

While we've all heard about the man in the moon, the heavenly light is also linked with the three faces of the goddess—the maiden, mother, and crone. It's no coincidence that the three faces of the goddess correspond to three distinct phases in a woman's life. Storytellers embodied all three forms in the tale of Proserpina, a young woman who was kidnapped by the lord of the underworld. Her mother, Ceres, was the goddess of the harvest—but while her daughter was missing, she refused to give life to the earth. Eventually, Proserpina was rescued by Hecate, the withered crone who had the power to travel between this world and the next.

The Moon is constantly changing form—as Moon goddesses often do—so her legend also varies. In ancient Greece, Selene was the goddess of the Moon. She would rise from the oceans each night, freshly bathed and crowned with a crescent Moon. In ancient Rome, she was Luna, Latin for "Moon."

The Greeks knew her as Artemis, the goddess of the hunt. In that role, Artemis could take life, cleanly and without reservation. She wasn't a goddess of death, however. In fact, she was the goddess of childbirth, and she was dedicated to shepherding new life into the world. As legend has it, she helped deliver her own twin brother, Apollo, immediately after she was born.

The Romans knew Artemis by the Latin name Diana. She was a hunter and an archer; the crescent Moon was her bow, and she could take life to preserve it. During childbirth, women in labor would cry out to her for relief; they believed that she could either kill their pain or kill them to end their suffering.

It all comes back to positioning: Luna and Selene were representations of the Moon in the sky. Diana and Artemis were her incarnation on Earth. And as the goddess of the underworld, Proserpina was the dark Moon who slipped periodically from our view.

Her rescuer, the wise old Hecate, was darker yet. In myth and legend, Hecate had the power to summon demons and phantoms from the bowels of the earth. She taught sorcery and witchcraft. She could be found wherever two roads crossed, on tombs, and near the blood of murdered persons. She herself traveled with the souls of the dead, and her approach was announced by the whining and howling of dogs.

The Astrology of the Moon ☽

The glyph for the Moon looks like a crescent Moon.

While the Sun lights the sky by day, the Moon rules the night. It's the guardian of dreams, the keeper of secrets, and the silvery orb of reflection and intuition.

Just as the Moon reflects the Sun's light, it also reflects our unconscious needs and desires. Because the Moon is shrouded in shadows and darkness, it represents secrets and mysteries that may not be understood—or even recognized.

In astrology, the Moon represents the emotional landscape. It symbolizes inborn and innate needs and desires. The Moon symbolizes the rocky landscape of memory and feeling—brilliantly illuminated when the Moon is full, but mysterious and enigmatic whenever it's hidden from view. Even though she's an intimate companion, the Moon keeps part of her face veiled, shrouding herself in shadow and refusing to reveal her dark side to the world.

The gravitational pull of the Moon symbolizes the irresistible force of our memories, dreams, and reflections. The tug of the past is irresistible—and easily repressed. The emotions that rise up at night usually don't make sense until the bright light of day.

Astrologically, the Moon symbolizes the depths of personality. The Moon reflects our fears and insecurities, as well as our desire for nurturing and safety. It describes our sensitivities: our inborn responses to emotional triggers, our instinctive responses to threats, and our immediate reactions to predatory behavior.

The Moon has ties to memory, mood, and motherhood—along with corresponding issues of creativity and the need to nurture our creations. The Moon symbolizes fertility and rhythm, because its 28-day cycles are typical of most women's monthly cycles. The Moon is also linked to pregnancy and childbirth, because its phases so clearly match the pregnant female form: slim, then round and full, then slim again. Its circular shape can suggest a reservoir, a womb, a cauldron, or a chalice.

The phases of the Moon are closely linked to the cycles of life: maiden, mother, and crone.

The Moon is also a symbol of public perception and popular opinion, because it represents how we're seen when we're projected into the sky.

Creative Guidance

What's your story really about? What message and meaning do you want to convey? What is your life's purpose? What is your character's purpose?

The theme of a story is often directly connected to the Sun and the Moon in astrology: the burning desire of the Sun combined with the reflection and understanding of the Moon.

Theme, however, is subtle—both in life and in fiction. When astrologers sit with their clients during an astrological consultation, the themes usually unveil themselves slowly and symbolically, in bits and pieces, as they discuss the highlights of the horoscope, and the highs and lows on the road map of life.

The Astronomy of the Moon

The Moon was our first calendar, and its cycle is a graphic reminder of the cyclical nature of existence—and it's a useful marker that helps us chart the cycles of our lives.

The Moon moves through all of the signs every month, and it's full in one sign each month of the year. Because the lunar and solar calendars aren't perfectly synchronized, the Moon makes a complete orbit around the earth every 28 days, and catches up with the Sun every 30 days.

It is interesting to note that from our vantage point on Earth, the Sun and Moon appear to be exactly the same size. Symbolically speaking, they are a matched set. Like Selene and Helios, Luna and Sol, or Diana and Apollo, they are a cosmic pair, equal in size and engaged in a perpetual race through the heavens. Where the Sun is masculine and active, the Moon is feminine and receptive.

The Moon is an irresistible force; its gravity helps stabilize Earth's orbit and produces the regular ebb and flow of the tides.

The Moon's orbit around the earth is synchronized with the earth's orbit around the Sun—so synchronized, in fact, that the bright side of the Moon always faces Earth and the dark side of the Moon always turns toward space.

Archetypal Roles

- In astrology, the Moon often represents a woman—a wife, mother, sister, or friend.
- The Moon's rule of the night sky could suggest a queen, a first lady, or a woman in authority. In practical terms, the Moon is an equal—a wife, partner, or better half.
- A woman's life experience unfolds in three phases: maiden, mother, and crone.
  - A maiden is pure, innocent, virginal, and self-possessed.
  - A pregnant woman carries the hope of the future. A mother can be loving and caring, willing to defend her children with her life—or a dark mother who systematically destroys her children.
  - A crone can be a wise and trusted grandmother, or a wicked witch—a dangerous woman who knows too much.
- The Moon's connection to nurturing and children can also symbolize a midwife, nanny, or nurse.
- Women are often categorized by extremes: they can be virgins or whores, or saints or seductresses. While you wouldn't talk about

women that way in real life, you can use those characterizations for dramatic effect.

- The Moon might remind you of Eve, the first woman who cursed humankind with original sin.
- There's a mystical quality to the Moon that links it to psychics and mediums, high priestesses, and keepers of secret wisdom.
- The Moon's reflective qualities might prompt you to think of advisors, counselors, psychiatrists, and psychologists.

A Quick Guide to Character Creation with the Moon

As you look at the Moon for literary inspiration, keep these facts in mind.

Sign Rulership: The Moon rules Cancer, the sign of motherhood, as well as home and family life, inheritance, and security.

House Rulership: The Moon rules the fourth house of the horoscope, where astrologers look for information about nurturing and the foundations of early childhood.

Dignity: The Moon rules Cancer, the sign of motherhood, home, and family. The Moon is a symbol of nurturing and security—which makes it debilitated in Capricorn, the opposite sign of business, career, and high-profile, public visibility. The Moon is exalted in Taurus, a sign of comfort and security. It's in its fall in Scorpio, a sign of intense scrutiny and introspection.

Physical Associations: The Moon rules the breasts, stomach, ovaries, and womb—a reminder of the nurturing power expressed through mother's milk and comfort food.

Geographical Associations: Cold, moist, and damp places: lakes, oceans, seas, ports, docks, bogs, spas, and fountains.

Element: The Moon is associated with the watery world of emotions.

Masculine/Feminine: The Moon is reflective and receptive.

Metal: Silver.

Creative Guidance

The Moon offers the perfect opportunity to consider your characters' back-stories. When you look at your characters by the light of the Moon, you can glean amazing insights into their formative years, primary relationships, and personal development.

- *Who raised your character?*
- *What was her family like?*
- *Who nurtured her?*
- *Who disciplined her?*
- *How would you describe her childhood?*
- *What were her school years like?*
- *What did she learn about relationships from her parents and family?*
- *Was her home life calm or stressful?*
- *How did she perceive her home life?*

The Moon's Strengths and Weaknesses

When the Moon is round and high in the sky, it embodies the height of femininity and refinement. It's fertile, creative, reflective, meditative, contemplative, sensitive, well-mannered, soft-spoken, and mild.

When the Moon is dark and shadowy, however, it's prone to fits of lunacy and unbridled passion. It's uncontrolled and uncontrollable, drunk with power, disconnected from reality, irresponsible, and lazy.

The Moon's Goals and Motivations

If you're creating a character based on a birth chart, look for the position of the Moon. The luminary's position will show you where your character will invest most of her emotional energy, both in her relationships and in her quest to prove herself.

With the Moon in ...	Your character will invest most of her emotional energy in ...
Aries	Establishing her importance, leadership, and drive
Taurus	Ensuring her own safety, security, and stability, and creating a comfortable environment

With the Moon in ...	Your character will invest most of her emotional energy in ...
Gemini	Presenting herself as clever, smart, and well-informed
Cancer	Nurturing others, in an effort to guarantee her own emotional security
Leo	Garnering respect, love, and admiration
Virgo	Analyzing, assessing, and organizing her world
Libra	Gaining and retaining popularity
Scorpio	Gaining a sense of mastery and control over life's deepest, darkest mysteries
Sagittarius	Acquiring worldly experience and proving her credentials and expertise
Capricorn	Climbing the ladder of success and worldly accomplishments
Aquarius	Devising life-changing innovations and improvements
Pisces	Immersing herself in the watery world of spiritual existence and alternate realities

Creative Guidance

A Blue Moon is a rare occurrence, resulting from the fact that the lunar calendar isn't perfectly aligned with our Gregorian calendar. There are thirteen full moons in a year. What rare event—happening once in a Blue Moon—will move your story forward?

Twenty Questions

1. *The Moon is a partner to the Sun. Describe a conversation between the Sun and the Moon.*

2. *Write about how the Sun and Moon characters met.*

3. *Outline an argument between the Sun and the Moon.*

4. *Describe how they feel during their time apart, and how they grow close, then separate.*

5. *Write a passage in first-person plural: "We ..."*

6. Is your character's strength waxing or waning?

7. The Moon experiences the cycle of birth and death on a monthly basis. What would it be like to be continually reincarnated?

8. What moments does your character relive, either consciously or unconsciously?

9. Does your character ever experience déjà vu? Work an example into your story.

10. What cycles does she repeat?

11. What words or expressions have become catchphrases?

12. How does your character grow, change, and then return to her starting point?

13. Who is your hero's companion?

14. How does she reflect your hero's strengths?

15. How does she reflect your hero's weaknesses?

16. What secrets could she reveal?

17. What facts does she conceal?

18. What is her dark side?

19. What are your hero's memories, especially of childhood? Describe your hero's mother. How does your hero relate to his mother?

20. The Moon is perpetually young—and preternaturally old. She's an old soul who celebrates her youth, but she's comfortable with the aging process. She's seen the world cycle through periods of growth and change for eons. She's almost impossible to shock—but you can try. Devise a scene or a scenario that would make your grandmother blush.

Mercury

The Great Communicator

There was no lack of material; boys happened along every little while; they came to jeer, but remained to whitewash. By the time Ben was fagged out, Tom had traded the next chance to Billy Fisher for a kite, in good repair; and when he played out, Johnny Miller bought in for a dead rat and a string to swing it with—and so on, and so on, hour after hour. And when the middle of the afternoon came, from being a poor poverty-stricken boy in the morning, Tom was literally rolling in wealth.

—Mark Twain, *The Adventures of Tom Sawyer*

The Traveling Companion

Mercury is the smallest planet, but it plays the largest number of roles in astrology. From friend, to neighbor, to spirit guide, the messenger planet constantly runs circles around the Sun.

Mercury is, at heart, a traveling companion. The planet has the smallest, fastest orbit, which makes it a steady, reassuring presence in the sky.

Archetypally, Mercury is well suited to the role of a neighbor, roommate, brother, sister, or cousin. Mercury can also make an appearance as a mail carrier, newsboy, or gossipy neighbor. He can even offer some comic relief.

Mercury can also be a herald of coming events. In fact, a lot of stories start when a messenger delivers a call to action—an offer that can't be refused, or a warning that can't be ignored.

In fact, Mercury, the winged messenger of the gods, conveys more information than you can imagine. He's the courier of the accumulated wisdom of all of time and space.

Mythic Models: Messenger of the Gods

Mercury was a heavenly messenger, a high-flying, fast-moving, winged spirit who could ferry communications between gods and men at the speed of light. He shuttled between Earth and Mount Olympus in the blink of an eye. He wore wings on his feet, so he never touched the ground, and his winged helmet was proof of his airy, intellectual nature. In fact, the glyph for Mercury looks like a stick-figure sketch of the young god, crowned with those wings. Mercury also carried a magic wand—a caduceus of gold, given to him by Apollo, who taught him the art of prophecy.

As the god of communication, Mercury was also the god of commerce, which connects him to fast talk and clever sales pitches. At times, he crossed over into the realm of the con man. He was the god of tricksters and thieves—but in all honesty, that wasn't a deal-breaker: the gods aren't bound by the same moral code as men.

Like Hecate, the dark goddess, Mercury was also one of the few souls who could cross the invisible boundary between life and death. He could travel in and out of the underworld at will. Most of the souls who passed through the portals of darkness were condemned to dwell there forevermore—or until they could be reborn, when memories of their previous incarnations would be wiped clean. Given his power as a psychopomp, Mercury occasionally served as an emissary and a guide to the spirits of the dead, ensuring their safe passage into Hades' realm.

In Greece, Mercury was also known as Hermes, and the Hermetic Maxim—"As above, so below"—has been a philosophical inspiration for centuries. Not only does it cast light on the premise that life on Earth is a reflection of a greater reality, it also suggests that the mind truly is more powerful than matter, and that an imaginary world, cloaked in the power of words, has the power to transform reality. Mercury has always been an emissary between the airy realm of ideas and the earthy world of physical existence.

There is a trickster element to Mercury that can't be overlooked. Not only did Hermes lie, cheat, and steal with impunity, but he also raised misinformation to an art form. He offered some information on a need-to-know basis, and occasionally he left out the most important parts. He could wrap his mind around any number of contradictions, inconsistencies, and incongruities, and convince his audience to accept any explanation for any story.

In literature, Hermes can be the antagonist who is so complex and multifaceted that he becomes more interesting, more intriguing, and more fascinating than the protagonist—because he embodies all of the protagonist's qualities, and their opposites. Does he contradict himself? Yes. He contains multitudes.

The Astrology of Mercury ☿

The glyph for this planet looks like Mercury, messenger of the gods, in his winged helmet.

Named for the fleet-footed messenger of the gods, the planet Mercury rules quick errands and short neighborhood jaunts. He rules the things we learn as children, when we first start to explore the microcosmic world of our own neighborhoods. He rules the tasks that children are often appointed to execute, like delivering newspapers and feeding pets. Through Mercury, we learn how to work and sell ourselves, by trying our wings at odd jobs around the neighborhood: door-to-door cookie sales, lawn mowing, shoveling, babysitting—real jobs with real value, but that are often entrusted to the youngest and most inexperienced members of society. With Mercury's guidance and direction, we can test our wings.

In astrology, Mercury represents logic, reason, wit, writing, and speech. Its placement in a horoscope chart, by sign and by house, describes early schooling and primary education, as well as siblings, cousins, playmates, and neighborhood friends.

Mercury's close proximity to the Sun suggests a connection to one's immediate neighborhood, as well as close ties to neighbors on the family tree—brothers, sisters, and cousins. After all, the gods on Mount Olympus were related, and Mercury helped ensure that they could stay in contact.

Because Mercury dispatched his errands at the speed of thought, the planet also represents the thought process, intellect, and communication style. It symbolizes basic training in reading, writing, and arithmetic during the grade-school years.

Mercury was the god of communication. An airy intellectual, Mercury describes how you think and how you communicate those thoughts to others. It symbolizes reason and rationale, logic and loquaciousness, verbal ability, and communication skills. It's more than idle chatter: Mercury is the mechanism of reason.

Mercury is tasked with the day-to-day essentials: quick neighborhood trips and early primary education. How were you taught to think? Who were your role models? What did you learn to adopt—or reject—based on the communicators around you? It's the foundation of your relationships and your ultimate success in life, both in terms of relationship and career.

Mercury is often written off as glib and fleeting, but its position in the chart is of primary importance.

The Astronomy of the Planet Mercury

Mercury is the Sun's closest companion in space, so it has the shortest orbit of all the planets—just 88 days. Mercury's speed and agility mark it as the quick-thinking, versatile ruler of short trips, neighborhood errands, everyday commerce, and workday commutes.

Mercury's trickster aspect is also apparent in its astronomical circuit. The planet's orbit is so near the Sun, and so quick, that it seems to zigzag through the sky, changing its apparent direction six times each year. When Mercury goes retrograde, it seems to be moving in reverse. That's a phenomenon when Earth moves ahead in our orbit around the Sun, and we're forced to look back over our shoulders and wait for Mercury to catch up.

Astrologically, Mercury retrogrades mark periods of time when messages are delayed, misdelivered, or misconstrued. Communication breaks down, and the tools we rely upon for our daily routines tend to fall apart too. Computers crash, networks go down, hard drives fail, and e-mail gets lost in the ether.

Of course, for a writer, miscommunication is a gold mine. When you lead your characters through a series of misunderstandings and misadventures, your readers won't be misled. They'll keep turning the pages for more. Everyone loves a quirky comedy of errors.

Archetypal Roles

Mercury can be cast in any number of supporting roles, including:

- A student, who pursues learning as a vocation.
- A poet, writer, or scribe, who transforms reality with the power of words.
- A thief, who steals from others when their guard is down.
- A wanderer, who leaves the known world to explore new horizons.
- A messenger, like a mail carrier, delivery person, or page. Messages can come from any number of sources, however, including gossipy neighbors, family members, and strangers on the street.
- Sometimes a communicative friend knows what the hero is thinking—and says it before the hero can put his thoughts into words.
- A source of information: a researcher, a reference librarian, a clerk at an information desk.
- A trickster, who uses his power to manipulate and deceive. Tricksters relish the disruption of the status quo, turning the ordinary world into chaos with their quick turns of phrase and physical antics.
- Some tricksters pose as fools. Shakespeare's fools were witty and concise; many truths were told in jest. Historically, a fool was an inverse counterpart to a king. Fools were the only ones who could speak truth to power. Court jesters weren't simpletons, and they often served to remind the monarchs of their own folly and humanity.
- A trickster can also be a magician, who can bend the laws of nature to suit his needs. He can be a sorcerer, who harnesses the power of spirits and demons for his own ends, or a wizard, a wise old man who can transform reality.

- Mercury's occasional role as a psychopomp, a conductor of souls, can lend your story a supernatural twist. His appearance could signal a message to or from the spirit world. He can be a shaman, who journeys between the physical and spiritual worlds on a specific mission.
- He might serve as a link between the conscious and unconscious minds. He could also represent a guide to travel in an unfamiliar area.
- Your messenger could even be an unlikely herald—like an angel unaware—who comes into the story in the guise of something completely unexpected: a child, an anonymous message, or a snippet of overheard conversation.

A Quick Guide to Character Creation with Mercury

Here's what you need to know to assess Mercury in astrological terms.

Sign Rulerships: Mercury is a multitasker. The planet rules two signs: quick-thinking Gemini and analytical Virgo. They're both signs of airy intellectualism. Gemini is curious and wide-ranging, while Virgo is discriminating and precise.

House Rulerships: Mercury rules Gemini's third house of communication and Virgo's sixth house of work and service to others.

Dignity: Mercury, with its lightning-fast orbit around the Sun, rules short trips. That means it's debilitated in Sagittarius, the sign of long-distance travel. The intellectual Mercury is equally uncomfortable when it's forced to wallow in the depths of Pisces' watery emotions. Mercury is exalted in Virgo—one of the signs it rules—and Aquarius, the airy, thoughtful sign that's also associated with the technology of modern communication.

Physical Associations: Mercury rules the parts of the body we use to gather and convey information: the shoulders, arms, and hands that belong to Gemini. Mercury rules the parts of the body we use to analyze data, too—the brain and the central nervous system, which belong to Virgo.

Geographical Associations: Mercury is associated with cold, dry locations.

Element: Mercury corresponds to the element of air, like a thought, a whisper on the breeze, or a message broadcast across an open sky.

Masculine/Feminine: Mercury, like the trickster he is, embodies qualities that are both masculine and feminine.

Metal: This planet is associated with mercury, of course, which is also referred to as quicksilver. Mercurial matters are fast-moving and free-flowing. They seem solid, but they're almost impossible to grasp. They slip into liquid at a touch. Mercury, like the words and thoughts he communicates, is fleeting.

Mercury's Strengths and Weaknesses

At his best, Mercury is smart, clever, curious, and creative. He's adaptable, attentive, and reactive. He's perceptive and keenly intelligent. He's got a quick wit and a wicked sense of humor.

Sometimes Mercury is too clever by half. He's not just cunning—he's also crafty and confusing. He lies. He cheats. He gossips and he steals. When Mercury goes bad, he turns misdirection into an art form. He's so bad, he's good.

Creative Guidance

For a writer, Mercury embodies the writer's mind of grasping multiple storylines and weaving them together, deftly, cleverly, succinctly, and skillfully. He is the consummate storyteller, revealing neither too much nor too little, but exactly what the listener needs to hear at a particular juncture. He offers information on a need-to-know basis.

Mercury was a psychopomp, a conductor of souls. Writers are psychopomps in their own right. They lead readers down the path of adventure and excitement. They live vicariously through the experiences of others. They're willing to venture into an underworld under the safeguard and protection of a guide, knowing that they'll be safely delivered and ultimately returned to their own world—changed and made better by the experience.

Just as Mercury could cross between the land of the living and the land of the dead, he can move between the worlds of conscious awareness and unconscious revelations. His magic wand gave him mantic powers over sleep and dreams. If you want Mercury to visit you during the night, keep a notebook by your bed so you can record the messages he leaves for you in the early morning hours.

Mercury's Goals and Motivations

With Mercury in ...	Your character's communication style will be ...
Aries	Bold and direct
Taurus	Slow, careful, clear, and musical
Gemini	Quick and wide-ranging
Cancer	Kind and compassionate, but also prone to emotional outbursts
Leo	Dramatic and self-centered
Virgo	Measured and precise
Libra	Charming, gracious, and collaborative
Scorpio	Secretive, understated, and not very revealing
Sagittarius	Outgoing, humorous, curious, and philosophical
Capricorn	Businesslike, with glimpses of dry, subtle humor
Aquarius	Friendly, kind, but somewhat offbeat and eccentric
Pisces	Slow, gentle, flowing, and somewhat confusing

Twenty Questions

1. *Create a new character for your story, or choose an undeveloped character from your existing cast, and put words in his mouth. Make him an unlikely messenger—and to complicate matters, try to ensure that his message will be misinterpreted, either as a joke or an outright lie. Many a truth is told in jest.*

2. *Mercury is a trickster. How is your character not what he appears to be? Write a story in which Mercury deliberately deceives another character.*

3. *Play tricks on your readers. Move parts around. Plant false clues. Misdirect. Change the ending.*

4. *Write a story in which a Mercury-based character breaks boundaries, crosses borders, and enters and exits a world that's forbidden to*

the rest of us, like a prison or an asylum. You could also try sending your character into Mercury's own supernatural world—Mount Olympus, home of the gods, or Hades, the realm of the dead.

5. *How does your character think? What could impede his thinking?*

6. *How does your character express himself?*

7. *Where does he get his information?*

8. *How does he verify his sources?*

9. *What stumbling blocks does he have when it comes to communication?*

10. *What was your character like as a child?*

11. *Where did he go to school?*

12. *Who was his favorite teacher?*

13. *What was his favorite class?*

14. *How does your character dress?*

15. *What does your character drive? How does he travel?*

16. *What is your character's daily routine?*

17. *Describe your character's neighborhood.*

18. *Does your character have brothers, sisters, or cousins? How do they relate?*

19. *Is there a supernatural twist to your story?*

20. *Will your character receive a message from the spirit world?*

Venus

The Love Interest

But, soft! what light through yonder window breaks?
It is the east, and Juliet is the sun.
Arise, fair sun, and kill the envious moon,
Who is already sick and pale with grief,
That thou her maid art far more fair than she.

—William Shakespeare, *Romeo and Juliet*

Most stories aren't complete without a love interest—and no planetary player is more suited to the part than Venus, the goddess of love.

Mythic Models: Goddess Types

In mythology, Venus was an etheric beauty who was associated with all the pleasures of the flesh.

Some say Venus was the daughter of Jupiter and Dione. Others say she sprang from the foam of the sea. The zephyr winds wafted her along the waves to the Isle of Cyprus, where she was received and attired by the Seasons, and then led to the assembly of the gods. They were charmed, and each one demanded her for his wife. Jupiter gave her to Vulcan, the celestial metalsmith, in gratitude for the service he had rendered in forging thunderbolts. It was the height of irony: the most beautiful of the goddesses became the wife of the most ill-favored of the gods.

Venus's husband, Vulcan, the celestial artist, was the son of Jupiter and Juno. Some say he was born lame, and his mother was so displeased at the sight of him that she banished him from her sight. Other accounts say that Jupiter literally threw Vulcan out of the heavens for taking his mother's side in a quarrel, and that Vulcan was crippled by the fall.

Despite their marriage, Venus rejected Vulcan in favor of Mars, the god of war. She and Mars enjoyed a long love affair, and she bore his children. Their son Cupid, the god of love, was her constant companion. Armed with his mythical bow, Cupid shot arrows of desire into the bosoms of both gods and men.

To be fair, Vulcan was partly responsible for Venus's infidelities. He was married to his work, which didn't leave room for an intimate relationship with the goddess of love. When he discovered her betrayal with Mars, however, he captured them making love, and trapped them in a net of fine spun gold. He then called upon all the gods of Mount Olympus to witness his wife's shame. At Neptune's insistence, Mars and Venus were released from their bonds.

The Astrology of Venus ♀

Like its namesake, Venus is the planet of love, beauty, pleasure, and attraction.

Venus symbolizes charm and social grace, along with peace and harmony. She represents refinement and the sensual delights of music, art, and dance.

Venus can be vain and irresponsible, but her self-indulgence usually takes a more civilized course through sensuality and flirtation. She's romantic, idealistic, and kind, as well as gentle and sympathetic. She's fertile and creative, and she embodies the balance and perfection that can be attained through passion, partnership, and unity.

In an astrological chart, Venus graces everything she touches with ease, comfort, affection, and enjoyment. She is generous to a fault. Like Jupiter, she's a benefactor; ancient astrologers called her the Lesser Benefic. That's usually a good thing, but not always—especially if she overindulges her children and they grow spoiled.

The glyph for Venus looks like a woman's hand mirror, which Venus used to admire her own splendor.

The Astronomy of Venus

Venus is both the morning star and the evening star. She welcomes the dawn and embraces the night.

From our position on Earth, Venus seems beautiful beyond belief. It's the second-brightest object in the night sky, and it offers a romantic glimpse of a bright and shimmering foreign world.

Up close, however, Venus is a landscape of molten lava and noxious gas, covered by clouds of water vapor and sulfuric acid. It's too hot to sustain life, and too poisonous to maintain a breathable atmosphere. In real life, Venus is a planet of perpetual rage. Does she sound like any fictional characters you know?

Venus orbits the Sun in 225 days, spending almost 19 days in each sign of the zodiac.

Creative Guidance

Spend a few minutes describing the theme you'd like to explore in your writing. Keep it in the background, like a silver thread unifying the other parts of your story.

You might not recognize your theme until you start analyzing the astrological imagery in your work. Astrology is effective that way; you'll notice recurring signs and symbols. Once you spot them, you can expand upon them.

A good theme reinforces the action of a story. At its most basic level, a theme is an inner reflection of a character's outer goal. You might discover that your hero isn't really after money. Instead, he wants power. You might find that your heroine doesn't just want romance; she wants acceptance. A rising superstar doesn't just want the adulation of crowds; she craves the love she never had as a child.

In the end, a powerful theme will help you focus on your characters and their journey. It will help you understand their drives and motivations, and add depth and dimension to their experiences.

Archetypal Roles

The goddess of love is easy to cast—or typecast—in any romantic role. Consider her when you're writing about:

- The lover, the object of passion.

- The love interest, the object of desire.

- The love goddess—an intimate companion, but not a wife or mother.

- The mistress—the single woman who poaches another woman's husband, or the unfaithful wife.

- The whore, a woman who has compromised herself and her principles—but she sells what men value at a fair market price.

- The temptress and seductress.

- The unobtainable beauty.

- The tease, the flirtatious minx who toys with a man's affections.

- The girl next door, waiting in the wings.

- Because the path of love is almost never smooth, consider all the variations on the theme: former lovers, scorned lovers, unfaithful lovers, jealous lovers, misunderstood lovers, or unrequited love.

- Secret admirers—or psychotic or sociopathic stalkers.

A Quick Guide to Character Creation with Venus

Here's what you need to know to assess Venus in astrological terms.

Sign Rulerships: In keeping with her role as the morning and evening star, Venus rules a pair of partnered signs: Taurus, the sign of earthly pleasure, and Libra, the sign of partnership.

House Rulerships: As the ruler of Taurus and the second house, Venus shows us what we love. As the ruler of Libra and the seventh house, she describes how we share that love with others. Her involvement leads to strong attachments, both to property and to people.

Dignity: Venus is the natural ruler of Taurus and Libra—two signs of beauty, grace, and equanimity. She's the queen of their domiciles. Venus's basic nature, however, is at odds with Aries and Scorpio, the two signs traditionally ruled by Mars, the god of war. (Remember that Venus and Mars were lovers. Opposites attract.) Venus is exalted in Pisces, a sign of emotional partnership and connection, but the goddess of sexual passion is at odds with Virgo, the sign of the virgin.

Physical Associations: Venus rules the throat, which puts her firmly in control of sweet talk and love songs. As the planet of pleasure and sweet delights, Venus is also associated with blood sugar levels and venereal disease.

Geographical Associations: Venus is associated with warm, moist places.

Masculine/Feminine: Venus could only be a woman.

Metal: Copper, a shimmering, gold-colored metal, reflects Venus's cosmetic appeal.

Venus's Strengths and Weaknesses

Venus was beautiful, charming, and gracious. She could win any object of her heart's desire.

She was also fickle and notoriously unfaithful.

Venus's Goals and Motivations

With Venus in ...	Your character will love ...
Aries	New adventures, new challenges, and new beginnings
Taurus	Creature comforts, stability, and tradition
Gemini	Talking, studying, and learning
Cancer	Homemaking, cooking, and nurturing
Leo	Attention, admiration, performing, and playing
Virgo	Perfection, precision, order, and control
Libra	Parties, reunions, performances, and clever conversation
Scorpio	Mysteries and secrets
Sagittarius	Long-distance travel, foreign friends, philosophy, religion, and higher education
Capricorn	Business, building, commerce, organization, growth, wealth, and reward
Aquarius	Technology, social groups, and visionary causes
Pisces	Mysticism, alternate realities, escapist fantasy, drugs, and alcohol

Twenty Questions

1. *Venus is the goddess of love and attraction. Which people does your character love—and why does she love them?*

2. *Venus' reach extends beyond human relationships, into the realm of beautiful objects and treasured belongings. What possessions does your character love? What special significance do they hold for her?*

3. *Venus also rules pastimes and hobbies—especially if they can be linked to objects of grace and beauty. Does your character have any creative ability or artistic talent? How has she developed it?*

4. *How does your character fall in love? Does she jump into relationships headfirst, or take slow, measured steps? Describe your character's behavior and actions in the early stages of a romance.*

5. *What does your character find attractive, either in people or in her possessions?*

6. *How does your character show love and demonstrate affection?*

7. *We say that people fall in love, as if they simply stumble into a relationship. In real life, however, romance takes effort. What signals does your character send to others, either consciously or unconsciously? What kind of people does she attract as a result?*

8. *In a similar vein, what kind of experiences does she attract? If you were to study her daily routine and interactions with others, what sort of pattern would you see?*

9. *What does your character desire?*

10. *What would she never admit to desiring?*

11. *What does she value? If the list seems too long, narrow it down to three.*

12. *The apostle Matthew once wrote, "For where your treasure is, there will your heart be also." Where does your character keep her most treasured possessions?*

13. *Where does she invest her time and energy?*

14. *What are her hobbies?*

15. *Where does she invest her money?*

16. *What does she have of value, to sell or interest others?*

17. *What is your character's single most attractive characteristic? How has it affected her?*

18. *Even beautiful people have flaws. Could anything about your character be described as repulsive? Does she know it's off-putting? If so, how does she try to keep it from view?*

19. *How does your character care for her possessions? Is she dutiful and responsible, or careless and lackluster in managing her belongings? Describe her outlook.*

20. *How does she care for people? Is there any similarity between the way she treats things and the way she treats those around her?*

Mars

The Warrior Spirit

And to the fire-eyed maid of smoky war,
All hot and bleeding, will we offer them;
The mailed Mars shall on his altar sit
Up to the ears in blood.

—William Shakespeare, *King Henry IV*

Fighting Words

Most stories open with drama and action—which is just what you'd expect from Mars, the ancient god of war. When he steps into the line of fire, guns blazing, you can expect crisis and conflict.

No one wants to read about an ordinary day in an ordinary life. The heart of any story is conflict, and Mars delivers by offering us a wide range of tragic accidents, crimes against humanity, and physical and psychological attacks.

Mars is the planet of energy, aggression, action, assertion, strategic offense, and self-defense.

Mythic Models: Gods of War

In myth and legend, the god of war was mated with Venus, the goddess of love, so he was both a lover and a fighter.

Mars was also the god of agriculture, who could turn swords into plowshares. He encouraged farmers to plant and tend their crops—because he knew that an army marches on its stomach.

Mars was the son of Jupiter and Juno. He had five attendants in his body guard: Eris (Discord), Phobos (Alarm), Metis (Fear), Demios (Dread), and Pallor (Terror).

The glyph for Mars looks like a spear and a shield—a reminder that war can be defensive as well as offensive, and that aggression and self-protection are two sides of the same coin.

The Astrology of Mars ♂

Mars is the red planet of courage and conflict, as well as passion and pain. Mars is colored by the blood that's spilled in pursuit of one's drives and desires.

Astrologically, Mars is associated with confidence and power. It symbolizes sexuality, stamina, and strength. It governs ambition, aggression, assertiveness, and impulse.

The planet suggests quick, sudden bursts of energy. It symbolizes potency and power. Mars is a marker of physical love, lust, and longing. It's also a sign of intensity, inspiration, and the impetus for change.

Mars also represents the machinery of war, sheer physical strength, and brute force. Mars rules sports and competitions—war games that take the place of battle during peacetime. It represents athleticism, training, and preparation for combat. Even today, the warlike god is remembered in military terms like martial arts and martial law.

Not surprisingly, Mars rules the weapons of war and conquest. Mars rules soldiers, surgeons, and metalsmiths. In short, Mars commands those who ride into battle to stem the red tide of death by conquering the forces of destruction with equal strength. Mars is the master of tools that can sever and pierce flesh, excise dead and unhealthy tissue, and make necessary sacrifices for the greater good. At times, the unrestrained warrior is also responsible for accidents, crashes, and careless cuts.

The Astronomy of Mars

Mars has always been an object of fascination, especially since astronomers first spotted its mysterious channels and canals in the 1800s. Mars has led science fiction writers to make fabulous conjectures about little green men and alien invasions.

Mars orbits the Sun in 688 days, spending about 57 days in each sign of the zodiac. It's also the first planet that orbits outside of Earth's orbit, making it something of a foreigner beyond our earthly realm.

Creative Guidance

Ancient astrologers called Mars the Lesser Malefic. His influence was never good. How can you follow in his footsteps to make your characters' lives harder? The best writers keep their stories moving with complications, subplots, and sidelines—each one linked to the main plot and the main theme of the story—to keep readers surprised, engaged, and wondering what will happen next.

Archetypal Roles

Mars is a bloodthirsty, primal warrior—but your soldier doesn't have to wear a military uniform. A businessman in a three-piece suit can do battle on Wall Street, and a woman in a little black dress is uniquely equipped to intimidate and conquer.

Mars can play any number of archetypal roles in a story.

- Mars can be a freedom fighter.
- He can be a knight, a rescuer, a defender of the weak and innocent, and a man on a mission.
- He might be a righteous defender—or a self-righteous zealot.
- At his worst, Mars can be a crazed attacker, intent on mutually assured destruction.
- In a storyline, Mars can represent a worthy opponent, a recruiting and training officer, or a sparring partner—anyone who helps the hero develop his or her fighting skills and reserves.
- Antagonist, adversary, opponent, warrior, patriot, compatriot, comrade-in-arms.
- A soldier, sailor, tinker, spy.
- A surgeon who removes diseased tissue to save the soul, or a medical specialist who works with the precision of the sword.
- Someone who works with iron: an auto mechanic, a racecar drive, a welder, or a construction worker.

- A modern-day warrior: police, paramilitary.
- An athlete—because war is more than a conquest of strength. It's also a game of strategy and skill.

A Quick Guide to Character Creation with Mars

Here's what you need to know to assess Mars in astrological terms.

Sign Rulership: Mars rules Aries, the sign of leadership and action. Before the discovery of Pluto, Mars ruled Scorpio, the sign of sex and death—both of which are closely related to Mars's masculine energy.

House Rulership: Mars rules the first house, where astrologers look for information about self-image and physical appearance.

Dignity: Mars is the master and commander of both Aries and Scorpio. Mars isn't at ease when it's forced to embrace romantic Venus's signs, Taurus and Libra. Mars is exalted in Capricorn, where it can put its executive experience to good use in business. It's in fall when it tries to apply those same skills to Cancer's realm of nurturing and homemaking.

Physical Associations: Mars presides over blood and the male sex organs. It's also connected to high fevers, violent accidents, trauma, pain, and surgery.

Geographical Associations: Mars is associated with hot, dry places.

Element: Fire.

Masculine/Feminine: Mars is a masculine planet.

Metal: Iron. Both the soil of Mars and the hemoglobin of human blood are rich in iron, and they share its distinct deep red color.

Mars's Strengths and Weaknesses

Mars is a confident, courageous warrior, who embodies the strength of a sound mind in a sound body. He can outthink, outwit, and outmaneuver any opponent. He's passionate and persevering, and he'll fight for victory at any price. When he's fighting for a cause he believes in, Mars is loyal and true.

Mars also loves to fight for fighting's sake. He's fiery and impulsive, and he doesn't need a reason to wage war or wreak havoc. He's quick to anger, and quick to rise to his own defense—just as he's quick to mount an aggressive offense. He's brash, bold, and argumentative; he can be both a bully and a braggart. He can be treacherous and untrustworthy, and dangerous and unreserved. He's ready, willing, and eager to do battle, and he's prepared to fight to the death.

Conflicting Opinions

Every story is based on conflict—a dramatic struggle between two opposing forces. The conflict could be as simple as a clash of personalities, or it could detail a complicated series of interactions as characters battle over incompatible goals, actions, and desires.

There are five types of conflicts in fiction. Each one serves as a barrier that keeps characters from reaching their goals.

- Man versus self—a story that forces a character to face his own inner demons.
- Man versus man—a story that pits an antagonist against a protagonist.
- Man versus nature—a story that puts human life in perspective and illustrates a character's courage and strength.
- Man versus circumstance—a story that forces a character to fight circumstances and fate.
- Man versus society—a story that pits a single individual against society's norms, customs, expectations, values, and mores.

You can use astrology to explore those conflicts thematically and symbolically from your characters' points of view.

Creative Guidance

Conflict, the core of any story, demands an antagonist who is as strong and compelling as the protagonist. The two must be evenly matched, or there is no contest.

An antagonist is often a complement to the hero's strength or a projection of his weaknesses. In fact, an opponent is often a projection of opposition—a complement to the hero's strength or a projection of his weaknesses. When your character looks into his opponent's armor and shield, who does he see looking back?

The interaction between a protagonist and an antagonist is usually a dance, an ongoing interaction in which both partners thrust and parry. Each one must anticipate the next move and capture the element of surprise. But in that duel to the death, your characters will feel most alive.

Mars's Goals and Motivations

If you're creating a fictional character, planet by planet and sign by sign, Mars will show you what your characters are willing to fight, kill, and die for.

With Mars in …	*Your character will fight for …*
Aries	Command and control. He'll make himself a general and organize the troops.
Taurus	Physical and emotional security. She'll prepare carefully for battle, and stockpile weapons and supplies.
Gemini	Information. He's ideally equipped to wage a Cold War of subterfuge and misinformation. He's an expert in intelligence gathering and reconnaissance. He might also be a double agent.
Cancer	Her family, home, and country. No sign is more patriotic than Cancer.
Leo	Dignity and honor. Leo is the king of the castle and the living embodiment of his realm.
Virgo	Duty and principles. Virgo fights out of a sense of obligation.
Libra	Peace. Libra is the sign of diplomatic negotiations, mediations, and treaties.
Scorpio	Power. Scorpio knows that all is fair in love and war, and that love is a battlefield.
Sagittarius	Philosophical principles and beliefs, religious tradition, and authority.

With Mars in ...	Your character will fight for ...
Capricorn	Success. He'll take any measures necessary to build and expand his empire.
Aquarius	The future. He'll use technology to fight a cold and impersonal war, far removed from the blood and gore of a battlefield.
Pisces	Escape from the harsh realities of the everyday world.

Twenty Questions

1. *Mars is a symbol of our passions and pursuits. What do your characters want with every fiber of their being?*

2. *What keeps them from getting what they want? Most people experience some frustration in achieving their dreams and desires—and Mars can symbolize the obstacles they face, as well as the energy it takes to overcome them.*

3. *What will your characters do to get what they want? How far will they go?*

4. *How does that change them?*

5. *What will your character fight and die for?*

6. *Is your character equipped to lead an army—or to march in one? If he's pressed into service, how will he respond?*

7. *What makes your character see red? What makes his blood boil?*

8. *What "fighting words" will propel him into action?*

9. *How does your character prepare for battle?*

10. *What weapons does he have at his disposal?*

11. *What battles has he lost?*

12. *Mars is responsible for battle wounds and bloodletting of all types. What physical injuries has your character suffered?*

13. *On a symbolic level, what war wounds has he experienced?*

14. *Everyone has some remnant of an old injury, either physical or emotional. What are your character's battle scars? Are they visible to a casual observer, or does it take a trained eye to see them? Develop*

at least one way to make your character's wounds apparent to your readers, through dialogue, description, or demeanor.

15. What is your character's greatest weakness? Was it the result of a wound, or the cause?

16. Mars rules mock battles of athletic competition, as well as training. What sports or physical activities does your character enjoy?

17. Does he compete? How does he train, and what sort of competitor is he?

18. Mars' warrior energy even reaches into the bedroom. Describe your character's sexual energy and proclivities.

19. Send a confrontation your character's way, and thwart any efforts he makes to deal with it according to custom. Make him transform weakness into strength. Force him to face his fears.

20. Villains are usually the source of conflict in a story—and they're often more interesting to write about than heroes. Switch gears, just as an experiment, and make your villain the hero of a story.

Jupiter

Larger Than Life

His eyes—how they twinkled! His dimples, how merry!
His cheeks were like roses, his nose like a cherry!
His droll little mouth was drawn up like a bow,
And the beard of his chin was as white as the snow.

—Clement C. Moore, *The Night Before Christmas*

When the hero of your story needs a lucky break, look for Jupiter. He's the god the ancients called the Greater Benefic. He's the giver of good fortune, and the guarantor of prosperity and growth.

When all hope seems lost, Jupiter will step in to save the day. He might arrive in the guise of a rich uncle, a kindly grandfather, or a man with a million-dollar check. He might be even come in female form, like a fairy godmother who can make dreams come true.

Of course, every present comes with a price. Fame and fortune are not free. Most special offers have some sort of strings attached. And on a personal level, the expansion that Jupiter brings to your story will also entail a fair amount of creative chaos.

That's okay. Jupiter is kind, and together, you'll work it out.

Mythic Models: Celestial Kings

Jupiter was the king of the gods, the ruler of Mount Olympus, and the master of both mortal and immortal subjects. He had the ultimate power of life and death, and he's the cosmic ruler who put many of the constellations in their heavenly homes.

That's not to say that Jupiter lived an exemplary life himself. He was a notorious adulterer who carried on with a wide range of goddesses and mortal women, and he fathered more children than you can count.

His wife Juno gave birth to his children Aries, the god of war, and Hebe, the Greek goddess of youth. His affair with Leto led to the births of Apollo, the sun god, and Artemis, goddess of the hunt. His affair with Themis, the goddess of justice, created the three Fates. And Athena, the goddess of wisdom, sprang full-grown from his head.

Jupiter himself was the child of Saturn and Rhea. They were Titans, the children of Earth and Heaven that sprang from Chaos. Saturn was the god of time, who managed to preserve his rule for years by eating his own children. He was repeating a family pattern: ages before, Saturn had usurped his own father. He feared that his offspring would do the same, so each time Rhea gave birth, he snatched up the child and ate it.

Eventually, Rhea tricked him by hiding Jupiter in a safe place and wrapping a stone in a baby's blanket. Cronos swallowed the stone without a second thought, and Jupiter was saved.

When Jupiter was grown, he drugged his father, forcing him to throw up all his other children. They'd been sitting in Saturn's stomach all along. Jupiter and his brothers dethroned their father and divided his holdings among themselves. Jupiter claimed the heavens, Neptune took the oceans, and Pluto seized the realms of the dead.

As fate would have it, Jupiter—known as Zeus in Greek mythology—would soon be threatened by his own child. After Zeus heard a prophecy that his first wife, Metis, would give birth to a god "greater than he," he swallowed her. She was already pregnant with Athena, however. Zeus's undigested pregnant wife and unborn child made him miserable with a pounding headache until Athena eventually burst forth from his head, fully grown and dressed for war.

The Astrology of Jupiter ♃

Jupiter is the god of good fortune. The planet's glyph looks like the numeral 4, which sounds like "fortune."

Like a cosmic Santa Claus, Jupiter bestows blessings, honors, and acclaim. He's larger than life—just as you'd expect from the largest planet in the solar system. Jupiter represents growth and expansion, as well as abundance and prosperity. Jupiter symbolizes luck, opportunity, prosperity, and success. Jupiter favors gambling, and he encourages his subjects to take chances.

Jupiter also encourages free trade and free thought. He promotes personal growth through advanced education, long-distance travel, and the free exchange of ideas with foreigners and fellow travelers. Jupiter rules the world of higher thought, higher education, philosophy, and spiritual tradition.

Writers have a special connection to Jupiter, because he also rules publishing. That's an offshoot of his role as the king of the gods, and his responsibility for the fair exchange of ideas. He's the father of philosophy and civilization—which means that he's also a symbol of the rule of law and order.

Jupiter is enthusiastic and exorbitant, excitable and energetic. He sees promise and possibility in a world without limits. He's a fan of unbridled growth and uncontrolled expansion, and he pays no heed to the thought of any bubbles bursting. He recognizes no boundaries; his world is one of open borders. As far as Jupiter is concerned, the more, the merrier.

Jupiter's greatest gifts are wisdom and success, long life, good health, and all the uplifting experiences the world has to offer: family, friendship, travel, philosophy. Jupiter gives you the good fortune to experience all that life has to offer—along with the depth to remember what you've been, the insight to realize what you are, and the imagination to visualize what you'll be. Jupiter melds the memory of the past with a vision of the future.

The Astronomy of Jupiter

Jupiter is a regal planet, with rings of brightly colored clouds flashing with giant electrical storms. It's also a protector; scientists say its massive gravity captures and deflects comets and asteroids that would otherwise threaten Earth and the inner planets.

Jupiter takes about 12 years to orbit the Sun, spending almost a year in each sign of the zodiac.

Archetypal Roles

When you create a character based on Jupiter, he could be a:

- Benefactor
- Favorite uncle
- Giver of gifts
- Game show host
- Lottery winner
- Gambler
- Mentor
- Fairy godmother
- Vote-buying politician
- Guardian angel
- Magical helper
- Supernatural being
- Priest
- Philosopher
- Politician

Creative Guidance

We usually think of a benefactor as a good thing—but Jupiter's gifts may not live up to their promise. Lottery winners often find their lives destroyed, not enhanced. A genie's three wishes almost always come at a price. Jupiter presents the perfect opportunity for a plot twist. We're always being told to be careful what we wish for. What gift can you offer your characters—and how can that gift go horribly wrong?

A Quick Guide to Character Creation with Jupiter

From a writing perspective, Jupiter illustrates the joy of creative writing, the act of brainstorming, free writing, and the unabashed flow of ideas. Here's what you need to know to assess Jupiter in astrological terms.

Sign Rulership: Jupiter rules Sagittarius, the sign of philosophy and adventure, long-distance travel, exploration, and philosophy. Traditionally, it also rules Pisces, the sign of mysticism and cosmic awareness.

House Rulership: Jupiter rules the ninth house of the horoscope, where astrologers look for information about higher education and long-distance travel.

Dignity: Jupiter, the king of the gods, is also the natural ruler of Sagittarius. Jupiter's broad vision is debilitated in Gemini and Virgo, two signs that demand precision and attention to detail. Jupiter is exalted in Cancer, because Jupiter is the Greater Benefic and loves to shower his loved ones with gifts; Jupiter is in fall in Capricorn, the sign of business and industry, where every reward must be earned.

Physical Associations: Jupiter, like Sagittarius, is associated with the hips and thighs.

Geographical Associations: Jupiter is associated with hot, moist environments.

Element: Fire.

Masculine/Feminine: Jupiter is masculine.

Metal: Tin.

Jupiter's Strengths and Weaknesses

At his best, Jupiter is generous and fair. He's gregarious, optimistic, honest, and sincere. He's enthusiastic, and determined to promote the best qualities of humankind.

On the other hand, Jupiter is also prone to exaggeration, overconfidence, and conceit. He can be overindulgent. He can also be hypocritical and pious.

Jupiter's Goals and Motivations

How will Jupiter bless your characters' growth and development? Check the planet's placement.

With Jupiter in ...	Your character will be blessed with ...
Aries	Leadership ability
Taurus	Money and property
Gemini	Intelligence and wit
Cancer	Nurturing parents, a large family, and beautiful children
Leo	Charisma, celebrity status, recognition, and admiration
Virgo	Dutiful servants, committed helpers, good health, intelligence, and a sense of order
Libra	Beauty, grace, charm, and style; attractive partners and faithful friends
Scorpio	A rich and rewarding sex life and a promising inheritance
Sagittarius	Opportunities to travel and learn
Capricorn	A Midas touch in business and administration; patience, perseverance, and financial success
Aquarius	A gift for innovation, visionary thinking, and a touch of genius
Pisces	Psychic ability, a clear and steady intuition, and a wholeness of body, mind, and spirit

Twenty Questions

1. *Jupiter, the Greater Benefic, is the bearer of gifts, the fountain of plenty, and the king of largesse. Think about your character in terms of his own generosity as well as the recipient of generosity from others.*

2. *Jupiter can represent excess—like someone who can't stop talking, shopping, or eating. In what way is your character prone to excess?*

3. *Jupiter rules growth and expansion. How has your character grown and changed over the years? What growth must he still experience?*

4. *How will your character's growth and change parallel the growth of your story?*

5. *What opportunity does your character hope for?*

6. *What opportunity will present itself?*

7. *They say fortune favors the brave. How does your character respond to opportunity?*

8. *Is your character naturally lucky or unlucky? How has that affected him over the years? How will it play out in your story?*

9. *Jupiter rules gambling and games of chance. Does your character take chances? Why or why not?*

10. *Jupiter is called the Greater Benefic. Has your character ever had a benefactor? Can you give him one?*

11. *Does he have a beneficiary? Describe their relationship.*

12. *What gifts has your character received? Conversely, what gifts has he given to others?*

13. *What is the greatest gift your character could receive?*

14. *What gift has your character always been denied?*

15. *Jupiter is optimistic and enthusiastic. He doesn't suffer from fear or self-doubt. When does your character feel most confident?*

16. *How does your character enter a room? Describe his body language, gestures, and mannerisms, as well as any greetings or phrases he tends to repeat.*

17. *How does your character make other people feel? Describe a typical interaction between your character and one of his friends, family members, or co-workers.*

18. *Jupiter rules the acquisition of property and physical possessions. What does your character collect?*

19. *What would your character never throw away?*

20. *Think about the alchemical metals assigned to the seven ancient planets. What can they tell you about any characters who have a strong link to those spheres? The Sun, for example, is connected to gold. Do your characters have a golden touch? A golden glow? How can you illustrate and describe that association?*

All creations are born from chaos. It's the writer's job to make sense of the free flow of ideas and events that come when pen meets paper. You won't have any luck trying to organize them, however, until Saturn gets in the game. Happily, he's up next.

Saturn

Authority Figures

Oh! But he was a tight-fisted hand at the grindstone, Scrooge! a squeezing, wrenching, grasping, scraping, clutching, covetous, old sinner! Hard and sharp as flint, from which no steel had ever struck out generous fire; secret, and self-contained, and solitary as an oyster. The cold within him froze his old features, nipped his pointed nose, shrivelled his cheek, stiffened his gait; made his eyes red, his thin lips blue; and spoke out shrewdly in his grating voice. A frosty rime was on his head, and on his eyebrows, and his wiry chin. He carried his own low temperature always about with him; he iced his office in the dogdays; and didn't thaw it one degree at Christmas.

—Charles Dickens, *A Christmas Carol*

The Cosmic Teacher

Saturn is the cosmic teacher—the universal taskmaster who insists that we learn life's lesson on a strict timetable. If we cut class, forget to turn in our homework, or cheat, he forces us to repeat the class.

Saturn doesn't accept excuses. He doesn't grade on a curve, and he doesn't offer partial credit. He is open to remedial lessons, however.

In literature, the Saturn figure might look like a formidable opponent. He seems to be an adversary, determined to thwart a hero through obstacles and interference. The hero of your story might even see Saturn as an enemy.

In reality, though—and Saturn is all about reality—Saturn only has your hero's best interests at heart. The challenges he poses are tests of stamina and merit, designed to help a true hero prove himself and prepare for a position of power, leadership, responsibility, and acclaim. Like a drill sergeant who trains soldiers to survive, Saturn can help your hero live to fight another day. Far from being an enemy combatant, Saturn becomes a teacher, a mentor, and a guide, a trusted advisor and confidant, a fellow traveler on the path of self-development.

Creative Guidance

From a writing perspective, Saturn is the editor. He forces writers to kill their babies and finish their work on deadline. He's cruel to be kind, and he offers his own rewards in the fullness of time.

Mythic Models: The Harvest Gods

Saturn may seem like a formidable foe. In fact, ancient astrologers referred to him as the Greater Malefic, and he stands in stern contrast to the benefic nature of his son, Jupiter.

Saturn is a fearsome figure, by any definition. He's the god of time—another version of Cronos—who ate his children, just as the years eventually destroy all of the world's creations.

We're used to seeing Saturn depicted as an ancient figure, garbed in a hooded robe and carrying a sickle. In more modern depictions, Saturn resembles the Grim Reaper; he's a skeletal figure who cuts short the lives of the young and harvests the souls of the old. He's measured, distant, cold, and calculating.

In Roman mythology, however, Saturn was the god of agriculture. He taught the ancients how to trim the vine and the olive, and his civilizing influence helped establish societal order and control.

Once a year, during the festival of Saturnalia, that social order was upended. Slaves were treated like royalty, and their masters dressed in rags to wait on them. Children received presents, and everybody feasted.

Saturn's mythology is a valuable reminder that not every hero is entirely good, and not every antagonist is entirely bad. Real people—and realistic characters—are more complex than that. In fact, it's usually a hero's own weaknesses that put him in jeopardy, and a hero's tragic flaw will often be his own undoing.

Story Structure

Saturn loves a good framework. Thousands of years ago, the Saturnian philosopher Aristotle described the perfect story model: beginning, middle, and end.

Over time, that simple framework evolved into a three-act structure. You might have learned about it in a literature or writing class. Characters face a crisis, confront their opposition, and take an active role in the consequences and conclusion.

The three-act structure usually breaks down into setup that introduces the characters, the setting, and the premise of the story; a second act filled with escalating threats and confrontations; and finally, a climax at the peak of the action, followed by a quick and clean resolution.

Theorist Gustav Freytag described the same basic narrative structure by expanding it to five acts: exposition, rising action, climax, falling action, and resolution. It's plotted like a mountain top; the characters fight their way to the peak, and then quickly descend as the story concludes.

Along the way, however, even the simplest stories keep readers engaged by continually ramping up the drama and intrigue, and raising the stakes for their favorite characters. For every step forward, the good guys are pushed two steps back. And while the heroes eventually learn from the experience, the villains use that time to sharpen their skills.

Creative Guidance

Just as an astrologer looks at a horoscope chart and then focuses on telling details, you can move from the general to the specific over the course of a story to orient your readers and then invite them to move deeper into the story. Start with an establishing shot, then zoom in for a series of close-ups and vignettes. Give them a sense of time and place that helps reveal the characters and the experience.

You can also start your story at any point on the horoscope wheel. You could start at the beginning and work your way through chronologically, or you could start in medias res, *in the middle of things. Use flashbacks and fast-forwards to reveal the fullness of your story in bits and pieces. Short, simple transitions, like "Meanwhile, back on the farm," will help your readers follow you through space and time.*

Experiment. You can arrange and rearrange the chronology of your story as much as you'd like.

The Astrology of Saturn ♄

Saturn, the ringed planet of boundaries and limitations, symbolizes discipline, boundaries, clear-cut definitions, and tradition.

Most people, of course, rebel at boundaries. They like to feel free and unencumbered. Saturn brings us down to earth and teaches us the practical realities of material existence. It proves that what doesn't kill us makes us stronger.

Saturn reminds us that reasonable people recognize their limits and make wise choices to make the most of the time and space they're allotted. Time is the best teacher, and most people are willing to trade youth and innocence for the wisdom and experience of age.

Even though Saturn's rings imply a certain number of limitations and restrictions, they also delineate boundaries that can help us define our position and relate to other people without losing our own individuality. Boundaries keep outside forces out and contain what belongs inside. In other words, Saturn's boundaries don't merely confine us: they define us.

The glyph for Saturn looks like a church and steeple—a bastion of tradition. It's a very Saturnian symbol.

Creative Guidance

Saturn is the ringed planet of limitations and restrictions, so it often signals physical problems that correspond to its zodiac sign. You can exaggerate those traits to come up with health issues for your most memorable characters. Someone with Saturn in Leo, for example, might have a weak heart—or a hunchback. A character with Saturn in Virgo might suffer from a nervous stomach; be sure he's got access to plenty of antacids. And someone with Saturn in Scorpio could be sterile or frigid or suffer from venereal disease.

The Astronomy of Saturn

Saturn, the ringed planet, is bounded by an ethereal perimeter of cosmic debris—remnants of past interstellar collisions and lunar dustups.

The ringed planet, encircled by the remnants of a shattered moon, has come to symbolize the very thing that makes us human—our vulnerability—and our defenselessness against the ravages of time.

Saturn is the slowest of the inner planets, and it takes almost 30 years to orbit the Sun. Is it a coincidence that so many literary characters face their greatest conflict and crisis as they reach their thirtieth birthday? Probably not.

The Saturn Return

Have you ever wondered why so many fictional characters seem to be just shy of thirty? It's not simply that they're attractive and at their physical peak—although that doesn't hurt.

Astrologically, everyone hits a crisis point as they reach age twenty-nine.

The Saturn Return is one of astrology's best-known milestones. It's an astrological phenomenon that occurs every 29 years, which is the time it takes Saturn to make one orbit around the Sun. When Saturn returns to the degree it occupied at the time of someone's birth, the person crosses over a major threshold and into the next chapter of life.

In fact, most people will experience two or three Saturn Returns during their lifetime.

The Saturn Return symbolizes three distinct stages of experience. For women, it marks the transitions from maiden, to mother, to crone. For men, it denotes the process of growing from scout, to soldier, to chief.

During the first Saturn Return, a person leaves youth behind and enters adulthood. By the second return, the person has matured. And with the third return, he or she has become a wise, experienced elder, who's learned from each stage that has come before.

The first Saturn Return is usually the hardest, because it's the first test of character and strength. Saturn insists upon strong structures and foundations. If there is weakness to be found, the first Saturn Return will mark a period of upheaval and rebuilding. It's not uncommon to lose bad relationships, unfulfilling jobs, or tenuous living situations during any Saturn Return.

The result is worth it. Sometimes, a Saturn setback is just the impetus we need to move forward.

Archetypal Roles

In the cosmic drama of the night sky, Saturn is Father Time, the Grim Reaper, and Dear Old Dad—all rolled into one. Saturn is ideally suited for any archetypal roles based on age and authority, including:

- The wise old man, a scholar, teacher, sage, and philosopher, willing to share his knowledge, guidance, and advice.
- The father figure, a leader and voice of collective authority; a provider and protector who can also be stern, powerful, and controlling.
- The leader, chief, king, or administrator.
- The Grim Reaper—the harvesting henchman.
- The destroyer, who clears away anything that has outgrown or outlived its usefulness.
- The master of the harvest, who tills the old crop under and prepares the field for a new crop.
- The dictator; the domineering, controlling ruler.
- The hermit, a recluse whose solitude inspires others to join him.
- The judge, the enforcer of the rule of law.
- The miser, who would rather live in squalor than part with his money.
- The teacher, who passes knowledge on to successive generations.
- The mentor and the guide.

A Quick Guide to Character Creation with Saturn

When Saturn shows up, the party's over. His disapproving stare makes everyone want to curl up and hide—because he forces them to think more critically of themselves. Saturn makes an ideal villain and an excellent foil, because it's so easy to project our failings and insecurities on him. Here's what you need to know to assess Saturn in astrological terms.

Sign Rulership: Saturn, the planet of structure and boundaries, rules Capricorn, the sign of business, career, and social standing. It is also the traditional ruler of Aquarius, the sign of social groups and causes.

House Rulership: Saturn rules the tenth house of the horoscope, where astrologers look for information about discipline, career success, public image, and social standing.

Dignity: Saturn is at home in Capricorn. Its strict disciplinarian side doesn't mesh well with Cancer's empathic sense—or with Leo's valiant individualism. Saturn is exalted in Libra, where its sense of law and order finds perfect balance on the cosmic scales of justice.

Physical Associations: Saturn is associated with the bones and skin, which provide structure and stability to the human form.

Geographical Associations: Saturn is linked to cold, dry, underground places, like caves, pits, caverns, and mines.

Element: Earth.

Masculine/Feminine: Saturn is masculine.

Metal: Lead.

Saturn's Strengths and Weaknesses

Saturn has a bad rap. Traditionally, it's been called the Greater Malefic, because of its proclivity for limitations, restrictions, constraints, and delays. On the other hand, Saturn is also the civilizing force that provides structure and foundation for growth and development.

Saturn can be cold, calculating, reasoned, and unemotional. It can contribute to feelings of loneliness and isolation. It can seem overly serious and severe—even punishing and oppressive.

Saturn can also be practical, frugal, patient, and profound.

Saturn's Goals and Motivations

Saturn's placement in a chart will show you where your characters will find themselves compelled to respect boundaries, limitations, and restrictions. They'll usually have to learn their lessons the hard way. If you're looking for conflict and drama in a character's life, Saturn delivers.

With Saturn in ...	Your character will struggle with ...
Aries	Leaders and authority figures. They'll also have to fight for their own independence.
Taurus	Money and property. Their sense of security—and self—will be challenged.
Gemini	Miscommunication and troubled thoughts. Your character might suffer from learning disabilities, developmental delays, speech impediments, and language difficulties.
Cancer	Unresolved issues from childhood. Your character might have an abusive or absent parent, or thankless, troublesome children.
Leo	Appreciation and acclaim. Your character will have to fight for recognition and reward.
Virgo	Duty and responsibility. Your character's good deeds will go unnoticed, and he'll have trouble getting his own needs met by others.
Libra	Unhappy partnerships and unfulfilling friendships. Your character might seem clumsy, graceless, unattractive, and unpopular. Your character might also find himself entwined with people who are old and sick.
Scorpio	Sex, death, and other people's money. He'll either get too little—or too much.
Sagittarius	Philosophical conundrums, oppressive religious traditions, and a lack of opportunities to travel and learn.
Capricorn	Career success and social status. Saturn in Capricorn makes young people seem old before their time. It can also be a marker of wide-ranging scandal and personal destruction.

With Saturn in …	Your character will struggle with …
Aquarius	Friends, social groups, and causes.
Pisces	Drugs, alcohol, and escapist tendencies.

Twenty Questions

1. *Saturn is the ringed planet of limitations and restrictions. Boundaries are definitions, and Saturn's influence will force you to define your characters. Who are they? What are they?*

2. *Saturn often represents a disability of some sort. Find a way to demonstrate the physical weakness of your character. Give him a limp, for example, or a stutter.*

3. *In a similar vein, demonstrate an emotional frailty. Does your character hesitate to cross the street? Obsessively wash his hands, or check the lock on the door? Stare longingly at the phone or the street outside his window?*

4. *Saturn rules structure and foundations. What is the foundation of your character's worldview? Can you connect it to a single person or experience?*

5. *What boundaries has your character established for himself? How does he enforce those boundaries?*

6. *What limits has he experienced, and what obstacles has he overcome?*

7. *What boundaries will your character refuse to cross? Which ones will he ignore?*

8. *Saturn is said to be the taskmaster of the zodiac. What life lessons has your character learned, and how did he learn them?*

9. *On the other hand, what lesson has he refused to learn?*

10. *Saturn is the planet of discipline and responsibility. What responsibility does your character shirk?*

11. *Saturn also enforces limits and restrictions. Who—or what—has limited your character's growth? How was that limitation enforced?*

12. *What structure does your character need?*

13. *What structure can you strip away?*

14. *Saturn is linked to authoritarian structures and leaders. What authority does your character respect?*

15. *How is he an authority in his own right?*

16. *How does he assert his power and authority?*

17. *What does he expect from himself?*

18. *Why does your character need to be taught a lesson?*

19. *How does your character take direction?*

20. *Most writers have a tendency to reveal too much. Once you finish the first draft of a story, read through it with an eye for details and descriptions that can be cut.*

Uranus

The Unexpected

"It was much pleasanter at home," thought poor Alice, "when one wasn't always growing larger and smaller, and being ordered about by mice and rabbits. I almost wish I hadn't gone down that rabbit-hole—and yet—and yet—it's rather curious, you know, this sort of life! I do wonder what CAN have happened to me! When I used to read fairy-tales, I fancied that kind of thing never happened, and now here I am in the middle of one! There ought to be a book written about me, that there ought!"

—Lewis Caroll, *Alice's Adventures in Wonderland*

Insight and Inspiration

Originally, the seven visible planets were the only representatives of the celestial pantheon of gods. As technology expanded our vision of space, however, the gods extended their reach—and as astrologers incorporated Uranus, Neptune, and Pluto into their work, they discovered that the new planets had symbolic significance that closely matched their namesakes.

Uranus, the ancient god of the sky, was reborn in 1781, when astronomers were finally able to peer beyond the reach of the visible planets into a universe that only time and technology could reveal.

Scientifically speaking, Uranus was the first of the modern planets, and its discovery changed what we know about the universe.

True to form, Uranus never steps into a story without delivering a plot twist—a sudden, unexpected change of course. He's a rebel, a revolutionary, and an instigator of change. He's unusual and unconventional. He doesn't live up to the expectations of others—instead, he exceeds them. He's a free spirit who marches to the beat of a different drum.

He's a visionary, with a far-seeing eye, in search of utopian vision, and he'll make use of whatever resources he finds at his disposal. He's ready to work with new technology and break the bounds of convention and time.

When you choose to base a fictional character on Uranus, you'll never know what to expect. Uranus is eccentric. He's unorthodox, unafraid, and unstoppable. He's innovative and inventive. Uranus has an unquenchable desire for experience and adventure.

In short, Uranus can be a gold mine for storytellers.

Mythic Models: The Sky God

Even though ancient legends are full of unusual stories, nothing can top the legend of Uranus.

In Greek mythology, Uranus was the personification of the heavens and the night sky. He's sometimes called the son of Gaia, and sometimes he's her husband. Together, he and Gaia had many children, including Saturn and Rhea.

Uranus hated his children, and immediately after they were born he confined them to Tartarus, the realm beneath the sea. Saturn rebelled, and castrated his father. Giants and nymphs sprang from drops of his blood, and Venus was born from the sea foam where he fell.

The Astrology of Uranus ♅

Everyone has a rebellious streak—a line that can't be crossed. When it's breached, revolt and revolution follow. Uranus is the celestial homeland of freedom, revolution, rebellion, and reform.

In society, Uranus rules radical ideas and people, as well as revolutionary events that upset established structures. It displaces and overthrows any establishment that has outlived its useful life span. It's the planet of revolution and progress.

Astrologers associate Uranus with genius and individuality. Uranus was discovered at the dawn of the Industrial Revolution, so it's associated with electrical energy and modern technology. It governs new ideas, inventions, and discoveries. Uranus also governs social groups that are dedicated to humanitarian ideals.

Uranus is associated with science and technology, and its glyph looks like a satellite.

The Astronomy of Uranus

Uranus is an unconventional planet in our solar system, too. It literally spins sideways on its axis. It's horizontal, not vertical. It rotates on its side, so that its two poles face the Sun in turn. During its revolution, one hemisphere is bathed in light while the other lies in total darkness.

Uranus is the first of three outer planets that are invisible to the naked eye, so they could only be discovered with the aid of telescopes and modern technology. Before 1781, when Uranus was discovered, the seven visible planets were the only players in the night sky.

Uranus takes 84 years to orbit the Sun, so it spends about 7 years in each sign of the zodiac.

Archetypal Roles

While it's hard to categorize the unconventional and eccentric, you can cast Uranus in any role that allows him to express his individuality. Try these on for size:

- The fool, an untested spirit, willing to trade innocence for experience.
- The outlaw, a spirited nonconformist.
- The martyr, who sacrifices himself for a cause.
- The rebel, who questions his society and culture.
- The inventor, innovator, explorer, and pioneer.
- The philosopher, who seeks answers to life's greatest mysteries.
- The alchemist, who seeks the elixir of life.

A Quick Guide to Character Creation with Uranus

Uranus is best suited to wacky, unconventional characters. Here's what you need to know to assess Uranus in astrological terms.

Sign Rulership: Uranus rules Aquarius, the sign of futuristic thinking.

House Rulership: Uranus rules the eleventh house of the horoscope, where astrologers look for information about social groups and idealistic causes.

Physical Associations: Like Aquarius, Uranus is associated with the lower legs, the ankles, and the circulatory system.

Element: Air.

Masculine/Feminine: Uranus is a masculine planet.

Uranus's Strengths and Weaknesses

It's hard to judge or hold a grudge against Uranus. He's just too offbeat.

At his best, Uranus is kind, caring, and humanitarian. He's dedicated to serving his fellow man, and he's constantly on the lookout for new tools, techniques, and technology to further his cause. He's inventive and ingenious. He's charming, clever, and creative.

When Uranus isn't functioning at full capacity, however, he's unpredictable, unreliable, and forgetful. He's prone to accidents and sudden outbursts. He can even be violent. At his most radical, Uranus is simply unappealing, unapproachable, and unpleasant to be around.

Creative Guidance

Combine the best—and the worst—characteristics from two planets or two signs. For maximum drama and conflict, pit the strong against the weak. Make sure your hero is out of his element. Raise the level of discomfort. Build some contradictions into his basic nature.

Uranus's Goals and Motivations

If you're creating a fictional character based on a horoscope, you can use Uranus's position to make him a true eccentric.

With Uranus in ...	*Your character will display an eccentric or rebellious streak by refusing to conform with ...*
Aries	Authority figures and societal norms
Taurus	Money and property

With Uranus in ...	Your character will display an eccentric or rebellious streak by refusing to conform with ...
Gemini	School systems and conventional methods of communication
Cancer	Parental and family expectations
Leo	Public opinion
Virgo	Customary standards of cleanliness and hygiene
Libra	Social norms and standards
Scorpio	Sexual mores and conventions
Sagittarius	Rules, laws, and religious tradition
Capricorn	Business and career expectations
Aquarius	Social groups
Pisces	Ordinary forms of spirituality

Twenty Questions

1. *How will your characters set the world on fire? How will they reshape the world, realign their thinking, and revolutionize the status quo? Look at Uranus, the rebel planet with or without a cause. Uranus simply wants to stop the world, change it, break the mold, and remake it—better and stronger than before.*

2. *What makes your character different and unique?*

3. *Is that quality obvious or hidden?*

4. *How could you incorporate it into your story?*

5. *Small details often suggest major characteristics. Name one unusual thing your character does before breakfast.*

6. *How does your character rebel against everyday authority, structure, or tradition?*

7. *Follow your character around for a day, and note any rules or regulations that he breaks.*

8. *Why does he rebel? Can you trace it back to a single experience or encounter?*

9. *What makes your character angry? How does he express it?*

10. *Does anything fill your character with rage? Describe it.*

11. *Most people go through predictable periods of rebellion and change. These are actually a requirement for growth and development. To pinpoint your character's most rebellious feature, describe his toddler years, when he was in the throes of the "terrible twos."*

12. *Fast forward a few years, and describe your character as an adolescent. If you need inspiration, you might like to observe real-life teenagers at a bus stop, restaurant, or store.*

13. *Describe a time your character did something unexpected.*

14. *Your fictional characters can experience the unexpected from outside forces, too. What would your character never expect?*

15. *How does your character view rebellious people?*

16. *How does your character accept radical ideas?*

17. *How does your character adapt to technology?*

18. *Has anyone ever told your character he's crazy?*

19. *Describe your character's peace of mind.*

20. *Send a shock your character's way, and thwart any efforts he makes to deal with it according to plan. Compel him to come up with an inventive solution to an unexpected problem. Make him transform a weakness into strength.*

Neptune

Daydream Believer

Call me Ishmael. Some years ago—never mind how long precisely—having little or no money in my purse, and nothing particular to interest me on shore, I thought I would sail about a little and see the watery part of the world. It is a way I have of driving off the spleen and regulating the circulation. Whenever I find myself growing grim about the mouth; whenever it is a damp, drizzly November in my soul; whenever I find myself involuntarily pausing before coffin warehouses, and bringing up the rear of every funeral I meet; and especially whenever my hypos get such an upper hand of me, that it requires a strong moral principle to prevent me from deliberately stepping into the street, and methodically knocking people's hats off—then, I account it high time to get to sea as soon as I can.

—Herman Melville, *Moby Dick*

Glamour and Illusion

As a writer, you have a secret weapon: when you sit down to tell a story, you can invoke the power and beauty of Neptune.

Neptune is the planet of glamour and illusion. It dissolves the boundaries between reality and fantasy. It casts a mesmerizing glow, and it makes readers more than willing to suspend their disbelief.

In Neptune's bubble, one can find shelter and escape from the harsh light of everyday reality. It's a place for pleasure seekers and escapists who choose altered states of consciousness to soothe their weary souls.

Neptune is alluring and enchanting—and like the shimmering planet, you too can cast a spell with every word you write.

Mythic Models: The God of the Sea

In Roman mythology, Neptune was the god of the sea. He ruled the tides and the tide pools, as well as the dark, mysterious world of the ocean's depths. Seas would rise and fall at his command, and he could drown his opponents in an uncontrollable swell of unfathomably violent emotion. A stormy sea will calm—or be stirred into a tempest of unimaginable depth. A pounding surf will crash into the shore, or retreat, quietly and without fanfare, back into the dark black murky depths of the sea.

Neptune's symbol of his power was the trident, which he used to shatter rocks, raise or subdue storms, and shake the shores. He could raise storms and hurricanes, and stir whirlpools of grave confusion. He could also raise his trident above the surface and call on the forces of air and fire to bear down upon the waves.

All the animals of surf and sea respond to his call. Oddly enough, Neptune also created the horse, and he was the patron of horse races. His own horses had brazen hooves and golden manes. They drew his chariot over the sea, which became smooth before him, while the monsters of the deep gamboled about his path. He also rode a dolphin.

Water takes the shape of its container, which means it has shapeshifting properties. When a woman in distress called out to King Neptune, he would change her form so she couldn't be recognized by her pursuers.

The Astrology of Neptune ♆

In astrology, Neptune dissolves barriers between this world and the next, and demonstrates that the spirit realm is as real as the physical world. It's the planet of dreams and illusions, as well as daydreams and spiritual release.

Despite being named for a king, Neptune is a feminine planet.

Neptune, true to her watery nature, is compassionate and intuitive. She embodies mysticism and psychic enlightenment.

Neptune also seeks pleasure and escape, through altered consciousness and altered states. The real world can be a dark and dangerous place, and Neptune quickly learns to flee from her fears through meditation, prayer, sleep, and dreams. If she can't slip the surly bonds of Earth by natural means, she'll find an outlet through drugs, alcohol, or even food. Neptune will get her fix any way she can.

Neptune can inspire creative visualization and visionary thinking. The planet is associated with fantasy, imagination, and art. It's idealistic, sensitive, and exceptionally psychic.

Neptune herself is gauzy and ill defined. She's got no sharp corners and no rough edges. She's soft and soothing, lovely to look at, and delightful to behold. She shades us from the harsh light of reality.

She can also bewilder and confuse anyone who happens to spend too much time in her orbit.

The Astronomy of Neptune

The planet Neptune is just as ethereal as you'd expect from its astrological symbolism. It's composed mostly of ethereal mist and gasses.

Neptune takes 165 years to orbit the Sun, so it spends about 14 years in each sign of the zodiac.

Neptune was discovered in 1846.

Creative Guidance

Neptune's glyph looks like King Neptune's trident. Have you ever noticed how many gods, like Neptune, wield a staff of power as an emblem of their authority and expertise? Think of it the next time you pick up your favorite pen.

Archetypal Roles

In astrology, Neptune is a planet of dreamlike illusion. In literature, Neptune is the character who's clearly not grounded in reality. She's a free spirit, a visionary, and she walks a fine line between inspiration and insanity.

- Neptune embodies the archetypes of psychics and psychotics.
- Neptune can be a celebrity, hidden behind a veil of glamour and artifice.

- She might be an addict, compelled to drown her sorrows and her fears.
- Neptune may be a psychic, who can tap into supernatural forces far greater than herself.
- She might also be a visionary, who sees a brighter, better future for humanity.

A Quick Guide to Character Creation with Neptune

Here's what you need to know to assess Neptune in astrological terms.

Sign Rulership: Neptune rules Pisces, the watery sign of intuition and emotional connection.

House Rulership: Neptune rules the twelfth house of the horoscope, where astrologers look for the mysteries and secrets most people prefer to hide away.

Physical Associations: Neptune rules the places where those secrets are confined, including hospitals, prisons, and mental institutions. Neptune also rules the glamour of Hollywood and the silver screen, where audiences can find brief interludes of escape in the darkness of a movie theater.

Element: Neptune corresponds to the element of water.

Masculine/Feminine: Neptune's energy is feminine and receptive.

Neptune's Strengths and Weaknesses

At her best, Neptune offers us an otherworldly vision of compassion and creativity. She embodies the best that spirituality has to offer. She's empathic, telepathic, intuitive, and kind. She doesn't just dream of liberation for herself—she wants to share her freedom with the world.

At her worst, Neptune is addicted to dreams that simply can't come true. She frustrates herself and everyone around her. She's out of touch with reality, neurotic, and confused. She might be able to fool herself, but she can't convince too many others to join her in her misery.

Neptune's Goals and Motivations

Even strong characters have weaknesses. Because Neptune dissolves the boundaries between reality and illusion, Neptune's position in a chart can show you where your characters can't see clearly—and where they're most prone to misunderstandings, misconceptions, and unreliable sources of information.

With Neptune in …	*Your character will be confused by …*
Aries	Leaders and authority figures
Taurus	Money and property issues
Gemini	Fast-talking salespeople and con men
Cancer	Family relationships
Leo	Celebrities and charismatic personalities
Virgo	Health, nutrition, diet, and exercise
Libra	Partners, close friends, and open enemies
Scorpio	Sex, death, and shared resources
Sagittarius	High-minded philosophy, long-distance travel, foreign people, and alien cultures
Capricorn	Business matters, career developments, and societal expectations
Aquarius	Technology, social groups, and casual friendships
Pisces	Psychic flashes, intuitive glimpses, dreams, drinking sprees, and drug addiction

Twenty Questions

1. *Neptune is the planet of glamour and illusion. In fact, a glamour is a magic spell—and in many ways, Neptune describes the way in which writers cast a spell over their readers. Think about the way you write. How do you pierce the veil between your everyday world and the world of your imagination? How do you wrap your characters in a cloak of illusion? How do you cloak the harsh realities of everyday life in the veil of a story?*

2. *How does your most glamorous character cast a spell over those around her?*

3. *What mask does your character wear, literally or figuratively, when she faces the world? Does she slather herself in a layer of makeup, or hide behind dark glasses? How does she present herself?*

4. *Neptune rules the realm of visions and imagination—especially at night, when we enter the land of dreams. What does your character dream about? Does she have any recurring dreams? What are they?*

5. *Dreams aren't always relegated to the night. What daydreams distract your character from her daily life?*

6. *Neptune often symbolizes a break or diversion from responsibility. How does your character escape from reality?*

7. *What alternate reality has your character created for herself?*

8. *What illusions does she accept as real?*

9. *What illusion has she created for herself?*

10. *During the height of drama and conflict, most people will seek a quick exit. What is your character's escape plan?*

11. *Neptune rules the shadow world of drugs, alcohol, and other mind-altering substances. What is your character's favorite drink?*

12. *How does your character act when she's drunk?*

13. *What drugs does she take? Does she get them by prescription, over the counter, or on the street?*

14. *Why does she take them, and what would happen if she stopped?*

15. *What does it take to get your character high? Is she willing to loosen her grip on reality, or does she fight to stay in control?*

16. *Alternately, is your character sober and responsible? Take that away, and plunge her into a period of substance use or abuse. How does her behavior change? How do those around her react?*

17. *Is your character an alcoholic? Clean her up—and write about the effect her transformation has on her daily life and her relationships.*

18. *We all have weaknesses, and we all make periodic resolutions for self-improvement. What has your character tried to change about herself? Did she succeed, or did she fail?*

19. *How did the experience change her?*

20. *A young woman's glamour is often abandoned, lost, or repressed as she ages. Write about an older woman who rediscovers her innate sense of beauty and style. How—and why—does she make the change?*

Pluto

The Dark Lord

Pluto, the grisly god, who never spares,
Who feels no mercy, who hears no prayers.

—Homer

Power, Passion, and the Prince of Darkness

Pluto makes an appearance in every story. It's only a matter of time.

Pluto is the god of the netherworld. He's Hades, the king of the dead, and Lucifer, the fallen angel. He's Satan, the prince of darkness and commander of legions of demons. He's the Devil, torturer of the damned, and the dark lord of the realm of shades.

His role isn't hard to define. Pluto is a monster, a demon, and a vampire. He's a kidnapper, rapist, and murderer. He's a hideous creature of the night. He's the thief of souls. He tortures his victims, and then leads them, silent, mute, and robbed of their voices, into the next life.

If you try to deny Pluto his status and power—as astronomers did recently, when they demoted his planet—you're in for a rude awakening.

Some of your characters will meet Pluto sooner than others. Others will stave off his appearance for hundreds of pages. But as a writer, you know he's coming; you've built him into the plot. And as a reader, you might even jump to the last chapter, just so you can gauge his approach.

Mythic Models: The God of the Underworld

In ancient Greece, Hades was the god of the underworld. In ordinary life he was usually called Pluto, because no one wanted to say his real name aloud.

Pluto was the son of Saturn and Rhea, an early form of Mother Earth. He was one-third of a triumvirate of power: his brother Jupiter ruled the heavens, and his brother Neptune ruled the seas.

Pluto's ensign of power was a staff, which he used, like Mercury, to drive the souls of the dead into their new life in Hades. Pluto also owned a helmet of invisibility, which he sometimes lent to other gods and men. The gateway to his realm was guarded by Cerberus, the three-headed hound from Hell.

Pluto took his wife, the maiden Persephone, by force. As she picked flowers in a meadow, Pluto opened the earth beneath her feet. Eventually, the dark goddess Hecate rescued Persephone and returned her to her mother, Ceres. The God of Death couldn't be completely stripped of his prize, however, so Persephone was still condemned to spend a third of each year in Hades.

Apparently, her life there wasn't a living hell. She adapted to her otherworldly position and became the powerful Queen of the Dead.

Pluto wasn't a faithful husband; during one of his affairs, he fathered the Furies. When he carried on with a nymph named Mintho, Persephone turned her into the mint plant. Pluto loved a nymph named Leuce, too; when she died, Pluto himself turned her into a white poplar.

Pluto was fiercely hated by mortal men. Even so, they treated him with respect, and they even sacrificed black sheep to appease him. Whoever actually offered the sacrifice had to turn away his face.

Pluto did have one redeeming quality, as far as the ancients were concerned: as king of the lower world, he was the giver of all the blessings that came from Earth, including precious gems and metals.

The Astrology of Pluto ♇

In astrology, Pluto symbolizes death and resurrection, forgiveness and release. It can indicate areas of testing and challenge, power struggles, and resistance. It's a planet of evolution and unavoidable change.

Pluto compels us to release anything that's no longer living up to our needs or expectations, so we can recycle and reuse that energy in better ways. Pluto teaches us that endings are merely part of the cycle of regeneration and rebirth, and inevitably lead to a second chance at a new life.

Pluto typically calls for the release of old habits, old patterns, and old relationships that have served their purpose and now should be relegated to the pages of history. He has a shadowy partnership with Saturn, the god of time.

Pluto will take your youth and beauty, either in one lump payment or in a series of installments.

The symbolism of Pluto also hints at the myth of the Phoenix, the mythical bird that burns and then is reborn from its own ashes. The bird is a symbol of destruction and purification by fire and subsequent rebirth from the ashes. It's a metaphor for transformation and change, metamorphosis and rebirth. It doesn't represent the loss of energy; instead, it symbolizes a conversion.

The glyph for Pluto looks like someone rising from the dead; technically, it's a coin and a chalice, symbols of payment for everlasting life. An alternate version of the glyph (♇) combines the letters *P* and *L*, which also happen to be the initials of the planet's discoverer, Percival Lowell.

The Astronomy of Pluto

Pluto is a controversial planet. Not only is it a misshapen ball of rock and ice, but it's also smaller than an asteroid—which compelled scientists to reclassify it as a planetoid a few years ago.

Pluto's power, however, cannot be denied. Since it was discovered in 1930, it's been an object of fascination for students and scientists alike.

Pluto is an outlier in our solar system; it gets practically no light or heat from the Sun. It travels in an eccentric, 248-year orbit.

As isolated and withdrawn as it is, Pluto doesn't travel alone. The planet has a satellite companion, a moon called Charon. Pluto and Charon are locked in a dumbbell-shaped orbit around a common point in space, perpetually locked in a mutual embrace. More often than not, that cosmic embrace looks like a power struggle, as the two orbs struggle for position.

Archetypal Roles

In literary terms, Pluto is a monster. It's the sum of all fears, and the specter of death and destruction. As every storyteller knows, however, monsters don't always reveal their true forms. Some can even survive in the sunlight.

- In myth and legend, Pluto embodies the archetype of a gate-keeper or a guardian. The souls who were consigned to his realm had little chance of escape.
- Pluto can symbolize the dark shadow of human existence, and the dark side of any personality. Most people project their own dark side onto others; you might want to determine where your characters cast their longest shadows.
- In contemporary astrology, Pluto often symbolizes the power of transformation. In a story, Pluto's position by sign and house could suggest your character's ability to change and grow in monumental ways.

A Quick Guide to Character Creation with Pluto

Here's what you need to know to assess Pluto in astrological terms.

Sign Rulership: Pluto rules Scorpio, the sign of mystery and secrets. After the planet was discovered in 1930, Pluto usurped that power from Mars, the traditional ruler of the sign.

House Rulership: Pluto rules the eighth house, where astrologers look for information about sex, death, and inheritance.

Physical Associations: Pluto rules the reproductive organs, which ensure the survival of the species. As each successive generation dies, a new generation is born to replace it.

Geographical Associations: Pluto is associated with the cold, dry element of earth. Pluto rules buried treasures, including metals and minerals, and is associated with any effort to bring secrets to light.

Element: Pluto can also be associated with the fires of Hell.

Masculine/Feminine: Pluto's energy is masculine and direct.

Metal: Pluto is linked to lead, the basest, heaviest alchemical metal. During medieval times, alchemists tried desperately to transform lead into gold in an effort to prove that the human spirit could be refined and elevated beyond the bounds of physical existence.

Pluto's Strengths and Weaknesses

While Pluto is an ominous figure in anyone's book, Pluto also possesses an unwavering ability to see every individual for what he or she is: a soul trapped in physical form. Pluto doesn't pull punches: he gets right to the point, and makes people face their darkest fears. Pluto can be violent and even terrifying. He's an irresistible force. He's undeniably powerful—but those who rise to the challenge and confront that power can claim it for their own. It's only when Pluto's power is subjugated or denied that he becomes a monster.

Pluto's Goals and Motivations

Pluto, the planet of death and resurrection, has the power to transform your characters. The process, however, is fraught with danger. Pluto's position in a horoscope chart will show you where your characters will face their greatest challenges—and discover their greatest opportunity for growth.

Creative Guidance

William Faulkner didn't mince words. "In writing," he said, "you must kill all your darlings."

Writing isn't just a matter of planting words on paper. It's also a process of culling the ideas that don't take root. Every writer overseeds a first draft, but overgrowth will overtake a story like weeds in a garden.

As you survey the landscape of your work in progress, look for words, descriptions, and scenes that you can eliminate. You might even be able to kill a few characters. Some can be reborn, combined into single composite characters that can do the work of several men. Kill your darlings, and streamline your story.

With Pluto in ...	Your character will be forced to assert his power by taking control of his ...
Aries	Freedom. Your character will be forced to assert his independence, defend his choices, and take responsibility for his own decisions.
Taurus	Money and property. Your character might have to lose everything he owns in order to appreciate what he really has.
Gemini	Thoughts and communication. Your character will have to learn to think and speak for himself.
Cancer	Parents and children. Your character will have to set boundaries and establish firm foundations for a healthy family life.
Leo	Creativity, recreation, and procreation. Your character will learn that all play and no work is no way to succeed in life.
Virgo	Duty, responsibility, dedication, and service. Your character will have to assess his strengths and weaknesses, and determine what goals he wants to reach.
Libra	Marriages, partnerships, romantic relationships, and friendships. Your character will be forced to cut ties with friends and foes who sabotage his relationships.
Scorpio	Sex, death, and shared resources. Your character won't be allowed to be a passive observer in the drama of life. He'll be forced in as an active participant.
Sagittarius	Higher education, philosophy, and long-distance travel. Your character will be sent packing, ready or not, on a journey of experience.

With Pluto in ...	Your character will be forced to assert his power by taking control of his ...
Capricorn	Career, status, and public recognition. Your character could face public exposure, scandal, or ruin.
Aquarius	Innovation, technology, and visionary thinking. Your character will be cast out of a starry-eyed realm of idealism, and cast headfirst into the down-and-dirty world of everyday existence.
Pisces	Metaphysics, mysticism, and psychic awareness. Your character won't be able to find an escape in drugs, alcohol, or dreams. He'll have to come to terms with earthly reality.

Twenty Questions

1. *Pluto is the god of the underworld—a dark and foreboding realm that most people dread. The underworld is one location, though, where a writer can mine for treasure. Without wasting any time, send one of your characters into an underworld, real or imagined. Force him there against his will.*

2. *Once he's acclimated, give him power. How will he use it?*

3. *Pluto rules the forces of death, destruction, and unavoidable change. Who—or what—has the power to destroy your character? How can you work a character's death and resurrection into your story? It can be literal or figurative.*

4. *Rework the Pluto and Persephone myth, from either character's point of view.*

5. *Has your character had a near-death experience? What happened to him, and what does he remember?*

6. *How does your character face death and deal with his own mortality?*

7. *Who could rescue your character from certain death? How could your character save himself?*

8. *Write about someone who has an obsession with youth, beauty, sexuality, and control.*

9. *Do any of your characters frighten you? Why or why not?*

10. *What's the most frightening thing your character can imagine? How can you turn that fear into a reality, and bump up the intensity of your story?*

11. *Pluto symbolizes power over life-and-death issues. What power does your character hold?*

12. *How does he assert his power?*

13. *How does he manage his power?*

14. *What would he trade in exchange for power? Would he sell his soul to the Devil? How would he negotiate the deal?*

15. *Think back to other stories you've heard about playing cards or gambling with the Devil. What stakes would drive your character to the table? Why would he risk it all?*

16. *How does your character control his temper?*

17. *What has your character lost during the course of his lifetime? Has he lost a valued possession, a much-loved parent or child, or something more intangible, like his sense of self? Develop a character who has lost something irreplaceable.*

18. *How does your character deal with grief—and how does your character react to other people's grief?*

19. *How can you make your character more compelling?*

20. *How will you conclude your story?*

Auxiliary Lights

While the planets are the major players in the drama of the skies, they're not the only heavenly bodies in the cosmic cast of characters.

Asteroids, for example, are planetoids—cosmic boulders—that orbit the Sun between Mars and Jupiter. The first four asteroids to be discovered were named after ancient goddesses: Ceres, the mother; Pallas Athena, the daughter; Juno, the wife and partner; and Vesta, the virgin priestess. The feminine energy of the goddess asteroids provides some balance to the patriarchy of the planets—most of which are decidedly male.

The goddess asteroids were joined, in the 1980s, by Chiron, a comet named after the wounded healer and teacher of the gods.

Astrologers also work with several other key points in the chart that can be just as intriguing for a writer looking for creative inspiration. They include the Black Moon Lilith, a mathematical point in space that illustrates the dark side of female power, as well as the North and South Nodes, which are indicators of past-life karma and current life lessons.

All told, that's good news for writers who want to round out their cast of characters. In the next few pages, you'll learn how you too can add astrology's finer points to round out your creations.

Ceres

The Earth Mother

Earth's increase, foison plenty,
Barns and garners never empty,
Vines and clustering bunches growing,
Plants with goodly burthen bowing;
Spring come to you at the farthest
In the very end of harvest!
Scarcity and want shall shun you;
Ceres' blessing so is on you.

—William Shakespeare, *The Tempest*

The Goddess of Prosperity

Ceres was the goddess of nature and the harvest. For centuries she ensured the prosperity of the earth and the well-being of humankind. She was the goddess of grain and prosperity. In fact, her name is the root of the word cereal, and her glyph is a variant of the harvest sickle.

When her daughter, Proserpina, was kidnapped, however, Ceres' grief almost destroyed the world. Her child's disappearance plunged the world into a long winter of bitter cold and deprivation.

When the story started, Proserpina—the goddess of spring—was a beautiful young woman. She was innocent, carefree, and unaware of the dangers that lurked beneath her feet. When she left her mother's side to pick flowers in a meadow, she was fair game for Pluto, the lord of the underworld. He reached up, pulled her down into his realm, and forced her to become his bride.

As Ceres searched desperately for her lost daughter, life on earth came to a standstill. At that point, Jupiter stepped in. He forced Pluto to relinquish Proserpina—but not before Pluto had tricked the young woman into eating four pomegranate seeds, which condemned her to remain in the underworld forever. After some negotiation, the gods decided that Proserpina would simply be compelled to return to Hades for four months each year—one for each seed she had consumed. The dark goddess Hecate crossed into the underworld to retrieve her, and Proserpina was allowed to spend eight months a year with her mother.

Every winter, when Proserpina is once again lost to the dark and foreboding land of the dead, Ceres grieves and the earth grows cold. But when Proserpina returns, Ceres—and the earth itself—spring back to life.

The Astrology of Ceres ⚵

While the story of Ceres is ostensibly a simple explanation for the seasons, it's more than a story about the cycles of life. There's a deeper message in the myth. It's also a useful marker for understanding the mysteries of life and death, as well as the corresponding emotions of grief and loss.

Ceres also helps us understand the rhythms and milestones of motherhood and parenting. The myth describes the principles of unconditional love, and the blessings of fertility and creativity.

In a horoscope chart, Ceres' placement can provide detailed information about the responsibilities of family life. It pinpoints how parents try to nurture and protect their children. It describes how they deal with the loss of their children's innocence—as well as their own. It also reveals issues of attachment and dependency, as well as separation and rejection.

From a literary standpoint, Ceres offers a compelling look at the dark side of motherhood. Her myth demonstrates how some characters will lash out when they're most grievously wounded.

The glyph for Ceres looks like a harvest sickle.

The Astronomy of Ceres

Asteroids are tiny planetoids orbiting the Sun in a belt between Mars and Jupiter. There are thousands of these cosmic boulders. Some are the size of cars. Others, like Ceres, are huge. In fact, Ceres measures about six hundred miles across—which makes it slightly larger than France.

Ceres was first discovered in 1801. For a time, it was thought to be a planet, but it was demoted in the 1850s. More than 150 years later, that demotion led to another, when scientists compared Ceres to Pluto, and then classified them both as dwarf planets.

Astronomers say that asteroids could be the shattered remains of a larger planet, or simply cosmic debris left over from the creation of the universe. Ceres, however, is its queen: she's the largest asteroid, and she alone is responsible for about a third of the mass in the asteroid belt.

Archetypal Roles

When you create a fictional character based on the myth of Ceres, you'll probably find that she fits into one of several categories:

- The young mother
- The overprotective parent
- The guardian
- The grieving parent
- The wounded warrior
- The vigilante
- The goddess of justice
- The queen of retribution
- Victims of assault, rape, kidnapping
- Prisoners of war

Creative Guidance

Ceres is a goddess most people can understand. Most women have children, and everyone has had a mother. With that being said, it takes almost no imagination to picture a dark mother who punishes those who displease or dishonor her, and rewards those who do.

It's also relatively easy to exaggerate the characteristics of any mother in your story. Don't worry that she won't be believable. When it comes to relationships between parents and children, truth is stranger than fiction.

Twenty Questions

1. *Ceres' story is one of loss and rediscovery. When her daughter was stolen, her sense of safety and security was destroyed, along with her daughter's innocence. How did—or how will—your character lose her innocence?*

2. *Compare one of your character's experiences to Ceres' story. What was the most meaningful possession your character ever lost or misplaced? What did that object represent?*

3. *Has your character ever been the victim of a theft? What was stolen from her?*

4. *How did she react?*

5. *Was her loss recovered? How?*

6. *How did the experience change her?*

7. *Ceres found advice and assistance from other mythic figures in the pantheon of gods. Who will fill that role in your story? Who will witness your character's loss and help her through it?*

8. *Devise a brief scenario in which your character is the victim of a crime. It doesn't need to be a violent crime—although that's certainly an option. You can also consider white-collar crime, organized crime, or a personal, moral, or ethical wrong.*

9. *Now turn the tables and create a storyline in which your character must commit a crime.*

10. *Not every loss in life is as dramatic as Ceres' bereavement. The steady passage of time strips everyone of youth, beauty, and vitality. Those losses are unavoidable, except through an early death. How does your character deal with change?*

11. *How does she cope with the passing of time?*

12. *Describe how your character acknowledges loss, whether it's her own or that of someone she knows.*

13. *How does your character grieve? Does she bury her pain or, like Ceres, lash out at the world? Write a short snippet of dialogue in which your character describes her experience with grief.*

14. *Build a scene or a story based on Elisabeth Kübler-Ross' five stages of grief: denial, anger, bargaining, depression, and acceptance.*

15. *What one thing does your character love more than life itself? What would happen if it were stolen from her?*

16. *What person, place, or principle is central to your character's self-image? How would your character react if she lost it? Try stealing it from her yourself, in the course of your story. What short- and long-term ramifications will result?*

17. *Try to develop a scenario in which your character's loss stems from her own actions. How will she cope with the guilt that results?*

18. *List three lessons your character has learned so far, whether they're life-changing or not.*

19. *List three lessons your character still needs to master.*

20. *Finally, develop the ending to a story in which your character is restored to wholeness after a loss.*

Pallas Athena

Goddess of Wisdom

A royal maiden who reigned beyond the sea:
From sunrise to the sundown no paragon had she.
All boundless as her beauty was her strength was peerless too,
And evil plight hung o'er the knight who dared her love to woo.
For he must try three bouts with her; the whirling spear to fling;
To pitch the massive stone; and then to follow with a spring;
And should he beat in every feat his wooing well has sped,
But he who fails must lose his love, and likewise lose his head.

—Brünhild, in the *Nibelungen*

Justice Is Served

Have you ever had a character spring, fully formed, into your mind's eye? Check her I.D. You're probably dealing with Pallas Athena. She's the warrior goddess who sprang fully formed from the head of Zeus.

Pallas Athena was a warrior queen. She's a female counterpart to Mars, but she was also the goddess of wisdom, justice, and culture.

The Mythic Model

Athena was the daughter of Jupiter and Metis, the guardian of Mercury's wisdom. Jupiter, however, had swallowed Metis to ensure that their unborn child wouldn't threaten his reign.

It didn't work. Athena continued to grow, until finally, Jupiter came down with a pounding headache. The ever-helpful god Hephaestus turned it into a splitting headache. He used an ax to cut Jupiter's head wide open, and Athena was freed.

She bounded into the world, fully grown and dressed for battle. In fact, the glyph for Pallas Athena is a representation of her spear. She was a goddess of wisdom, and she fought for justice and truth.

As the daughter of an immortal, Athena could be in several places at once. She could fly through the air, and she didn't eat, drink, cry, or bleed.

In time, Athena became the patron goddess of Athens, a city she won in a contest with Neptune. The gods decreed that Athens would go to that one who produced the gift most useful to mortals. Neptune created the horse; Athena produced the olive.

Athena advised city leaders. She helped protect her people from outside enemies, as well as anyone who would destroy it from within. She gave men courage and led armies of defense—but she had no sympathy for Mars's savage love of violence and bloodshed. She was efficient and organized, and she helped bring law and order to her people.

As the goddess of justice, Athena was frequently involved in legal decisions—but she was also a goddess of mercy. When the other judges' decisions were split, she usually broke the tie by voting in favor of freeing the accused.

Athena usually had an owl on her shoulder. It became her trademark, and a symbol of her wisdom and intelligence.

It's not clear why Athena also went by the name Pallas Athena. Some say Pallas was a friend of Athena. When Pallas died, Athena honored her by taking her name.

Athena also presided over the useful and ornamental arts, both those of men, such as agriculture and navigation, and those of women, like spinning, weaving, and needlework. She's credited with inventing the flute and the trumpet, the plow, the rake, the ox-yoke, the bridle, the chariot, and the ship. She also made mothers fertile, helped children grow, protected crops from damage, and guided travelers safely over sea and land.

The Astrology of Pallas Athena ⚴

The glyph for Pallas Athena looks like a spear.

Astrologically, Pallas Athena describes how we face the issues of learning, creativity, the arts, politics, healing, alienation from relationships, competition, and the fear of success.

The Astronomy of Pallas Athena

Pallas was the second asteroid to be discovered. It was first spotted in 1802, and it's the third largest in size.

Archetypal Roles

When you create a fictional character based on Athena, she could be:

- A daughter
- A crusader
- A motherless child
- A child without a childhood
- A daughter who derives most of her identity from her father

Creative Guidance

Myth and legends of astrology can serve as a framework for your story—a skeleton that you can flesh out with muscle and skin. You can also turn to myths and legendary events for themes and subplots. You don't have to be blatant. Use a deft hand and a soft touch, and your readers won't know or guess the source.

Twenty Questions

1. *Pallas Athena was a goddess of many gifts. Is your character intellectually gifted, socially savvy, or street smart? What special skills does she possess?*

2. *What useful talent does your character have to offer the world?*

3. *Pallas Athena was born fully grown. Describe several ways in which your character might seem wise beyond her years.*

4. Write about a child who seems like an old soul. What sets that child apart?

5. Athena was the patron goddess of Athens. What city or town does your character like best? Why is that place a good fit for her personality?

6. Pallas Athena was also the goddess of justice. Put your character in a courtroom, either as a claimant, a defendant, or a member of the legal profession. Why is she there?

7. How does she interact with the other players?

8. How does her presence change the courtroom's atmosphere and the course of events?

9. How would your character explain the concept of truth?

10. How would she describe the concept of justice?

11. What injustice would your character fight to correct?

12. Whom might your character feel duty-bound to protect?

13. Pallas Athena was a warrior goddess, willing to fight for humanity. Is your character naturally courageous? Why or why not?

14. Write a scene that forces your character to be courageous—even if she has to fake it.

15. Write a scene in which your character loses her courage and suffers a setback as a result.

16. Give your character a supportive friend or ally who can give her courage.

17. Pallas Athena was prized for her invention of the olive. As you write, remember that necessity is the mother of invention. Give your character an unusual problem, and force her to devise an inventive solution.

18. What contests or prizes has your character won?

19. How did she win them?

20. Give your character a hobby, and then devise an unexpected use for that hobby.

Juno

The Faithful Partner

Penelope, daughter of Icarius, heard his song from her room upstairs, and came down by the great staircase, not alone, but attended by two of her handmaids. When she reached the suitors she stood by one of the bearing posts that supported the roof of the cloisters with a staid maiden on either side of her. She held a veil, moreover, before her face, and was weeping bitterly.

"Phemius," she cried, "you know many another feat of gods and heroes, such as poets love to celebrate. Sing the suitors some one of these, and let them drink their wine in silence, but cease this sad tale, for it breaks my sorrowful heart, and reminds me of my lost husband whom I mourn ever without ceasing."

—Homer, *The Odyssey*

A Jealous Wife

Juno was one of the original literary inspirations. In fact, she was the reason for the Trojan War, which Virgil documented in the *Aeneid* and Homer described in the *Iliad*.

The Mythic Model

Juno was the wife of Jupiter, which made her the queen of the gods. Jupiter was notoriously unfaithful, and while Juno was bitter, jealous, and vindictive, she remained true to her vows. That made her the goddess of marriage and partnership.

Juno's wedding was one of the most auspicious events that ever took place on Mount Olympus. All the gods were present, and the festivities lasted for days.

It didn't take long for Jupiter to prove himself a faithless husband, though. His affair with Leto led to the birth of Apollo, the sun god, and Artemis, goddess of the hunt. His affair with Themis, the goddess of justice, created the three Fates. And after his affair with Metis, Athena sprang fully grown from his head.

Juno's probably not the kind of woman you'd want for a friend—but she would be fun to write about. She was notoriously cruel to anyone who crossed her path, particularly if they happened to be the lovers or children of her unfaithful husband. She routinely tried to kill them all, including Hercules and Dionysus.

Like Jupiter, Juno was the daughter of Saturn and Rhea. According to Homer, she was raised by Oceanus and Tethys, and afterward became the wife of Zeus, without the knowledge of her parents. Later writers add that she, like the other children of Saturn, was swallowed by her father, but afterward restored.

Juno and Jupiter fought constantly. At one point, Juno conspired with Neptune and Athena to put Zeus in chains. Zeus responded by beating her. He even hung her up in the clouds, with her hands chained and two anvils suspended from her feet. When Vulcan tried to help her, Zeus hurled him down from Olympus.

On a more charming note, Juno had a pet peacock, and her lady in waiting was Iris, the goddess of the rainbow.

The Astrology of Juno ⚵

The glyph for Juno looks like her scepter.

In astrology, Juno symbolizes faithful wives and partners, marriage contracts, and binding agreements.

Juno also reveals how your characters will feel about their partners and contractual obligations. She'll describe how they deal with jealousy and rage, as well as power and possessiveness. Juno colors romance and receptivity, along with mutual trust and security.

The Astronomy of Juno

The asteroid Juno was discovered in 1804. It was the third asteroid to be revealed, and it's the ninth largest in size.

Archetypal Roles

As a fictional character, Juno can play any number of wifely roles:

- A faithful partner
- A devoted wife
- A cheated spouse
- A vengeful woman
- An abused wife
- A murderous mate

Creative Guidance

How do your characters measure up?

The hero of your story—your protagonist—should be fully rounded and developed, like a three-dimensional character. To ensure that he has a worthy challenger, his opponent—the antagonist—should be just as well developed.

Your supporting players, however, can be flat and two-dimensional. You can draw them with bold strokes, and imbue them with exaggerated characteristics. They might surprise you—and occasionally, they might even upstage the stars—just enough to brighten the story for a moment or two.

Twenty Questions

1. *Juno was a jealous guardian of her marriage—her most treasured relationship. What does your character guard with her life?*

2. *What does she wish she possessed?*

3. *Conversely, which possessions would she like to rid herself of?*

4. *Despite her jealous rages and hostile personality—or, perhaps, because of them—Juno was worshipped as the goddess of marriage and partnership. Has your character ever been married?*

5. *Describe her wedding—and then describe her marriage. What did the wedding ceremony say about her relationship? What did it signal about the eventual course of the marriage?*

6. *Juno's husband was notoriously unfaithful. How has your character been betrayed?*

7. How does your character betray others?

8. How might she betray herself?

9. How would your character react if her betrayal were exposed?

10. How does your character feel about commitment? Does she fear it or yearn for it? Why?

11. Juno didn't hesitate to punish those who crossed her. Describe your character's dark side, and include an example that illustrates it.

12. Write a scene that forces your character to be cruel.

13. Devise a scenario in which your character is the victim of cruelty.

14. Write a scenario in which your character would seriously injure someone else.

15. Write a scene in which your character must kill. What consequences will follow?

16. Develop a scene in which your character is punished for her wrongdoing.

17. What would your character consider to be an unforgivable offense?

18. How does your character seek vengeance or retaliation?

19. What's the worst mistake your character ever made?

20. Describe something your character feels guilty about.

Vesta

Goddess of Hearth and Home, the Temple Virgin

I can live alone, if self-respect, and circumstances require me so to do. I need not sell my soul to buy bliss. I have an inward treasure born with me, which can keep me alive if all extraneous delights should be withheld, or offered only at a price I cannot afford to give.

—Charlotte Bronte, *Jane Eyre*

The Mythic Model

Vesta just called—and she'd like you to write a chick lit story about her.

Vesta is the prototype of the strong single woman. Like so many gods and goddesses in the Greek and Roman pantheons, she was the daughter of Saturn and Rhea. According to the earliest myths and legends, however, she was Saturn's firstborn, so she was also the first child he consumed. For the rest of her life, she would continue to take a leading role in community life and culture.

Vesta was the guardian of the hearth and the keeper of the sacred flame. Her name means "essence" and "fire," and she was a central figure in everyday life and worship.

Every home in Rome kept a fire lit in her honor, all the time. In that capacity, as the guardian of hearth and home, she was the goddess of domesticity and devotion. When babies were born, parents prayed to her to bless each child and keep them safe. Whenever there was a sacrifice, Vesta got the first share.

Small communities are often like extended families, so the ancient cities all had a sacred hearth devoted to Vesta, too. Supplicants would go to Vesta's temple whenever they wanted to implore her protection or find sanctuary in her grace. When new communities were established, they would carry a spark from her sacred flame from their previous home.

Vesta was beautiful, of course, but when Apollo and Neptune both asked for her hand, she swore by the head of Jupiter to remain a virgin forever.

In each temple dedicated to Vesta, six vestal virgins served as priestesses. They wore white robes and veils, and it was their duty to keep her sacred flame alive, to offer sacrifices, and to pray for the protection of her people. The vestal virgins were chosen as children, and they were sworn to remain chaste and serve for thirty years.

The Astrology of Vesta ⚶

The glyph for Vesta looks like a flame.

Vesta's position in a horoscope chart will reveal your character's work and devotion—which are very similar to Virgo traits. Its position will show you how your characters integrate a sense of duty with their sense of self. Vesta offers insight into isolation and intimacy, as well as alienation, sacrifice, and sacred sexuality.

Vesta symbolizes how your characters will give themselves to others. Her placement will reveal how they offer hospitality to strangers, and how they guard their most precious possessions.

The Astronomy of Vesta

Vesta is the second-largest asteroid. It was the fourth to be discovered, and it's the second largest in size.

In keeping with its mythical role as the keeper of the sacred flame, Vesta is also the brightest asteroid. When the conditions are just right, you can actually see it with your own eyes.

Archetypal Roles

Vesta can help keep your story burning, by playing a wide range of single women. Vesta can be the model for:

- A virginal young woman
- An innocent maiden
- A priestess
- A nun
- A career woman
- A charity worker
- A saint
- A shy, reserved, and colorless creature
- A sacrificial lamb
- A stranger
- A loner
- A servant
- The keeper of a sacred flame

Creative Guidance

Vesta's temples and altars have become key components of her myth. In fact, it's almost impossible to imagine Vesta anywhere but in a temple. The association could inspire you to experiment with the settings that correspond to your characters. What scenery is an essential part of your characters' existence? What backdrop is familiar to them, and what props do they need to function? More importantly, what will happen to them if—and when—they find themselves in new surroundings?

Twenty Questions

1. *What does your character believe is holy?*
2. *What secret does she guard?*
3. *Whom does she protect?*
4. *What sacred fire burns within her?*
5. *Describe her closest circle of friends.*
6. *What part of your character is sacred and pure?*
7. *What does she pray for—and to whom does she pray?*
8. *What is she devoted to?*

9. In what way does she feel isolated?

10. How does she give of herself to others?

11. How does she show her devotion?

12. What sacrifices has she made?

13. What services does she perform for others?

14. What was she trained to do as a child?

15. What expectations did her family have for her?

16. What color of clothing does she prefer? Why? Does that color hold special significance?

17. Is your character a virgin? If not, how did she lose her virginity?

18. Imagine a scenario in which your character sits by a fire. What does she see? What does she think about?

19. What does your character still have from her childhood home?

20. What would your character save if her home were on fire?

The Black Moon Lilith

The Woman Scorned

I saw that the bride within the bridal dress had withered like the dress, and like the flowers, and had no brightness left but the brightness of her sunken eyes. I saw that the dress had been put upon the rounded figure of a young woman, and that the figure upon which it now hung loose, had shrunk to skin and bone.

—Charles Dickens, *Great Expectations*

She-Devil

For 5,000 years, Lilith has lingered in the shadows of myth and history. She's one of the most fascinating characters in story or astrology.

The Mythic Model

Obviously, Lilith is a dark goddess. In the best-known version of her story, Lilith was Adam's first wife, created at the same time and in the same place in the Garden of Eden. They were equals—but Adam insisted that she submit to his demands.

Lilith refused. Instead, she spoke the secret name of God, sprouted wings, and fled into exile in a Sumerian cave, somewhere along the shores of the Red Sea.

Once Lilith had established a home of her own, far from her former husband, she became her own woman. She turned her back on the life that had been preordained for her, mated freely with monsters and fiends, and gave birth to hundreds of demon children a day.

Adam complained bitterly about his fate. God sent angels to retrieve her, but Lilith refused to return. Adam was forced to accept a second wife—one who was not his equal, but who was torn from his side.

At that point, Lilith was demonized by the husband and the civilization she had rejected. When her children were condemned to death, Lilith killed them herself.

In later retellings of the myth, Lilith was portrayed as a vengeful succubus who sapped men of their strength while they slept and murdered other women's children in their cribs. Some even say she became the mother of all vampires. According to one version of the story, Lilith and Adam had a child together: Cain, the cursed. When Cain murdered his brother, Abel, he found refuge at Lilith's side, and the two of them established a race of the living dead.

For centuries, Lilith has been maligned as a monster, a witch, and a whore. Contemporary analysts, however, see a compelling second storyline in her myth—that of a strong-willed, independent woman, willing to take any steps necessary to ensure her own survival.

Both viewpoints come into play when we examine Lilith's place in astrology.

The Astrology of the Black Moon Lilith ⚸

The Black Moon Lilith symbolizes personal power—especially in a world that sometimes seems determined to crush individuality, creativity, and personal expression.

Lilith refuses to be repressed, contained, or managed. She rejects limitations, conditions, or expectations imposed by outside forces, whether they happen to be friends, family members, or authority figures.

Lilith demands the freedom to express herself creatively—and she insists on the corresponding freedom to control her own creations. She would rather destroy what she loves than have it used, abused, stolen, or misappropriated by someone else.

Lilith can't be convinced or cajoled to get with the program, go with the flow, or go along to get along. She draws a line in the Mesopotamian sands of time. There is no room for negotiation when Lilith is involved; she's the final authority on matters that pertain to her own life and existence.

The Astronomy of Lilith

The Black Moon Lilith isn't a point of light in the sky, like the Moon, or a center of gravity, like the earth. The Black Moon Lilith isn't a tangible cosmic body at all. Instead, the Black Moon Lilith is a ghost moon—an ethereal, mathematical point on a horoscope chart, derived from the real Moon's position in the sky.

In simple terms, the Moon moves around the earth in an elliptical pattern—so when you see it diagrammed, the earth looks off-center. The Black Moon Lilith fills the void that's left—and in the process, the Black Moon Lilith symbolizes the nature of spirit caught in the web of a physical universe.

For a time, some astrologers were actively engaged in speculation about a hypothetical "Dark Moon" that could be spotted only rarely in the dark night sky. As it turns out, the earliest reports of a Dark Moon Lilith were based on a flawed telescope lens back in the 1700s.

Today, the Black Moon Lilith is a focal point for the study of personal power. She represents the deepest, darkest mysteries of physical existence, and of a soul that's trapped in a material world.

Archetypal Roles

The Black Moon Lilith can be the model for:

- The woman scorned
- The wild woman
- The demon
- The Wrath
- The Destroyer
- The enraged feminist
- The bitch
- The banshee

Creative Guidance

Think about the angriest woman you know. What made her that way? Would telling her story put her rage in context? You might find that you become more sympathetic—or that you simply generate more material for a character based on Lilith.

Twenty Questions

1. Try to incorporate elements of the Lilith myth into one of your characters. Start by picturing the angriest woman you can imagine. (She might be based on someone you know in real life.)

2. What—or who—made her so angry?

3. How does she demonstrate that anger? Is it publicly visible, or simmering beneath the surface?

4. What was she like before she was angered?

5. What was her life like then?

6. Does your character repress her emotions, or express them openly? Describe one example of how she makes her feelings known, either covertly or overtly.

7. How do other people treat your character?

8. How does your character treat other people?

9. How does your character approach partnerships?

10. How does she feel about love and marriage?

11. How does your character demonstrate her personal power?

12. What is one thing your character refuses to do?

13. Describe a simple, everyday way in which your character demonstrates control of her life.

14. How has your character been demonized?

15. How has your character been marginalized?

16. How has your character been maligned?

17. How could your character seek revenge?

18. Imagine a scenario in which your character could be forced into exile.

19. Imagine a scene in which your character isolates herself.

20. How could you bring her back into the fold?

Chiron

The Wounded Healer

When Mary Lennox was sent to Misselthwaite Manor to live with her uncle everybody said she was the most disagreeable-looking child ever seen. It was true, too. She had a little thin face and a little thin body, thin light hair and a sour expression. Her hair was yellow, and her face was yellow because she had been born in India and had always been ill in one way or another. Her father had held a position under the English Government and had always been busy and ill himself, and her mother had been a great beauty who cared only to go to parties and amuse herself with gay people. She had not wanted a little girl at all, and when Mary was born she handed her over to the care of an Ayah, who was made to understand that if she wished to please the Mem Sahib she must keep the child out of sight as much as possible. So when she was a sickly, fretful, ugly little baby she was kept out of the way, and when she became a sickly, fretful, toddling thing she was kept out of the way also.

—Frances Hodgson Burnett, *The Secret Garden*

The Key to Wisdom

In the cosmic drama of the skies, Chiron is a mentor and a guide. He can lead your characters to greatness, if they'll only follow his advice.

The Master Teacher

Chiron, the wounded healer of myth and legend, learned his lessons the hard way.

Chiron was a centaur—half-human, half-horse. He was a magical blend of man and beast, so he symbolized spirit and intelligence in animal form.

The Mythic Model

Chiron was the son of Saturn and Philyra. He lived on Mount Pelion, and he learned the art of divination from Apollo and the skill of hunting from Diana. In turn, he served as a teacher to the ancient Greeks and Romans. He taught Jason, Achilles, and the legendary hero Hercules. When Hercules accidentally shot him with a poisoned arrow, however, Chiron's immortal essence condemned him to suffering without end. As Chiron sought relief for his crippling injuries, he accumulated a vast store of medical knowledge. He shared that wisdom with others, which led to his legendary reputation as a wounded healer. Eventually, the gods took pity on Chiron's suffering. He was allowed to give his immortality to Prometheus, who had stolen fire from the gods, and Zeus placed Chiron among the stars as Sagittarius.

The Astrology of Chiron ⚷

Modern astrologers look to Chiron for information about the wounded healer that resides in every person's horoscope chart, along with corresponding efforts toward healing and recovery. Its position often reveals a karmic wound that can be almost impossible to heal.

Astrologers think of Chiron as a bridge between the inner and outer planets. It serves to connect the known and unknown, and helps us cross from sickness into health.

The glyph for Chiron looks like a key.

The Astronomy of Chiron

In astronomy, Chiron is a comet with a unique and erratic orbit. It travels between Saturn and Uranus, and occasionally crosses into Jupiter's orbit.

Chiron takes more than 51 years to orbit the Sun. At that time, when it returns to its original position in our birth charts, most people experience some sort of midlife crisis. As they face the old age and mortality of their parents, they also recognize that their own children are adults now, too. It's a good time to come to terms with life, to forgive their parents, and to release the dreams they had for their own children so that everyone can get on with their lives.

Archetypal Roles

Chiron is one of the greatest archetypal figures of all time. He lends himself to characterization as a:

- Teacher
- Tutor
- Professor
- Healer
- Caregiver

Creative Guidance

Everyone has some sort of physical weakness, whether it was inherited at birth or is the remnant of an old injury. Find a way to demonstrate the physical weakness of your character. Give him a limp, a stutter, or an obvious disability. Then go a step further, and connect it to a deeper meaning, on a spiritual, emotional, or psychological level. Someone whose feet hurt all the time, for example, may have issues with feeling safe and grounded; he lacks a foundation, or a solid footing. Someone with a sore throat might be afraid to speak.

You can also use hidden disabilities to demonstrate emotional frailties. Does your character hesitate to cross the street? Obsessively wash his hands or check the lock on the door? Stare longingly at the phone or the street outside his window? What do those symptoms suggest about your character's psychological makeup?

Twenty Questions

1. *If your character were a magical meld of man and beast, what would it be? Include some of those animal characteristics in your description.*

2. *Chiron was one of mythology's most heralded instructors. Even the gods trusted him to train their children. Who was your best teacher—and how could you incorporate him or her into one of your stories? You might want to consider casting your favorite teacher as a mentor or a guide for one of your characters.*

3. *Alternately, work on some backstory for one of the characters you're developing. Who was his best teacher? What lessons did your character learn from that teacher, and why were they important?*

4. *What lessons does your character teach others?*

5. *Chiron suffered for years from a wound that was inflicted by one of his students. What's the deepest wound your character has suffered?*

6. *How has he tried to heal those wounds? Has he sought professional help, or has he tried to self-medicate?*

7. *What has he learned from his injuries?*

8. *What is your character's physical weakness? How will that play into the story?*

9. *Send your character to a doctor, a clinic, or a hospital. How is he treated, and how does he treat those who try to help him?*

10. *Now send your character in search of alternative healing. Describe the experience.*

11. *Imagine a scenario in which your character is gravely wounded, or devise a storyline in which your character falls desperately ill.*

12. *Imagine a scene in which your character hurts himself.*

13. *Describe the symbolic significance of his illness or injury. A sore throat, for example, could illustrate your character's unwillingness to speak up for himself, or chest pains could suggest a broken heart.*

14. *Why might your character resist getting well?*

15. *What are your character's weaknesses and limitations?*

16. *What purpose do they serve?*

17. *How will they play into the story?*

18. *Devise a scenario in which your character tries to hide his weaknesses.*

19. *How can you turn his weaknesses into strengths?*

20. *The gods gave Chiron a place of honor in the skies at the end of his days. How would your character like to be remembered?*

Behind the Scenes: A Planetary Casting Call

It's possible to develop an entire cast of characters based solely on planetary archetypes. Take, for example, Shakespeare's *Macbeth*. It's easy to imagine how the players could fall neatly into orbit.

The Sun: While Macbeth is the star of the show, he's a tragic hero—a bloodthirsty, ambitious general who murders King Duncan in pursuit of power. In the process, he seals his own doom.

The Moon: Lady Macbeth is her husband's partner in crime. Her involvement in Macbeth's misdeeds illustrates the dark side of the Moon. She spurs her husband to kill King Duncan—and when he fails to follow through with the conclusion of their plan, she finishes the job herself. Eventually, her involvement in the treacherous crime drives her mad. She sleepwalks by moonlight, and in one of the most famous dramatic scenes of all time, she tries desperately to wash the blood from her hands, crying, "Out, damned spot!"

Mercury: Three witches open the show by telling Macbeth that he will be king, and that Banquo, Macbeth's traveling companion, will sire future kings. Like Mercury, the messenger of the gods, the three witches can move easily between this world and the next. They also have a trickster aspect: they deliberately leave their predictions open to interpretation, which fools Macbeth into a false sense of security.

Venus: Lady Macduff, the wife of the Thane of Fife, is a devoted wife and mother—the epitome of love and beauty. Macduff, however, suspects Macbeth of treachery. Macbeth seeks to quiet him by killing his family. In a gruesome scene, Lady Macduff and her children are viciously slaughtered—and Macduff becomes a ruthless warrior determined to seek revenge.

Mars: Like Mars, the god of war, Macduff ultimately kills and beheads Macbeth.

Jupiter: Macbeth's first victim, the good King Duncan, embodies Jupiterian justice and moral order. His murder leads to chaos and destruction.

Saturn: When Macbeth murders King Duncan, the king's son Malcolm raises an army to overthrow Macbeth and restore order and control—two hallmarks of Saturn's rule.

Uranus: The planet of the unusual and the unexpected describes two of the prophecies that are Macbeth's undoing. The three witches told Macbeth that he would reign until Birnam Wood came to him in Dunsinane, and that no man of woman born could kill him. As it happened, Malcolm's soldiers camouflaged themselves with branches from Birnam Wood, and Macduff wasn't born from a woman, per se—he was born by Caesarian section.

Neptune: Shortly after the play begins, Macbeth and Lady Macbeth ply the king's guards with alcohol. When they pass out, Macbeth kills the king. Lady Macbeth takes the plot a step further: she leaves the bloody daggers with the guards, so they'll be blamed for the murder. Neptune is often linked to the negative effects of alcohol and drugs.

Pluto: Pluto's heavy hand is everywhere in the Scottish play, but the planet of death and destruction is best personified by Banquo—Macbeth's traveling companion. Banquo and Macbeth are together at the start of the show, when they meet the three witches. When the witches tell Banquo that he'll beget a line of kings, Macbeth starts to see him as a threat to his own ambition. Macbeth has Banquo killed—but Banquo's ghost returns to haunt Macbeth, and presage Macbeth's own downfall.

Behind the Scenes:
Astrology and Anatomy

When you're creating and describing your characters, remember that each sign of the zodiac rules part of the body, starting with Aries at the head and moving sequentially through all twelve signs to Pisces at the feet.

Aries—the head

Taurus—the neck and throat

Gemini—the twin embrace of the shoulders, arms, and hands

Cancer—the breasts and stomach

Leo—the heart and spine

Virgo—the nervous and digestive systems

Libra—the kidneys and lower back

Scorpio—the reproductive organs

Sagittarius—the hips and thighs

Capricorn—the skeleton and joints, particularly the knees

Aquarius—the shins

Pisces—the feet

Behind the Scenes: Generational Planets

Uranus, Neptune, and Pluto are generational planets, and they signify traits and characteristics that are common to entire age groups. That can be a useful tool for writers who are looking for insight into the politics and culture of a generation.

The three planets are at the fringe of our solar system. They have long-ranging orbits around the Sun, which means they don't change signs very often.

In the descriptions that follow, you might notice some inconsistencies in the dates that mark each planet's progress through the signs. That's because planets don't always move smoothly from one sign to another. Their orbits aren't steady and unswerving. In fact, from our perspective on Earth, planets often seem to cross tentatively into a sign, reconsider, and then back up for a short period of time. If you're dealing with a date that falls close to a transition point, you can always check an ephemeris—a table of planetary positions, online or in print—to determine a planet's exact placement in the sky.

Uranus

Uranus was discovered in 1781, shortly after the telescope was invented. The planet's discovery coincided with giant leaps forward in technology, along with radical change and revolution in the world's political landscape.

It's no coincidence that scientific innovation and political upheaval are closely connected. People who are fighting for their survival tend to devote all of their resources to new weapons and life-saving devices.

Uranus has an orbit of 84 years, which means it lingers in each sign of the zodiac for about 7 years. During each passage, it describes a generation's vision of freedom and change.

Uranus in Aries: (1927–1935) When Uranus traveled through Aries, the sign of leadership and initiation, its movement marked a crisis in the global economy. The Roaring Twenties came to a shocking end when the stock market crashed, and the Depression forced the United States into rugged self-sufficiency and global isolationism.

Uranus in Taurus: (1934–1942) Uranus reversed the downfall of the Depression when it moved into Taurus, the sign of stability, comfort, and security. In the United States, the New Deal promised a new path to stability and comfort. Unfortunately, Uranus's course through Taurus also marked the start of World War II, which forced Americans to deal with threats to their national security.

Uranus in Gemini: (1941–1949) When Uranus passed through Gemini, the sign of thought and communication, the study of psychology and sociology experienced a radical growth and transformation. Uranus also happened to be in Gemini during the start of the American Revolution, Lincoln's election, and the Civil War.

Uranus in Cancer: (1948–1956) Cancer is the sign of home and family life. When Uranus was in Cancer, America's post-war generation created a new, suburban way of life, focused on raising their Baby Boom offspring, watching a new invention called television, and eating precooked, factory-prepared TV dinners.

Uranus in Leo: (1955–1962) The television revolution changed everything in the worlds of entertainment and sports—both of which fall in Leo's realm. People expected to be entertained in their own domains, and celebrities and sports stars alike had to change their game plan.

Uranus in Virgo: (1961–1968) Uranus's passage through practical Virgo led to a series of improvements and inventions in cooking, cleaning, clothing, and personal care. Women stopped ironing, for example, and started dressing their families in permanent-press polyester.

Uranus in Libra: (1968–1975) Libra is the sign of marriage and partnership—so when rebellious Uranus passed through the sign, divorce rates skyrocketed, sex was freed from the bounds of marriage, and alternative lifestyles became more widely accepted.

Uranus in Scorpio: (1975–1981) When Uranus moved through mysterious Scorpio, the New Age took shape. Astrology became hugely popular for the first time in centuries. Entertainment technology also started being geared for private use. The Walkman was introduced, video games came home, and computers became more powerful and more manageable.

Uranus in Sagittarius: (1981–1988) We didn't know it at the time, but when Uranus was in far-reaching Sagittarius, university scientists were starting to weave the World Wide Web. Most of us were distracted by the escalation—and the eventual resolution—of a global arms race.

Uranus in Capricorn: (1988–1996) When Uranus was in Capricorn, the sign of business and convention, traditional values and conservative politics experienced a popular resurgence.

Uranus in Aquarius: (1995–2002) Uranus rules cultural innovation and scientific technology. The planet's passage through its own sign heralded the birth of the Internet and the arrival of affordable home computers.

Uranus in Pisces: (2002–2009) Pisces is the most mystical sign. Uranus's passage through Pisces prompted changes in spiritual beliefs, religion, and morals. Uranus also moved through Pisces from 1919 through 1927, a period marked by Prohibition, speakeasies, and the Roaring Twenties.

Neptune

Neptune was discovered in 1846, as a result of scientific theory and mathematical calculation. Astronomers knew it existed, because something was exerting a gravitational pull on the orbit of Uranus.

Because its presence was felt before it was seen, Neptune symbolizes the hidden realities of existence. Astrologically speaking, Neptune describes how generational groups experience and share their spiritual views.

Neptune has an orbit of 165 years. As you think about Neptune's place in your stories, consider the boundaries it has dissolved throughout history.

Neptune in Aries: (1862–1875) Neptune's passage through Aries marked pioneering efforts in chemistry, pharmaceuticals, and spiritualism.

Neptune in Taurus: (1875–1889) Neptune in Taurus marked an emphasis on physical growth and expansion. Millions of people emigrated to the United States and pushed west, in an effort to fulfill their destiny and live their dreams.

Neptune in Gemini: (1889–1902) Neptune, the planet of Hollywood glamour, moved into the sign of communication and started making movies.

Neptune in Cancer: (1902–1915) Neptune boosted an entire generation's sense of intuition and imagination when it moved into nurturing Cancer.

Neptune in Leo: (1915–1929) When Neptune was in Leo, everyone was a star. People lived vicariously through radio shows and Saturday-night movies. They set out to experience the same emotions first-hand, dancing their way through the Roaring Twenties and defying Prohibition.

Neptune in Virgo: (1928–1943) Reality came crashing down when Neptune passed through earthy Virgo. The stock market crashed, the Depression led to World War II, and families were forced to deal with the fundamental task of keeping body and soul together.

Neptune in Libra: (1942–1956) When Neptune was in Libra, the sign of the scales, people tried to put the world's battles behind them, and find beauty and balance in the simple pleasures of life.

Neptune in Scorpio: (1956–1970) Scorpio is fascinated with the dark mysteries of life—sex, and death, and other people's money. When Neptune moved through Scorpio, an entire generation began to explore sex, drugs, and rock and roll.

Neptune in Sagittarius: (1970–1984) In Sagittarius, Neptune continued its quest for higher learning by experiencing alternate realities—which caught the attention of politicians and preachers who wanted to regulate the journey.

Neptune in Capricorn: (1984–1998) Neptune is the planet of illusion. It dissolves boundaries and casts a shadowy veil over reality. Neptune's passage through Capricorn, the sign of business and finance, led to confusion in the world of commerce and capitalism.

Neptune in Aquarius: (1998–2012) In Aquarius, Neptune inspires a sense of spiritual connection and awakening.

Neptune in Pisces: (2012–2024) Neptune rules Pisces, the watery realm of the collective unconscious. As it passes through this sign, it will swim in dreamy visions of peace, love, and understanding.

Pluto

Pluto is our newest planet—or, if you subscribe to its scientific definition, Pluto is one of our newest planetoids.

Pluto was discovered in 1930, during a period of unprecedented war and upheaval. Metaphorically speaking, Pluto dropped a bomb in our lap; the faraway world was discovered at the same time people started to stockpile weapons of mass destruction that had the power to destroy our own planet.

Pluto is the farthest planet from the Sun, with an orbit of 248 years. Because that orbit is elliptical and erratic, Pluto's passage through each sign is anything but consistent.

Compare these Plutonian passages to the characters and time periods you write about:

Pluto in Aries: (1822–1852) Pluto stimulated pioneering ideas in the world of scientific theory and practice.

Pluto in Taurus: (1852–1883) Pluto changed how people thought about money, property, and power. Marx developed his communist political theory and economic philosophy.

Pluto in Gemini: (1883–1914) Pluto transformed the world of communication through telegraphs, telephones, newspapers, photography, and recorded music.

Pluto in Cancer: (1914–1938) Pluto changed the mood of the public, by shifting attention from the underworld of the Mafia to the underlying instability of the world economy and global politics.

Pluto in Leo: (1938–1957) Pluto's weapons of war trickled down, by delivering tools and technology that transformed awareness and communication. An entire generation slowly realized that they had the power to change the world, both individually and collectively.

Pluto in Virgo: (1956–1972) Pluto revolutionized medical science and technology. For the first time in history, immunizations and vaccines could ward off mass casualties, and transplant technology could extend life even in the face of certain death.

Pluto in Libra: (1971–1984) Pluto transformed family law and international diplomacy, and unified the people of the world through shared music, movies, and television drama.

Pluto in Scorpio: (1983–1995) Pluto's passage through Scorpio marked shocking developments in our obsession with sex and death. As the Cold War ended, Pluto dispatched a new plague, AIDS, to take the atom bomb's place in our litany of nightmares and fears.

Pluto in Sagittarius: (1995–2009) When Pluto passed through the sign of long-distance travel and higher education, it found a way to unite the world, by connecting everyone on the web.

Pluto in Capricorn: (2009–present) Pluto's entry into Capricorn marked an ongoing period of economic crises, political shakeups, corporate restructuring, and global revolutions.

Creative Guidance

While the generational planets can lend a touch of authenticity to your work, it's important to remember that you can mix and match the planets and signs to create characters that are believable and true to life. What's more, the signs provide a focus for your characters' drives and desires— which leads to plot and story development.

Planets in Aspect

Planets, like people, cross paths—and their geometric aspects in the houses of the horoscope can be a creative way to visualize relationships on terra firma, too. It's just another way that astrological terminology crosses over into real-life language.

You don't have to master the art of studying aspects, which involves seeing points on paper in terms of their spatial relationships to each other. After all, everyone knows that writers hate math.

Instead, think about how people relate to one another. Those who have nothing in common tend to square off. Those with diametrically opposed worldviews oppose each other. People who share the same viewpoint work in conjunction.

While some aspects don't have easy literary counterparts in simple language terms, you'll recognize their relationships.

Ptolemaic Aspects

Astrologers have been using five basic aspects since Claudius Ptolemy described them in the first century A.D.

☌ *Conjunction 0°*

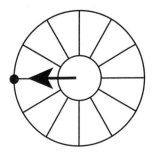

Planets in conjunction share the same position in a chart. As a result, they share a common focus and viewpoint. In most cases, each strengthens the other. They operate, in effect, as a powerful combined force.

Two characters who operate in conjunction might be lovers, partners, or best friends.

✶ *Sextile 60°*

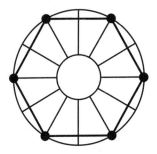

Planets in sextile are separated by 60 degrees. As a result, they'll share the same polarity—masculine or feminine—but they'll have different elements. They'll also have different modes. Some will be cardinal leaders, others will be fixed maintainers, and the rest will be flexible and mutable.

Even so, planets in sextile are comfortable with each other. When you think of sextiles, think of clubs and collections of close friends—like a group of women that get together for girls' night out.

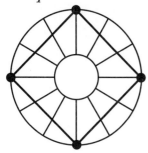

Any two planets that square off in a chart are 90 degrees apart. This aspect can be troublesome, because the planets work at cross-purposes. While they share the same modality—cardinal, fixed, or mutable—each has a different polarity. One will be masculine and active, while the other will be feminine and receptive. Their energy will be different, too, since they'll embody different elements of fire, earth, air, or water.

This is the aspect to think of when you're creating characters who rub each other the wrong way. They'll never see the world alike, and they'll never be able to come to a mutual understanding or agreement.

△ *Trine 120°*

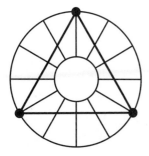

The trine is an easy combination in which two planets are 120 degrees apart. The planets share the same congenial element—fire, earth, air, or water—so their energy flows freely back and forth.

This is the aspect to think of when you picture teammates or collegial work associates.

☍ *Opposition 180°*

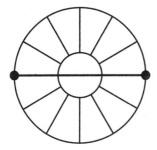

Two planets in opposition to each other are 180 degrees apart. That might seem confrontational, but there's also plenty of room for communication and agreement, because each has a clear view of the other's position.

Planets in opposition also share the same modality—cardinal, fixed, or mutable—and masculine or feminine polarity, which makes them both either active or receptive. You might think they'd never get along, but opposites attract. You won't be surprised to learn, however, that a relationship that's rooted in opposition can often be described as a love-hate relationship.

Interplanetary Communication

Any connection between planets, no matter what form it takes, is important. Here's how planetary contact typically plays out in a horoscope chart.

- The Sun can energize a fellow traveler—or overshadow him. The Sun tends to highlight and personalize everything it touches.
- The Moon's reflective and emotional energy helps other planets recognize their innermost feelings, connect to friends and family members, and boost their intuition. The Moon adds emotional depth and lends a compassionate ear.
- Mercury, the planet of speed and communication, can kick events into motion, deliver messages, and provoke thought and discussion. Mercury adds intellect, speed, and communication to everything it touches.

- Venus, the planet of love and attraction, enhances the beauty, charm, and creativity of every planet she graces with her touch.
- Mars, the warrior planet, sounds a call to action. It can be a battle cry, or a physical release through sexual or athletic conquest. Mars adds intensity, energy, and drive to every other planet it tackles.
- Planets that brush up against Jupiter, the Greater Benefic, find that their energy is magnified. They become more visionary, more philosophical, and more influential.
- Saturn is the planet of structure, boundaries, and foundations. When Saturn bumps into another planet, it starts building fences and imposing order.
- Uranus's impact is always unorthodox. Its contact with other planets invites innovation, revolution, and rebellion. It almost always disrupts or overturns the other planet's usual outlook and methodology.
- Neptune, the nebulous planet of glamour and illusion, dissolves boundaries. Neptune can shift another planet's viewpoint, and replace clarity of thought with a hazy view of reality.
- Pluto, the god of transformation, breaks other planets down. It destroys them so they can be remade and reborn, better than they were before.

Twenty Questions

1. *Use planetary strengths and weaknesses to describe your characters' strengths—and their tragic flaws.*
2. *Combine the strengths and weaknesses of two or three planets to create a character with built-in personality conflicts.*
3. *Write a character sketch based on two planets or two signs. Combine the fiery intensity of the Sun with the passion of Mars, for example, or the curiosity of Gemini with the mysticism of Neptune.*

4. *Traditionally, planets are either masculine or feminine. Use that association to write about a female planet as a male character, and vice versa.*

5. *Think about the symbolism of opposing planets, and stage a battle between good and evil—either internal or external. The battle could be waged in a character's mind, or it could unfold in his interactions with others.*

6. *Pit two planets against each other, and record their interaction. They'll probably argue—but how will they defend their positions?*

7. *When they've exhausted their arguments, write a scene in which they reconcile.*

8. *If the planets are more than platonic, turn their reconciliation into a romance. Send them out to dinner—or into bed. You can use aspects as indicators of attraction.*

9. *You could also use opposing planets as inspiration for a story about a love-hate relationship.*

10. *Write a scene in which your character doesn't say a word, but communicates through movement and action, just as planets quietly move through their orbits.*

11. *Conjoined planets share the same position in a horoscope chart— which means, from our perspective, they share the same place in the sky. Write about two characters who are alike enough to be twins, but devise a scene in which they drive each other crazy.*

12. *Use the symbolism of the square to describe two characters who simply rub each other the wrong way.*

13. *Planets in sextile share the same polarity—either masculine or feminine. Write about a friendship between two men or two women.*

14. *The trine is an easygoing combination shared by planets of the same element. Write about two people who seem to click the moment they meet.*

15. *Alternately, force two characters who have nothing in common to spend an afternoon together.*

16. *Use the imagery of a sextile or a trine to write about a group of co-workers who meet to socialize after hours.*

17. *Write about your character's relationship with his or her employer.*

18. *Play the party game "Two truths and a lie" with your planets. Get your characters to lie convincingly about themselves by mixing truths, believable half-truths, and outright falsehoods.*

19. *Planets are larger than life. Your characters can be, too. What mythical story has become interwoven with each character's own experience? Look for links to legendary figures from literature and from life, based on their names and personal stories.*

20. *Try to visualize your characters based on their planetary characteristics. Draw them as you see them in your mind. Alternately, look for images in magazines, art books, or museum galleries.*

Behind the Scenes:
The Seven Ages of Man

As you work to integrate the planets into the lives of your characters, consider how writers and philosophers have been linking the planets with the human lifespan for centuries. Shakespeare, for example, used the analogy in *As You Like It*:

> *All the world's a stage,*
> *And all the men and women merely players:*
> *They have their exits and their entrances;*
> *And one man in his time plays many parts,*
> *His acts being seven ages. At first, the infant,*
> *Mewling and puking in the nurse's arms.*
> *And then the whining school-boy, with his satchel*
> *And shining morning face, creeping like snail*
> *Unwillingly to school. And then the lover,*
> *Sighing like furnace, with a woeful ballad*
> *Made to his mistress' eyebrow. Then a soldier,*
> *Full of strange oaths and bearded like the pard,*
> *Jealous in honour, sudden and quick in quarrel,*
> *Seeking the bubble reputation*
> *Even in the cannon's mouth. And then the justice,*
> *In fair round belly with good capon lined,*
> *With eyes severe and beard of formal cut,*
> *Full of wise saws and modern instances;*
> *And so he plays his part. The sixth age shifts*
> *Into the lean and slipper'd pantaloon,*
> *With spectacles on nose and pouch on side,*

His youthful hose, well saved, a world too wide
For his shrunk shank; and his big manly voice,
Turning again toward childish treble, pipes
And whistles in his sound. Last scene of all,
That ends this strange eventful history,
Is second childishness and mere oblivion,
Sans teeth, sans eyes, sans taste, sans everything.

Shakespeare probably based his observations on the work of Claudius Ptolemy, whom we met in the last section. Ptolemy's texts were widely studied in Shakespeare's day.

Ptolemy described the seven ages of man, from birth to death, and linked them to the seven classical planets. Traditionally, those planets were listed by their speed: the Moon circles the zodiac in a month. Mercury takes 88 days. Venus completes the cycle in less than a year. From our perspective, the Sun moves through all twelve signs during the course of one year. Mars makes the trip in 2 years. Jupiter takes 12 years, and Saturn's journey takes about 29 years.

- *The infant.* The Moon, like an infant, grows quickly.
- *The schoolboy.* Mercury is linked to the formative years and primary education, when children learn to think and communicate. Mercury's influence isn't limited to childhood, however. Wherever it lands in a chart, it adds a measure of childlike innocence, curiosity, and enthusiasm.
- *The lover.* As youngsters hit the hormonal rush of adolescence, they come in contact with Venus, the planet of love and attraction. While passions might subside with time, Venus is always a blushing beauty, wherever she lands in a chart. By the time most people are young adults, they come into their full power, like the Sun.
- *The soldier.* With Mars and middle age, we're forced to reconcile our drives and desires with our responsibilities.
- *The justice.* As people approach retirement, they relax. Jupiter is the king of the gods, the founder of law and order, and the

bringer of gifts. When the Greater Benefic delivers the benefits he has promised, people enjoy the fruits of their labor.

- *The pantaloon—a comic character, and the victim of the clown.* Saturn, the ringed planet of limitations and restrictions, forces everyone to slow down and prepare for final endings. Saturn is always a mixed blessing: he can make young people seem old before their time, but he can also ensure that they have the fortitude and endurance it takes to reach their dreams.

- *The second childhood.* The oldest among us tend to slip into senility, and consciousness passes away as all the planets fade from view.

PART II

Signs and Stories

As the planets revolve around the Sun, your characters will move through the signs of the zodiac, and their stories will unfold. We'll follow the plot, and discover what obstacles and conflicts keep them from reaching their goals. We'll also study the ways that the symbolism of the same twelve signs can be the foundation of story structure, theme, and symbolism.

The Signs
of the Zodiac

Thousands of years ago, when astrologers were first developing the principles of the art, they saw the planets rise and set against the backdrop of a different constellation each month.

There were twelve prominent constellations that resembled animals—one for each month of the year. Curiously enough, children who were born when each constellation was at its peak tended to embody the qualities of those stars—almost as if they were under the influence of a celestial spirit animal. The word *zodiac,* in fact, is Greek for "circle of animals."

Eventually, twelve of those constellations became the twelve signs of the zodiac.

The signs aren't literal. The constellations vary in size, and our view of them is always shifting. Instead, the signs are simply equal divisions of space, compartmentalized for convenience and symbolic significance.

The Circle of Animals

The zodiac's signature animals can tell you a lot about each sign. Here's a quick overview.

1. Aries, the ram—determined and headstrong
2. Taurus, the bull—confident, earthy, and strong
3. Gemini, the twins—curious and conversational
4. Cancer, the crab—hard-shelled, but softhearted
5. Leo, the lion—regal and brave; the king of the jungle
6. Virgo, the virgin—pure and self-controlled

7. Libra, the scales—constantly striving for balance
8. Scorpio, the scorpion—focused and intense
9. Sagittarius, the archer—driven to run and explore
10. Capricorn, the goat—a social and career climber
11. Aquarius, the water bearer—a visionary in service to a higher calling
12. Pisces, the fish—swimming in an alternate reality

Creative Guidance

Write about your characters as though they really were the animals that signify their signs. Refer to them not by name, but as animals. Describe their movements, physical characteristics, and interactions with others. Once your description is drafted, replace the animal references with your characters' names.

Common
Characteristics

In this section, you'll learn the specific characteristics of each sign. First, however, let's take a look at the general characteristics they share: the elements and the modes.

The Elements

For centuries, scholars and philosophers believed that the entire world consisted of just four elements: fire, earth, water, and air. Most also believed that the human body was made up of the four elements as well. Some people, for example, have always been considered "fiery," while others can still be described as "earthy."

Even though modern scientists have moved beyond elemental physiology, the ancient elements still constitute a useful psychological model—as well as a handy formula for understanding your characters.

- Fire signs—Aries, Leo, and Sagittarius—are as mesmerizing as fire itself. They give off heat and light that's impossible to ignore and difficult to contain. They're energetic, enthusiastic, spontaneous, impulsive, and optimistic. They're dramatic, charismatic, and passionate. They're impulsive, spontaneous, and action-oriented. They burn with passion. They're spirited.

- Earth signs—Taurus, Virgo, and Capricorn—are as stable and supportive as the ground beneath your feet. They're solidly established in the physical and material realities of life. They're sensible and capable, shrewd and secure. They're practical and pragmatic. They're cautious, slow-moving, thorough, and unhurried. They know the world will wait for them.

- Air signs—Gemini, Libra, and Aquarius—are quick-witted, with thoughts that are as fleeting as the wind. They're curious and communicative. They rise above the mundane: they're high-minded visionaries. They're observant and well-informed. They're intellectual, too. Their heads are filled with ideas and imagination.
- Water signs—Cancer, Scorpio, and Pisces—are emotional and intuitive. Their moods can rise and fall like the tides. They can be turbulent and swirling, or deep and calm. They flow through the world of emotions and relationships. Water assumes the form of its container, and rises to its own level. Water signs are sensitive, sympathetic, nurturing, empathetic, compassionate, and instinctive.

The Drama and Conflict of Duality

In a world where opposites attract, all of the signs have characteristics that make them either masculine or feminine—or, in modern terms, active or receptive, extroverted or introverted, linear or circular, and yin or yang. They can complement each other, or they can clash, often in surprising ways.

- Fire and air signs are masculine. They're outspoken, confident, courageous, and bold. They're assertive. They don't wait for results: they make things happen.
- Earth and water signs are feminine. They're quiet and responsive. They're naturally intuitive and understanding. They're patient and strong, and they have the wherewithal to see events through to their conclusions.

In real life, of course, every individual embodies a blend of masculine and feminine qualities. In literature, however, it's more interesting to allocate those characteristics in unexpected combinations.

Creative Guidance

Create a character whose basic nature is torn between outgoing masculinity and receptive femininity. It's the type of conflict you often find in unwill-

ing heroes—quiet, unassuming characters who find that fate forces them into an active role they wouldn't choose for themselves.

In this case, however, you can create characters who don't conform to the usual standards and expectations. Try your hand at an outgoing hero who has to hide his true nature, for example, to effect change behind the scenes.

Modes: Beginning, Middle, and End

The twelve signs aren't just elemental. They can also be categorized according to mode—a technical way to describe their modus operandi, or their way of interacting with the world.

The modes are based on the fact that astrology is a calendar-based study. The twelve signs, just like the twelve months of the year, can be grouped into four seasons: spring, summer, fall, and winter.

The signs fall into three corresponding modes: cardinal, fixed, and mutable. The modes parallel the beginning, middle, and end of each season.

- Cardinal signs mark the first month of each season—which means that they're the signs that take charge, initiate change, and make new starts. Characters who embody a lot of cardinal qualities are leaders. It might help to remember that the first day of Aries marks the first day of spring. The first day of Cancer is the first day of summer. The first day of Libra is the first day of fall, and the first day of Capricorn is the first day of winter. Cardinal signs are courageous, energetic, and self-motivated. They're unstoppable forces of nature.

- Fixed signs mark the middle months, which are the high point of each season. Just as you know that midsummer days are hot and midwinter nights are cold, Taurus, Leo, Scorpio, and Aquarius are clearly defined. They're steady, persistent, and enduring. It's hard for fixed signs to change, which gives them a reputation for being stubborn, slow-moving, and deliberate, but they're respected for their sense of purpose, strength, and endurance.

- The mutable signs of Gemini, Virgo, Sagittarius, and Pisces bring each season to a close. Because they mark the change of seasons, they're flexible, adaptable, and versatile. They can be fickle and chaotic, but they're also friendly and cooperative. They can navigate through periods of transition and bring projects to a successful conclusion.

Pieces of the Puzzle

When you see the signs in order, it's easier to picture their modes—cardinal, fixed, and mutable—along with their elements and qualities.

Element/Quality	Cardinal Signs	Fixed Signs	Mutable Signs
Fire/Active	1. Aries	5. Leo	9. Sagittarius
Earth/Receptive	2. Taurus	6. Virgo	10. Capricorn
Air/Active	3. Gemini	7. Libra	11. Aquarius
Water/Receptive	4. Cancer	8. Scorpio	12. Pisces

Creative Guidance

You might notice that the cardinal, fixed, and mutable modes parallel the beginning, middle, and end of basic scene and story construction, or the first, second, and third acts of a three-act story.

In each case, characters are presented with a mission or a challenge. They encounter resistance when they try to make changes, and eventually they reach a resolution—which, more often than not, simply lays the groundwork for a new set of problems and obstacles.

Compatible Signs

Some signs are compatible. Others mix like oil and water—or, more technically, fire and water.

Ancient philosophers came up with a schematic to demonstrate the qualities of each element, to illustrate the interactions of the elements. It's based on four simple principles:

- Fire is hot and dry.
- Water is cold and wet.
- Air is wet and hot.
- Earth is dry and cold.

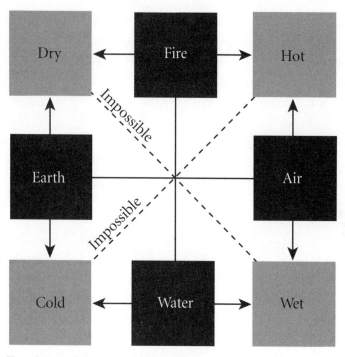

- Fire Signs: Aries, Leo, Sagittarius
- Earth Signs: Taurus, Virgo, Capricorn
- Air Signs: Gemini, Libra, Aquarius
- Water Signs: Cancer, Scorpio, Pisces

So what does that mean for your characters? To start, people who share the same element will always be compatible. They speak the same language, they share the same worldview, and they work with the same modus operandi.

Because opposites attract, you can also expect opposing signs—fire and water, and earth and air—to feel a certain attraction to each other, too. They see the world from completely different vantage points— which could lead to some great arguments—but they can also meet in the middle and come to a mutual understanding. In a sense, they complete each other.

But when you deal with impossible elemental combinations, you'll create characters who will struggle when they're paired off. Granted, they can meet and quickly find that each is an object of fascination to the other; that's a common finding in relationship astrology. They might even share some qualities: hot, wet, cold, or dry. But some qualities are simply impossible to reconcile. Watery characters will never be able to understand their dry, dispassionate opponents of earth. Air will only inflame fire. Fire can't touch earth, and air won't appreciate water.

Basically, when a hot-blooded, fiery character squares off against a cold, calculating adversary of air, conflict is inevitable.

As a writer, you can use that to your advantage.

Behind the Scenes: Temperament and Humor

You might have run across characters in medieval literature who were described in terms of their temperament and humor. It's a form of character analysis that dates back to ancient Greece and Rome. The temperaments were based on the elements, and the corresponding humors were based on bodily fluids.

The sanguine temperament corresponds to air. Sanguine characters are breezy. They're outgoing, friendly, talkative, impulsive, social, and charismatic. Like air, blood was warm and moist. (*Sanguineous* is derived from the Latin for "bloody.")

The choleric temperament corresponds to fire. Choleric characters are energetic, ambitious, passionate, domineering, and aggressive. Like fire, yellow bile was warm and dry. (*Chole* is Greek for "bile.")

The melancholic temperament corresponds to earth. Melancholic characters are obsessed with grave and heavy issues. They are quiet, thoughtful, introverted, and artistic, and are preoccupied with sadness and tragedy. Like earth, black bile was cold and dry. (*Melanchole* is Greek for "black bile.")

The phlegmatic temperament corresponds to water. Phlegmatic characters go with the flow. They're quiet, content, relaxed, kind, affectionate, and observant. Like water, phlegm was cold and moist. (*Phlegma* is Greek for "phlegm.")

Not surprisingly, individuals who were unbalanced in their makeup were often thought to be sick—sometimes dangerously so—and in need of remedies and healing.

Creative Guidance

Think back to a relationship you've experienced that went horribly wrong. You can recall a romance, a family connection, or a friendship.

What elemental traits did you have in common? What ultimately drove you apart? Were you calm, cool, and collected, while your partner was a hot-head? Were you temperamentally unsuited to each other?

Keep that relationship in mind, because it could be the foundation for a fictional tragedy that's a lot more fun to write about than your real-life heartbreak.

Now, on to the signs themselves.

Aries, the Ram

Would the world ever have been made if its maker had been afraid of making trouble? Making life means making trouble.

—George Bernard Shaw, *Pygmalion*

Characteristics

Invoke Aries, and you'll call upon the primal passions of human-kind—a hot-blooded, fiery-tempered masculinity, with a quick-trigger temper and an iron will.

Aries, the first sign of the zodiac, is the sign of leadership and initiation. That makes Aries adventurous, pioneering, and decisive. The typical Aries is a natural leader—but he rarely checks to make sure his followers are behind him. He's independent, self-reliant, impulsive, and in charge.

Fact Sheet

Ruling Planet: Aries' ruling planet, Mars, is the red planet traditionally associated with the unbridled energy and passion of war, aggression, action, and self-defense. In fact, Aries actually was the Greek god of war. The Romans called him Mars, and the two are practically insep-arable. When your character is an Aries, he'll be fearless, confident, courageous, and in control. Like a warrior, he'll need to prove himself on the battlefield, in the boardroom, and in the bedroom.

Physical Association: Aries rules the head, so an Aries character will be a hard-headed, determined, take-no-prisoners leader who will do whatever it takes to assert himself. In an argument, Aries can out-smart, outmaneuver, and browbeat almost any opponent with the battery of facts at his disposal. Occasionally, you might think he's got a thick skull, because it's almost impossible to get him to change his mind.

Signature Animal: People with a strong Aries influence in their charts can be a lot like rams. They're strong-willed, and they're not afraid to butt heads or to use their superior knowledge and intellect as a battering ram. They're fearless and competitive, and when they put their minds to something, they're an unstoppable force. A strong Aries character is even willing to die for a cause. After all, rams were sacrificial animals in the ancient world.

♈

Glyph: The Aries glyph looks like the horns of a ram.

House Rulership: Aries rules the first house of the natural horoscope, where astrologers look for information about first impressions and physical appearance.

Mode: Aries is a cardinal sign. The Sun is usually in Aries between March 21 and April 19, starting with the spring equinox. The sign marks the first month of spring and the first day in the astrological year. That starting position makes Aries a cardinal sign, too—a marker of change and individuation.

Element: Aries is a fire sign. It always runs hot; in fact, it's brash and downright brazen. Aries is impulsive, impatient, and impetuous. He's brave, bold, and adventurous. He's passionate about the causes he believes in. He doesn't doubt himself for a moment, or question the rightness of his cause. His confidence draws followers like moths to a flame. He's inspiring, mesmerizing, and charismatic. He's bright, optimistic, and direct. He takes direct, aggressive action, and he asserts himself in sudden, energetic bursts. He's optimistic, exuberant, and enthusiastic. He's ambitious and alert. He's energetic and impulsive, but he's got a short attention span, and he moves quickly from one goal to another.

Career Counseling

Characters with a strong Aries influence will be drawn to careers in the military, the paramilitary, and the police force. They also make excellent firefighters, mechanics, welders, and physical therapists.

Costume Department

Any character in Aries will don the uniform of a warrior and prepare to do battle. Sometimes the uniform is a suit of armor. Sometimes it's a three-piece suit. Sometimes it's a dress designed to lure men into submission. And sometimes it's simply a brave face or a false front.

Like a soldier, your Aries character will be tall and sinewy. When he stands, he'll stand at attention. Even when he's at ease, a part of him will remain on guard, constantly tracking the movements of his troops and watching the perimeter for approaching armies.

Because Aries rules the head, you can also expect an Aries character to wear headgear, whether it's a helmet, a dashing hat, or a crown. An Aries woman won't let her hair go unadorned; she'll be a trendsetter, and she'll wear a hairstyle designed to make a strong first impression.

Your Aries character will also have a prominent forehead, either because it's broad or high. He'll probably have a scar from an old fight, or a birthmark from a past life. And because Aries is ruled by the red planet, he might also have red hair.

Comfort

As the planets move through the signs, some will feel happy to reach Aries. Others will be looking for an early exit.

Mars, for example, feels perfectly at home in Aries. According to the ancient system of planetary dignities, he's in his own house, so he's in complete control of his surroundings.

When the Sun passes through the sign, it's an exalted visitor; both Mars and the Sun are fiery leaders.

Venus, on the other hand, is debilitated in Aries, because the goddess of love just doesn't belong on a battlefield. And when Saturn falls in Aries, he's an unwelcome guest; the independent, free-wheeling nature of the sign isn't suited to the limitations and restrictions imposed by Father Time.

Compatibility

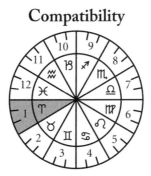

To determine how well your Aries characters will relate to other signs, consider the elements. When Aries joins forces with other fire signs, a few small flames can grow into a raging conflagration. Air feeds fire, and can lead to tremendous blowback. Water will either extinguish flames or dry trying. And while earth can offer up fuel for the fire, the land itself won't burn. In fact, a groundbreak is usually an effective way to stop fire in its tracks.

You can also look at Aries' position on the zodiac wheel. Aries and Libra are polar opposites, which mean they see the world from opposing points of view. Because opposites attract, however, the two signs will often meet in the middle. Aries squares off against Cancer and Capricorn; while they share the same cardinal drive for leadership, they tend to operate at cross-purposes. On the wheel, Aries, Leo, and Sagittarius form a triangular ring of fire; their shared element makes them kindred spirits.

The Aries Writer

If you have the Sun, Moon, or Mercury in Aries, you probably write like you're on fire. You're passionate and driven. You're direct and to the point. You can write to inspire, and you can lead your readers directly to the conclusions you choose.

You're smart. You base your work on sound logic and reasoning. Once you've finished your first draft, however, you don't enjoy the rewriting or editing process. You're impatient and you want to move on to the next project.

Twenty Questions

1. *How is your character like a ram?*

2. *Aries rules the head. Describe your character's head.*

3. *How does your character style his hair?*

4. *Does your character wear a hat? He should. Describe it.*

5. *Aries is a sign of confrontation. Write a scene in which your character confronts an opponent over an inconsequential activity or event.*

6. *Confrontation finds Aries even when they're not looking for a fight. They project an air of confrontation, so they seem to attract conflict, too. Have your character be attacked by a random stranger in a public place, like a coffee shop or a movie theater.*

7. *Put some fighting words in your characters' mouths.*

8. *Aries is ruled by Mars, the red planet. How does that play out in real life? What makes your character see red?*

9. *Play with this idea: What if your character perceived red in a way different from the rest of us?*

10. *Make the color red a focal point for your writing. Write as many synonyms as you can for red. Sprinkle them liberally throughout your story, without being too obvious.*

11. *Assume that love and hate are simply two sides of the same coin. Then write about the connection between red wine and blood.*

12. *Look around you. Where do you see the color red in your immediate environment? How does it affect you? How do you use the color red in your everyday life?*

13. *Do you edit with a red pencil or pen? Why or why not?*

14. *Think about sacrificial lambs. How does your character compare to them?*

15. *Aries expresses passion more readily than most. How does your character display passion?*

16. *Write a scene in which he reveals his passion without explicitly talking about it. Use body language, gestures, and understated remarks. Write between the lines. Make implications and suggestions.*

17. *Now let your character put his passion into words. Remember to write from his point of view, based on his experience and perspective.*

18. *Give your character a scar, birthmark, head wound, or head ailment. Describe it in detail. What's wrong with his head? How did it happen? How does it affect his daily life?*

19. *Aries rules the first house of self-image and public appearance. It's the face we show the world. Describe your character, in depth, physically, as a stranger would see him. Start at the head—an obvious Aries starting point—and work your way down.*

20. *Finally, describe how your character looks from behind, when he's not face to face with the public or an opponent. Put it in context. Who can see him from that vantage point, and why?*

Taurus, the Bull

He lay on his back in his blankets and looked out where the quartermoon lay cocked over the heel of the mountains. In the false blue dawn the Pleiades seemed to be rising up into the darkness above the world and dragging all the stars away, the great diamond of Orion and Cepella and the signature of Cassiopeia all rising up through the phosphorous dark like a sea-net. He lay a long time listening to the others breathing in their sleep while he contemplated the wildness about him, the wildness within.

—Cormac McCarthy, *All the Pretty Horses*

Characteristics

When you want to connect with your Taurus characters, simply think back to your high school years, when you longed for beauty and high fashion that were just beyond your reach. It doesn't matter how rich or stunning you actually were; inside every Taurus, there's a goddess struggling to break free.

Fact Sheet

Ruling Planet: Taurus is ruled by Venus, the goddess of love and the planet of beauty, grace, and charm. Any character with a strong Taurus connection will be driven to fulfill their soul's calling for elegance and refinement.

Physical Associations: Taurus rules the neck and throat, so Taurus characters have lovely voices. They're talented singers and musicians, with more than their fair share of rhythm and grace. They also make excellent dance partners.

Signature Animal: Like the sign's signature animal, the bull, Taurus characters are creatures of comfort. They're sensual. Beauty and splendor make them feel alive.

♉

Glyph: The glyph for Taurus looks like the head of a bull, or the ring in a bull's nose. Taurus can be bull-headed: stubborn, immovable, and almost impossible to placate. Taurus can also be bullish when it comes to the practice of their beliefs. Just remember that when you mess with the bull, you get the horns.

House Rulership: Taurus is the sign of security and stability. It rules the second house of the horoscope chart, where astrologers look for information about money and property, material resources, and spiritual treasures.

Mode: Taurus is a fixed sign. The Sun is usually in Taurus between April 21 and May 21—the second month of spring, when the season is in full flower.

Element: Taurus is an earth sign, which makes it practical, patient, and persevering. Taurus is grounded, stable, and reliable. The sign is also a mark of dedication, determination, discipline, and dependability. It's hard-working and industrious. Taurus will literally move heaven and earth to reach its objectives. Loyal and steadfast, Taurus is a rock of solidarity and comfort in difficult times. Taurus can be possessive and materialistic. Characters with a strong Taurus influence are conventional. They cling to tradition. They're slow to adapt to cultural trends, and they're not particularly fond of revolutionaries or eccentrics.

Career Counseling

Thanks to their fixed earth qualities, Taurus characters make excellent managers, bankers, bookkeepers, accountants, landscapers, farmers, and chefs. Add ruling planet Venus to the mix, and you could find yourself with a decorator, designer, beautician, or stylist. You can also put Taurus's beautiful voice to work with a career in music, theater, public speaking, public relations, or broadcasting.

Costume Department

Characters in Taurus automatically become creatures of comfort. Their energy is focused on earthy, grounded, physical realities. They dress themselves in classic styles, with elegant and long-wearing jewel-tone fabrics. They also make sure their surroundings are appointed in the finest style they can afford.

Taurus rules the neck and throat, so you'll find that characters with a strong Taurus influence have a lovely speaking voice, with words and whispers as pleasant as a song. They may have singing or musical ability. At the very least, they'll have an innate gift for choosing the perfect background song or setting.

Physically, Taurus characters are sturdily built, with muscular legs and shoulders. Their eyes are big and soft, with a placid, steady gaze. Taurus men have thick bull necks, while the necks of Taurus women are long and slender. Their hair tends to be naturally curly or wavy. In real life, you probably don't want to tell your Taurus friends that they look like contented cows, but you can certainly keep the analogy in mind when you're creating fictional characters.

Comfort

Some planets are more suited to the sign of Taurus than others. Venus rules Taurus, so when she's in the second house, she's the queen of the castle. The Moon is exalted in Taurus; the goddess's maternal qualities dovetail perfectly with the comforting, stable energies of the sign. Mars, on the other hand, is debilitated in Taurus; the god of war doesn't want to settle down.

Compatibility

To determine how well your Taurus characters will relate to other signs, consider the elements. When Taurus combines with other earth signs, they literally build on each other's strengths. When earth mixes with air, the combination usually stirs up some dust—and could even lead to a windstorm. Earth and water can be a nurturing combination; rain nourishes natural growth. Earth and fire are generally a neutral combination, unless the earth is used to break a firestorm or quench the flames of desire.

You can also consider Taurus's position on the zodiac wheel. Taurus and Scorpio are polar opposites, which means they see the world from opposing points of view. Because opposites attract, however, the two signs can meet in the middle. Taurus squares off against Leo and Aquarius; while they share the same fixed qualities of consistency and stability, they tend to operate at cross-purposes. On the wheel, Taurus, Virgo, and Capricorn form a supportive, earthy pyramid of power. Their shared energy makes them especially well suited to work on building projects together.

The Taurus Writer

If you have the Sun, Moon, or Mercury in Taurus, you're thoughtful and methodical in your work. You enjoy the creative process of thinking and creating. You prefer to read—and write—works of genuine substance and lasting value and importance.

You love beautiful language, and you might have a tendency to develop flowery prose.

Your physical environment plays a key role in your work. You probably enjoy listening to music while you write, and you like to be surrounded with your reference materials and resources.

Twenty Questions

1. *Astrology offers one of many mixed metaphors when it gives us a bull—a decidedly masculine creature—as the symbol of a feminine sign. Why do you think that is?*

2. *Taurus is ruled by Venus, the planet of beauty and attraction. Think about the inherent contradiction in describing a cow as a beautiful, feminine creature. Can a woman be one thing on the outside, and something else entirely on the inside?*

3. *Describe your character as if she were a bull—or, to be technically correct, a cow, or any large, plodding, heavyset creature.*

4. *Research the myth and legend of Europa. She fell in love with Jupiter when he turned himself into a bull and seduced her. Since Europa wasn't the first woman on Earth to fall for a line of bull, her experience should be easy to incorporate into a story.*

5. *Taurus rules the neck and throat. Describe your character's neck.*

6. *Now describe your character's voice.*

7. *Describe your character's speaking habits and patterns.*

8. *Give your character a verbal tic. Does she stutter? Clear her throat a lot? Does she whisper, shout, or use a sing-song lilt? Does she have an accent?*

9. *What does she say when she's surprised?*

10. *What does she say when she wants attention?*

11. *Historically, cattle were a measure of wealth, as valuable as real estate. A healthy herd of cattle represented a guarantee of prosperity—of food, and milk, and breeding. What does your character invest in? What security does it provide?*

12. *Taurus rules the second house, where astrologers look for information about values and possessions. What does your character prize the most?*

13. *How much money does she have in the bank?*

14. *How did she earn it?*

15. *As an experiment, strip your character of her wealth and worldly goods. How does she react?*

16. *Taurus characters have an innate need for beauty and style. Consciously or unconsciously, their craving for culture and sophistication enters into every decision they make. How does your character dress? How does she decorate her home?*

17. *What happens if your character is too poor to afford nice things?*

18. *What happens if she has the genetic misfortune of looking like a cow? What if she's a Minotaur—a pure and lovely soul trapped in the body of a monster? Well, then you know her secret drives, desires, and motivation.*

19. *In mythology, the Taurean Minotaur was a monster trapped at the center of a winding maze. Play with that idea as you write your next story. Think of your plotline as a maze of twists, turns, and unexpected developments.*

20. *Along those same lines, think of your story as a circular construction. Build a reference to the end of your story into the beginning. Your character will come back to his starting point, changed. What will still be recognizable? What will change?*

Gemini,
the Questioner

"My mind," he said, "rebels at stagnation. Give me problems, give me work, give me the most abstruse cryptogram or the most intricate analysis, and I am in my own proper atmosphere. I can dispense then with artificial stimulants. But I abhor the dull routine of existence. I crave for mental exaltation. That is why I have chosen my own particular profession, or rather created it, for I am the only one in the world."

—Sir Arthur Conan Doyle, *The Sign of the Four*

Characteristics

You probably won't have any trouble coming up with dialogue for your Gemini characters. In fact, you'll be lucky if they let you get a word in edgewise.

Fact Sheet

Ruling Planet: Gemini is ruled by Mercury, the planet of speed and communication—which means that Gemini characters are the great communicators of the zodiac. They are insatiably curious, talkative, flirtatious, and playful, with a wide range of thoughts, interests, and experiences to share and compare. They're quick-thinking and smart. Mercury was the messenger of the gods, but he was also the patron of salespeople, liars, and thieves. There's quite a bit of overlap in those three departments. There's a trickster aspect to Mercury's role.

Physical Associations: Gemini is ambidextrous: it rules the dual embrace of shoulders, arms, hands, and fingers. Gemini also rules the twin chambers of the lungs, which control the air we breathe and use to communicate. As luck would have it, those are the exact same body parts we use to reach out and touch someone—either in person or long-distance.

Signature Animal: The sign of the twins represents the duality of two separate individuals, working in tandem. The two kindred spirits make the most of two identities, two ideals, and the intersection of two points of view. The sign also describes the intersection of separate viewpoints, primarily through communication. People communicate in a variety of ways, and Gemini covers the spoken word, written word, and body language. After all, facial expressions are a universally recognized form of communication.

♊

Glyph: According to myth and legend, the glyph for Gemini depicts two brothers, Castor and Pollux. They were great warriors, noted for their devotion to each other, and Zeus created the constellation Gemini in their honor.

House Rulership: Gemini rules the third house of the horoscope, where astrologers look for information about communication, learning styles, and elementary education. It controls the free and open expression of ideas—and it lends a sense of magic to written and verbal communication. Gemini also rules short trips and sibling relationships. Gemini can be a Jack of all trades; its wide-ranging interests make it versatile, open to new experiences, and willing to try anything once.

Mode: The Sun is usually in Gemini between May 22 and June 21. The sign marks the third and final month of spring. That makes it a mutable sign: it's flexible, spontaneous, adaptable, and able to ease the transition from one season to the next. Gemini can also be scattered, fickle, nervous, restless, easily bored, and eager to move on to something new and exciting.

Element: Gemini is an air sign. The element of air symbolizes intellectual energy. It's curious, versatile, smart, and eager to learn. Gemini characters have lofty goals and aspirations, and they seek their fortune in the heady atmosphere of clouds and sky.

Career Counseling

Your Gemini character will always be Mercurial. He could be a professional communicator, engaged in broadcasting, journalism, marketing, or advertising. He could be a messenger, mail carrier, courier, or delivery person. He might also take the low road, and become a con man or a thief.

Costume Department

Any character in Gemini will be a messenger—either a bearer of glad tidings or a harbinger of doom. You can dress him in uniform, or simply let him freelance. Typically, that messenger will do double duty as a scholar or a hobbyist.

He'll be fidgety and restless: his mutable air sign can't be contained in a physical body or bound to Earth's gravity for too long at a stretch. He'll be light on his feet; he might be an excellent dancer. He'll be wiry and thin, with long legs, arms, and fingers. He'll have pointy facial features—and thanks to Mercury's trickster influence, he'll have a devilish grin.

Comfort

Mercury rules Gemini; it's one of the only signs where he truly feels at home. When Jupiter passes through the sign, however, it's debilitated; the expansive planet wants to see the big picture, but in Gemini, he's forced to deal with minutiae.

Compatibility

To assess how well your Gemini characters will relate to other signs, consider the elements. When airy Gemini catches up with other air signs, they can join forces in a whirlwind of shared ideas and communication—or collide, like two massive cloud forms, in a thunderclap of energy. Gemini's airy nature can feed and inspire fire—or blow it out. Gemini also stirs up trouble with water; the air will either evaporate water, or whip it into a frenzy of crashing waves. When Gemini's air brushes past the surface of the earth, it can either blow gently over the earth, raise clouds of dust, or twist and turn into a tornado.

You can also look at Gemini's position on the zodiac wheel. Gemini and Sagittarius are polar opposites. Gemini focuses on short trips, while Sagittarius is interested in long-distance travel. While their plans are diametrically opposed, there is room to meet in the middle. Gemini squares off at 90-degree angles to Virgo and Pisces; while they share the same easygoing flexibility, they tend to operate at cross-purposes. On the wheel, Gemini, Libra, and Aquarius are all air signs; their shared element helps them communicate on the same elevated level.

The Gemini Writer

If you have the Sun, Moon, or Mercury in Gemini, you were born to write. You can write about any subject under the Sun—and you can write quickly and intelligently. Your wide-ranging interests give you a head start in developing any subject. You also have a lot of sources at your disposal. You might specialize in journalistic reports, firsthand accounts, and true stories. You'll probably manage to be published and get paid for writing, because you know that a writer needs an audience, and you'll be frustrated if your message goes unheard.

Twenty Questions

1. *Gemini is the sign of the twins. Does your character have a secret double—or an alter ego, like Dr. Jekyll and Mr. Hyde? If not, give him one.*

2. *Gemini rules the arms and hands. Describe your character's hands. Are they long and graceful, or square and chunky? How would he describe his hands?*

3. *Palm readers note that the length of the fingers is directly related to the speed of thought. People with short fingers think quickly; it doesn't take long for their thoughts to travel. People with long fingers are more careful. The line of thought is longer. If you were a palm reader, what would you say about your character's fingers?*

4. *Gemini is a sign of communication. How old was your character when he learned to talk?*

5. *What were his first words?*

6. *Gemini is also the sign of siblings and cousins. Describe your character's immediate and extended family. He'll be heavily influenced by siblings and cousins—and if he's an only child, with no peers in his generation, he'll be notably affected by their absence.*

7. *Gemini rules elementary education. Describe your character's grade-school years.*

8. *Gemini rules the immediate neighborhood. Describe the places where your characters live.*

9. *Gemini also rules routine habits and daily routine. Describe a typical day for both your hero and your villain.*

10. *Any character with a strong Gemini component automatically becomes lighter than air, curious, inquisitive, charming, and chattering. He'll be talkative, curious, and quick-witted. His IQ rises, but his attention span gets shorter. Give your character a touch of ADD—and at least three hobbies.*

11. *Some Mercurial characters are too clever by half. They can be devious. Turn one of your supporting players into a trickster.*

12. *Play with the idea of parallel story construction. Tell the same tale from two points of view, or from two points in time.*

13. *Create a parallel universe for your character.*

14. *Write about two people who were switched at birth.*

15. *Write about someone who finds himself involved in a case of mistaken identity.*

16. *Write about a romantic hero who's fickle and inconstant.*

17. *Write about someone who's torn between two lovers.*

18. *Write about someone who's having an affair.*

19. *Gemini characters can read subtle clues in body language, because language and communication are their forte—no matter how the information is delivered. Write a scene in which few words are exchanged but much is said.*

20. *Write about a character who's of two minds on every subject.*

Cancer, the Crab

She had only to stand in the orchard, to put her hand on a little crab tree and look up at the apples, to make you feel the goodness of planting and tending and harvesting at last. All the strong things of her heart came out in her body, that had been so tireless in serving generous emotions. It was no wonder that her sons stood tall and straight. She was a rich mine of life, like the founders of early races.

—Willa Cather, *My Antonia*

Characteristics

It might take some time to get to know your Cancerian characters. As a rule, they'll be somewhat reserved, reclusive, and self-protective—much like their signature creature, the crab.

If you want your Cancer characters to reveal themselves, get them angry. Back them into a corner. Poke them with a stick. There's an element of danger involved, but you can't get close to a Cancer by keeping your distance.

Fact Sheet

Ruling Planet: Like her ruling planet, the Moon, the crab can be moody. Just as the Moon changes from day to day, and the tides rise and fall in response, Cancer can be imaginative and wildly responsive to fluctuations in the environment around them. She can be overpowering, suspicious, and, when she's living out the archetype of the dark mother, smothering with her affections.

Physical Associations: Cancer rules the breasts and stomach—which clearly indicates a mother's lifelong role as a nurturing presence in her children's lives. For most mothers, feeding their children is a primary part of their jobs—first by nursing their children as infants, and later by filling their stomachs with home-cooked meals.

Signature Animal: Crabs are designed to be defensive. Their hard shell offers a tough, nearly impenetrable barrier between the dangers of the outside world and the vulnerable creature inside. Crabs scuttle sideways when they move; they rarely take a direct course. They even put out feelers to sense the direction they should travel. When they sense danger, they lash out, with sharp, pinching claws that can amputate and maim their tormentors. At the same time, however, that drive for protection and defense makes watery Cancer one of the most nurturing signs of the zodiac. A typical Cancerian character is a caregiver. She's maternal, nurturing, and sensitive.

♋

Glyph: The glyph for Cancer looks like the claws of a crab, or the breasts that nurture and sustain a child's life.

House Rulership: Cancer rules the fourth house of motherhood, home, and family life—the foundation of the chart. Cancer is also one of the most patriotic signs: Cancer will fight for home and country.

Mode: The Sun enters Cancer on the summer solstice, which usually falls around June 21. The sign marks the first month of summer. That makes it a cardinal sign of leadership, initiation, and new beginnings.

Element: Because they're water creatures, Cancerians are sensitive and intuitive.

Career Counseling

Cancerians are maternal—but they're suited to a whole world beyond motherhood. Cancer characters are creative problem solvers. They know how to multitask, and they know how to manage people. Your Cancer character could stick with nurturing, and establish herself as a homemaker, caregiver, chef, or restaurateur. She could also be a small business owner, real estate agent, or interior designer. She could work with children as a teacher or a nurse. She could also be a counselor, therapist, psychologist, or public relations professional. Like her ruler, the Moon, a Cancer character will be tuned in to public moods and perceptions.

Costume Department

Any characters in Cancer might seem to shift shape, like the Moon. They could have a secret dark side. They'll probably seem a little ethereal—especially since they favor silver and white.

Cancer rules the breasts and stomach, so look for big breasts, a barrel chest, or a pot belly. A Cancerian might also have a beaming face and broad smile, round and full like the Moon.

Subconsciously, Cancers tend to hide beneath a shell and dress defensively. There is always something between them and others, whether it's a suit of armor or an apron.

Cancerian characters have round faces, wide eyes, and innocent expressions. They typically have crooked teeth and short, upturned noses, with pale skin and rosy cheeks. They tend to daydream a lot. They're short, soft, and round, and they tend to be top-heavy. In fact, they always seem a little shorter and a little heavier than they really are, and even thin Cancerians will be curvy.

Comfort

Even though Cancer is the sign of home and family life, the planets don't always feel comfortable and at home when they pass through the sign.

The Moon, of course, is most at home in Cancer, the sign of its own domicile. Mars, on the other hand, is in its fall in Cancer. Mars is the warrior planet, and no one wants their home to be a battlefield or to find their home at Ground Zero in an attack. Jupiter is exalted in Cancer, because Jupiter is the Greater Benefic, and it loves to shower its loved ones with gifts. Saturn, however, is debilitated in Cancer. Saturn wants to create order, but Cancer prefers a gentler form of discipline than Saturn can provide.

Compatibility

How do the signs relate to one another? When water nourishes earth, it nurtures the soil and promotes growth. When Cancer combines with fire, however, it either quenches the flames or sizzles, steams, or evaporates. Water will dampen air; it could even lead to a downpour of torrential proportions. And when one body of water flows into another, it takes the shape of its container and rises to its own level.

You can also consider Cancer's position on the zodiac wheel. Cancer and Capricorn are polar opposites, which means they see the world from opposing points of view. Capricorn is in a position of public visibility, while Cancer is safely ensconced at home. Because opposites attract, however, the two signs complement each other. Cancer squares off against Aries and Libra; while they share the same cardinal signs of leadership and initiation, they tend to operate at cross-purposes. Cancer, Scorpio, and Pisces are all water signs, so their shared emotional energy makes them especially well suited to friendship and bonding.

The Cancer Writer

If you have the Sun, Moon, or Mercury in Cancer, you write to help and advise others. You might specialize in writing about subjects that enhance home and family life, like parenting, cooking, and interior decorating. You have an intuitive sense about the information your readers want, and a special skill for presenting that information in language they understand.

You have a gift for making money at whatever you do, so writing could be a perfect second job for you. You might even do most of your writing after dark. After all, you're ruled by the Moon, so moonlighting seems only natural.

Unfortunately, you're extremely sensitive to criticism, so you're probably better off not reading your reviews unless they've been pre-screened by someone who loves you.

Twenty Questions

1. *How is your character like a crab? Does she hide within her shell, or does she go on the offensive? Is she easily frightened or provoked? Describe how she acts with family and friends. Compare that behavior to her demeanor at a party, or in a crowd.*

2. *Cancerians are extremely sensitive. How does your character protect herself emotionally?*

3. *How does she defend herself when she's attacked?*

4. *Cancer rules the breasts and stomach. How does your character feel about her figure?*

5. *What does your character like to eat?*

6. *What does she like to cook? Is she a good cook?*

7. *Describe your character's kitchen.*

8. *Symbolically speaking, how does your character feed herself—not just physically, but spiritually and intellectually?*

9. *Cancer is also a sign closely associated with motherhood. Describe your character's mother.*

10. *What lessons did your character learn at her mother's knee? Were they helpful? Were they true?*

11. *Create a character based on your mother's astrological signature.*

12. *Write what you know about your mother's childhood, and then compare it to your own.*

13. *If you have brothers or sisters, call them and ask them to describe their childhood perceptions of your mother. The differences might surprise you. Incorporate them into a profile of a completely fictional character.*

14. *Write about a grandmother—either one you had or one you wish you had.*

15. *Cancer is ruled by the Moon, which means that Cancerian characters are constantly cycling through emotions and experiences. What cycles does your character continually repeat?*

16. *As the Moon pulls at the earth, the lives of Cancer-based characters seem to ebb and flow like the tides. Describe your character's highest highs and lowest lows.*

17. *The crab carries its home on its back. What does your character always carry with her to remind her of home or to make her feel at home? What does she keep in her purse? What's in the glove box of her car?*

18. *The Moon is associated with silver, prized not only for its intrinsic value but also its reflective properties. When your character is deep in thought, what's on her mind?*

19. *Cancerians can be reflective—but they can also be distracted by shiny trinkets and baubles. When your character looks around, what catches her eye?*

20. *Write about a baby who's abandoned on a doorstep.*

Leo, the Lion

When he shall die,
Take him and cut him out in little stars,
And he will make the face of heaven so fine
That all the world will be in love with night
And pay no worship to the garish sun.

—William Shakespeare, *Romeo and Juliet*

Characteristics

Be very careful when you add a Leo to your cast of characters. Leos love the limelight—which means you might have a hard time convincing your supporting players that they're not the stars of the show. After all, everyone is the hero of their own story, with goals and motivations, drives and desires, and inevitable conflicts that threaten to thwart their objectives. Every individual has a life of their own, even if most of the action happens behind the scenes.

Fact Sheet

Ruling Planet: Leo's ruling planet, the Sun, is also used to being the center of the action. It's the center of the solar system, and every other heavenly body revolves around it. In astrology, the Sun symbolizes the ego and individuality of the self. Apollo, the god of the Sun, embodies the regal qualities of both the planet and the sign. He's fiery and charismatic. He's mesmerizing and dramatic. He's a majestic source of light, heat, and inspiration. He's spontaneous, gregarious, and outgoing. He's daring and determined, powerful, and born to lead.

Physical Associations: Leo rules the heart and spine. It's no accident that we use the terms *heart* and *backbone* to describe the bravery and courage of heroes—as well as those they inspire.

Signature Animal: The lion is the king of beasts, which is one reason so many kings seem to display lions on their coat of arms.

♌

Glyph: The glyph for Leo looks like a lion's tail or a lion's mane. Leo is represented by a lion, the king of beasts, who hunts and dispatches his prey without bitterness, recrimination, or regret. The lion is also an alchemical symbol for the Sun—Leo's ruling planet—along with gold and sulphur.

House Rulership: Leo rules the fifth house of the horoscope, where astrologers look for information about recreation, procreation, and creativity. It's a playful sign that ultimately leads Leo to the joys of fatherhood and family life.

Mode: The Sun is usually in Leo between July 21 and August 23. Leo, the fixed fire sign of the zodiac, rules the hottest month of summer, when the earth is closest to the Sun, the days are long and scorching, and the season is at its peak.

Element: The sign is unmistakably fiery.

Career Counseling

Any characters in Leo will automatically assume the mantle of a king. They might shine as a business executive, a leading man, or a politician. Leos make excellent models, movie stars, and media personalities, too.

Costume Department

Any planet or personality in Leo becomes regal, like the king of beasts. They're dramatic and showy. They dress for success—and attention.

Because Leo rules the heart and spine, you can expect a Leo character to be confident, brave, and fearless. He'll wear fiery colors that can't go unnoticed, like red, orange, and gold. In fact, Leo expects to be seen and admired. Expect them to wear athlete's clothing or uniforms; they love to play for pay.

Leo personalities typically have thick manes of hair, with large, catlike eyes and a graceful way of walking. They carry themselves with pride. They're usually tall, with thin waists and trim legs. They move slowly but dramatically, and they speak loudly, with bearing and authority.

Comfort

The Sun rules Leo, so when it passes through this sign, it once again returns to its proper place at the center of the solar system. Mercury, the sign of speed and communication, doesn't mind delivering messages to the Sun; in fact, he's always in close proximity. Mercury is in fall when he's forced to stay for an extended visit in the Sun's house, however. He doesn't have time to linger. Saturn is also debilitated in Leo, because the planet of structure and stability doesn't mesh well with valiant individualism.

Compatibility

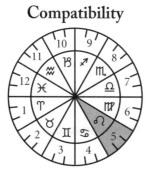

To determine how well your Leo characters will relate to other signs, consider the elements. When fiery Leo joins forces with other fire signs, the conflagration can only grow—or even explode. Fire is fueled by air signs. Water will either extinguish fire or be evaporated by the encounter. And while fire can burn growth and structures to the ground, pure earth will extinguish flames.

You can also consider Leo's position on the zodiac wheel. Leo is diametrically opposed to Aquarius; Leo's desire for individuality directly contradicts Aquarius's emphasis on friends and social groups. Leo squares off at a 90-degree angle to Scorpio and Taurus. They're all fixed signs, but they tend to work at cross-purposes. Leo's fellow fire signs, Sagittarius and Aries, can join forces to build a ring of fire, fueling each other's needs for adventure and exploration.

The Leo Writer

If you have the Sun, Moon, or Mercury in Leo, you have a flair for dramatic language and self-expression. You write to be noticed—and admired.

There's a playful tone to your writing, which translates into a love of puns and wordplay. You're a visual thinker, with an eye for descriptive phrasing. Your sentences are active, not passive—you specialize in being direct and to the point.

You probably like writing about children, sports, or hobbies.

Twenty Questions

1. *How is your character like a lion?*

2. *Leo characters typically have a thick mane of hair. Does your hero fit the bill? Describe his hairdo.*

3. *Is your hero naturally courageous, or is he a cowardly lion? How do you know?*

4. *Leo is the sign of showmanship. Put your hero on center stage. How will he perform? What will he perform?*

5. *How does your hero deal with stage fright?*

6. *Look up the Sun signs of your favorite celebrities. How do they remind you of your protagonist?*

7. *Write about a lion tamer or a circus.*

8. *Use all five senses when you write. Sight is the most obvious and most used. But how does a lion smell? Sound? Feel? While you can't exactly taste him literally, what taste does a lion's smell leave in your mouth? Work it in when you can. Hint at the taste of blood and raw meat. Keep your descriptions primal, like the lion himself.*

9. Leo is ruled by the Sun. What happens when your hero steps out into the light?

10. What would happen if he were cut off from the Sun, and trapped inside?

11. Write about a character who spends his nights awake. Why is he up? What does he do while the rest of the world is asleep?

12. Write a short story that describes a planetary or zodiacal character who's forced to spend time in an uncomfortable, unfamiliar place—like a god or goddess in exile.

13. Leo rules the fifth house, where astrologers look for information about creation, procreation, and recreation. What are your character's hobbies?

14. What does he do after work and on weekends?

15. Does your character have a secret skill that no one knows about? Describe it.

16. Does your character have children? What are their names and ages? What are they like?

17. Run through the list of signs for story ideas you can express in a single sentence. Imagine, for example, that Leo, the lion, is forced to fight for love, or that Cancer, the crab, must come out of her shell to nurse a stranger in a war zone. Consider what would happen if Gemini, the twins, were separated at birth—but they experience a series of mystical coincidences that draw them together at the worst possible moment.

18. Become a master of age progression and regression, and write about your Leo character at different stages of life. You can repeat the experiment with the rest of the cast, too. Astrology will help you discover how their innate personality traits rarely change.

19. Write a story about two people looking up at the night sky when the constellation Leo begins to move.

20. Rewrite a myth or fable about a lion.

Virgo, the Virgin

*Whenever you feel like criticizing any one ... just remember that all
the people in this world haven't had the advantages that you've had.*
—F. Scott Fitzgerald, *The Great Gatsby*

Characteristics

Your Virgo characters offer a fascinating study in character analysis.
When you create a Virgo character, you're actually creating a complement to Gemini, because both are ruled by Mercury.

Both signs are predominantly intellectual. While Gemini is curious and communicative, however, Virgo is conscientious and contemplative.

Virgos are patient, practical, and prudent. They're diligent, resourceful, and organized. They're dedicated to their work, and they're remark-
ably patient and calm. They can be demanding—but they expect more
from themselves than from others. In fact, Virgos often isolate themselves in an effort to live up to their own high standards.

Fact Sheet

Ruling Planet: Both Virgo and Gemini are ruled by Mercury, the god
of thought and communication.

Physical Associations: Virgo rules the nervous and digestive systems, and
most Virgos are keenly aware of their health and nutrition. They recognize the fact that they are what they eat. In fact, the Virgo virgin is
usually pictured holding a sheaf of wheat.

Signature Animal: Virgo is represented by a virgin—more spiritual
than physical. A virgin is wholesome, holy, and pure. That doesn't
mean that a Virgo character is destined for a life of celibacy. In

Latin, Virgo means "unmarried" or "self-possessed." Ultimately, most duty-bound Virgos give of themselves by choice, not out of a sense of obligation. They have integrity, and they always stay true to themselves. Historically, unmarried temple virgins served their communities by living exemplary lives of public service and personal responsibility.

♍

Glyph: The glyph for Virgo looks like a pair of angel wings, or a woman with her legs crossed.

House Rulership: Virgo rules the sixth house of the horoscope, where astrologers look for information about work and service to others.

Mode: The Sun is usually in Virgo between August 23 and September 23. The sign marks the third and final month of summer. That makes it a mutable sign: it's changeable and varied, to ease the transition from one season to the next.

Element: Virgo is an earth sign, grounded in the practical realities of physical existence.

Career Counseling

Virgos are analysts and problem solvers. They make excellent researchers, librarians, analysts, and statisticians. Their fascination with food may lead them into the field of nutrition, and their obsession with health makes them excellent nurses, therapists, medical technicians, and doctors. Their Mercurial skill with language also equips them for careers as writers, editors, and translators.

Costume Department

Any planets or personalities in Virgo pay close attention to detail. They don't dress to impress; they dress in fashions that serve a function. They're utilitarian and practical, prepared for emergencies, and, like Mercury, ready to travel on a moment's notice. They might seem dry and serious, but they have a droll sense of humor that passes over most people's heads. They might even seem to dress down so they won't be noticed, as if they're wearing a cloak of invisibility.

Your Virgo characters will probably have fair skin and doll-like features, including round eyes and delicate lips. Most people think they're beautiful, but Virgos will always be self-conscious and critical of their own appearance.

Because Virgo rules the nervous system, they'll have long arms and long fingers, and they'll seem to be perpetually in motion. Virgos look fragile, but they can surprise you with their strength.

Comfort

As the planets travel through the zodiac, some will settle into Virgo with a sigh of relief. Others will struggle to get comfortable.

Mercury, the ruler of the sixth house, is both dignified and exalted in Virgo. Jupiter, however, is debilitated there, because it's forced to narrow its focus and pay attention to detail. Venus, the goddess of love and affection, makes a poor choice of roommate for the virgin. Promiscuity and celibacy are a bad match.

Compatibility

To determine how well your Virgo characters will relate to other signs, consider the elements. When Virgo combines with other earth signs, they literally build on each other's strengths. When earth mixes with air, the combination usually stirs up some dust—and could even lead to a windstorm. Earth and water can be a nurturing combination; rain nourishes natural growth. Earth and fire are generally a neutral combination, unless the earth is used to break a firestorm or quench the flames of desire.

You can also look at Virgo's position on the zodiac wheel. Virgo and Pisces are polar opposites. Virgo wants to pay precise attention to detail, but Pisces wants to float through an alternate reality. Virgo squares off against Sagittarius and Gemini. While they share the same easygoing mutability, their missions are elementally at odds. Virgo has the most in common with her fellow earth signs, Capricorn and Taurus; all three are practical, grounded, and resourceful.

The Virgo Writer

If you have the Sun, Moon, or Mercury in Virgo, you're disciplined and determined. You're studious, too. You enjoy doing research, and you're methodical and analytical in your approach. You like to be precise, and you'll work long and hard to find just the right word.

You don't mind sharing your knowledge with other writers. In fact, you probably enjoy proofreading and copy editing as much as writing, whether you're checking your own work or acting on behalf of others.

Twenty Questions

1. *Virgo is ruled by Mercury—the same planet that rules Gemini. In Virgo, however, Mercury becomes serious and high-minded. How will that affect your heroine? Describe her in two different moods, one silly and one serious.*

2. *Virgo rules the sixth house of work and service to others. Write about someone who helps others at her own expense.*

3. *Write about someone who has a lot of servants. How does she treat them?*

4. *What do the servants think of her?*

5. *Virgo is the sign of the virgin. How did your heroine lose her virginity?*

6. *If she hasn't lost her virginity yet, would she like to? How can you make it come about in your story?*

7. *What part of herself does your character keep private even from her most intimate friends and romantic partners?*

8. Consider the possibilities of an interspecies romance, and write about the relationships between the signs of the zodiac. How do the signature animals interact? How do they form allegiances? How do they fight, and how do they make love?

9. Create a character who conforms almost completely to the description of a Virgo—but throw in one characteristic that's completely out of character for the sign.

10. Create a full-fledged horoscope for a Virgo character, or simply pick and choose the bits and pieces you'd like to explore. The process of researching and applying astrological traits is very Virgoan.

11. Draft a brief treatment for the same story as a short story, novel, movie, play, or poem.

12. Virgo rules the nervous and digestive systems. Write about a character who has an unusual diet.

13. Virgo is often associated with sickness and health. Describe the worst illness your character has ever suffered.

14. How can you tell when your hero is nervous or distressed?

15. Virgo also rules everyday duty and responsibility, like those associated with pets and plants. How does your character tackle her daily obligations?

16. How did she manage her chores as a child?

17. Describe your heroine's pets.

18. Review all the signs of the zodiac, and work the signature animals of each sign into the sequence of a story.

19. Research the myths and legends you associate with your characters. Remember that even a character's name is linked to ancient gods and goddesses, or their more modern incarnations, like biblical figures, saints, and historic figures.

20. Give your character a theme song, and explain why you chose it.

Libra, the Scales

It is a truth universally acknowledged, that a single man in posses-sion of a good fortune, must be in want of a wife.

—Jane Austen, *Pride and Prejudice*

Characteristics

Libra makes an excellent partner in crime—or in creative writing. She's a social creature, with a fondness for dialogue and expansive discourse. When you include her in your stories, you'll feel like you're writing about a friend.

Fact Sheet

Ruling Planet: Like Taurus, Libra is ruled by Venus, the planet of love and attraction. Both Libra and Venus represent the epitome of charm and grace, designed to attract and appeal.

Physical Associations: Libra rules the kidneys, which help keep the whole body in balance, as well as the lower back, the graceful seat of power.

Signature Animal: Libra is the only sign that's not represented by a living creature. That's odd, because Libra is probably the most social animal in the zodiac. Librans have an innate need to balance themselves through relationships with others. They also crave human connection through the beauty and harmony of art and culture. Libra is skilled at solving problems, compromising, and arranging diplomatic solutions for any conflict. Libra knows there are two sides to every story, and when called upon to mediate, can be an exceptional arbitrator. Occasionally, Libra's need to see both sides of any issue can make it seem indecisive. Libra's charm, however, makes up for it.

Almost everyone is familiar with the scales of balance, as well as the goddess of justice who's usually seen holding them. It's a reminder that your Libra character is dedicated to the pursuit of balance and equanimity—even if she struggles to achieve that balance for herself.

♎

Glyph: The glyph for Libra looks like a perfectly balanced set of scales.

House Rulership: Libra is the seventh sign. It rules the seventh house of the horoscope, where astrologers look for information about marriage and partnership—as well as open enemies. If that doesn't make sense at first, think about your ex-husband.

Mode: The Sun is usually in Libra between September 23 and October 22. The sign marks the first month of autumn. That makes it a cardinal sign: it takes a leadership position and initiates change and forward movement. Libra is a cardinal sign. Its start marks the first day of fall. Like Aries and Cancer before it, Libra is a leader and an initiator, an agent of change and decisive action.

Element: Libra is an air sign. In astrology, the element of air symbolizes intellectual energy—and Libra is intelligent. It's extroverted, communicative, and conversational. Libra is interested in others, and she's able to express that interest in an utterly charming fashion.

Career Counseling

Libra is the sign of grace and balance, which makes it uniquely equipped to serve as a judge, arbitrator, negotiator, mediator, marriage therapist, ambassador, artist, musician, or dancer.

Costume Department

Any planet or personality in Libra is automatically graceful, charming, and easy on the eye. Like Venus, her ruler, Libra will dress herself in fashion's most becoming styles, tailored to perfection and designed to attract admiration. Look for an engagement or wedding ring; partnership is important to a Libra.

Any character in Libra will be physically attractive, with or without clothing. Libra women have the figure of a dancer, with equally graceful movements and poses.

Most Librans have a matched set of dimples, either on their cheeks, noses, knees, or elbows. They have symmetrical, heart-shaped faces, with chiseled, refined features. They might not be classic beauties, but they're always physically striking.

Libra characters also have melodious voices and infectious laughter.

Comfort

As the planets move through the signs, some will feel comfortably at home in Libra. Others will be decidedly uncomfortable.

Venus is in dignity in Libra, her natural home. Mars, however, is debilitated there. The god of war doesn't necessarily want to devote himself to love and partnership. Saturn, the judge, is exalted in Libra, where he ensures that the scales of justice are evenly balanced. The Sun is in fall in Libra. As the king of the solar system and the center of attention, he doesn't share power well.

Compatibility

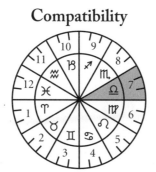

When airy Libra catches up with other air signs, they can join forces in a whirlwind of shared ideas and communication—or collide, two massive cloud forms, in a thunderclap of energy. Libra's airy nature can feed and inspire fire—or blow it out. Libra stirs up trouble with water, which can only react by quietly evaporating or being whipped into crashing waves. Air can blow gently over the earth, or raise clouds of dust.

To determine how well your Libra characters will relate to other signs, you can also consider their position on the zodiac wheel. Libra and Aries are polar opposites. Libra desires partnership, while Aries craves independence. Libra squares off against Capricorn and Cancer; although they share the same cardinal drive for leadership, they tend to operate at cross-purposes. Libra communicates best with the other air signs, Aquarius and Gemini. Their shared energy guarantees constant chatter and scintillating conversation.

The Libra Writer

If you have the Sun, Moon, or Mercury in Libra, you have a gift for understanding complex relationships. You're able to tackle difficult subjects with charm and grace, and balance both sides of any issue. While you might be good at writing about legal affairs and business arrangements, you'd probably rather write about the finer pleasures in life—especially love, romance, and culture. You're a fair-minded patron of the arts, and you'd make an excellent art, movie, or theater critic.

Twenty Questions

1. *Libra is the sign of balance and partnership. Is your character in a relationship? Describe his partner.*

2. *How did they meet?*

3. *Now describe the relationship. What does your character get from his partner, and what does he give?*

4. *What keeps them together?*

5. *How will your character cope when his relationship is threatened? Will he celebrate, or will he be unbalanced? Write it and see.*

6. *Describe a particularly bad breakup your character suffered in the past.*

7. *Send your character to a marriage therapist. What will he discuss?*

8. *Our most intimate partners also know our darkest secrets and our deepest fears. What secrets could your character's partner tell you about him?*

9. *Most Librans try to find themselves by comparing and contrasting their own experience with other people's. What does your character see when he looks into a mirror or catches his reflection in a store window?*

10. *Libra is an air sign, signifying its connection to intellect and thought. Does your hero follow his head or his heart? How so?*

11. *Think of the Libra signature as the scales of justice, and plunge your character into a legal nightmare. Divorce might work, or embezzlement, or any dispute that involves the betrayal of trust in a relationship.*

12. *Write about a lawyer, a judge, or an officer of the court.*

13. *What do you believe about justice? Is it a theme of your work?*

14. *Write about a character who must choose the lesser of two evils.*

15. *Now write about a character who must choose the greater of two evils.*

16. *Write about an unlikely partnership between good and evil.*

17. *Write about an arranged marriage.*

18. *Libra is ruled by Venus, the planet of love, beauty, and attraction. Unfortunately, the word Venus is the source of the word venereal. If you want to plunge your hero headfirst into drama and conflict, you might want to infect him with an unpleasant social disease.*

19. *Describe your character's musical tastes. What is his favorite song?*

20. *Libra is an artistic sign. Draw, paint, sketch, or create a collage about a character with all the attributes you can link to the qualities of a sign—whether that happens to be Libra or not.*

Scorpio, the Scorpion

My name is Sherlock Holmes. It is my business to know what other people don't know.

—Sir Arthur Conan Doyle, *The Adventure of the Blue Carbuncle*

Characteristics

If you're writing a mystery, a thriller, or a dark, gothic romance, you'll probably want to cast a Scorpio in a leading role.

While most people fear death, Scorpios are unafraid of darkness. In fact, they're fascinated by it. They're drawn to the dark rites of transformation, compelled by the mysteries of life and death, and propelled by the allure of sex and the aphrodisiac of power.

Fact Sheet

Ruling Planet: Scorpio's ruler, Pluto, is the planet of death, regeneration, and unavoidable change. In ancient myth and legend, Pluto was the lord of the underworld and the keeper of the souls of the dead. Before Pluto's namesake planet was discovered, however, Mars was Scorpio's ruler—and today, the sign is still colored by the passion of the god of war.

Physical Association: Scorpio rules the genitals. As a result, Scorpio characters are mesmerizing and seductive, and they're constantly in search of intimacy. Because so few people appreciate their fascination with power and control, however, they tend to scare off most prospective companions.

Signature Animal: The Scorpio glyph looks like a scorpion: a stealthy, hidden creature that defends itself with a poisonous barb. When Scorpios feel threatened or wounded, they lash out. They don't forget any damage that's been done. They can even be obsessive. Occasionally, Scorpio is represented by an eagle, a bird of prey, or a phoenix, the mythical bird that dies and is reborn from its own ashes.

♏

Glyph: The glyph for Scorpio is designed to look like a stick-figure scorpion, complete with a stinger on its tail.

House Rulership: Scorpio rules the eighth house of the horoscope, where astrologers look for information about shared resources and life-changing experiences.

Mode: The Sun is usually in Scorpio between October 23 and November 22. Scorpio rules the second month of autumn, when the days and nights are in perfect balance, and the season is at its peak. That makes it a fixed sign: established, clearly defined, and overflowing with emotional energy.

Element: Scorpio is a water sign—but because it's fixed water, it often seems to be preternaturally calm. Remember that you can't always gauge the depth of a Scorpio character by skimming the surface. Still waters run deep.

Career Counseling

Scorpio characters can pursue their darkest fantasies and fascinations in careers that count on research and investigation. They make excellent detectives, spies, psychiatrists, psychologists, coroners, and morticians.

Costume Department

Any planet or personality in Scorpio immediately takes on a brooding, dark, intense quality. While they might not lurk in shadows, they dress to recede into the background, where they can observe the world around them.

Scorpio characters are dark and strikingly handsome. Their eyes are piercing, with a gaze that can see into other people's souls. They have good bone structure, with high cheekbones and sculpted features. While Scorpios can seem brooding, they can also look like they've been carved from stone. When a Scorpio is observing the world, it's impossible to know what he's thinking behind his mask of impassive objectivity.

How does Scorpio dress? Sexy. Just for size, try slipping your character into a little black dress, in homage to Scorpio's contemporary ruler, Pluto, or a revealing red gown in deference to Scorpio's classical ruler, Mars.

Comfort

As the planets circle the zodiac, they'll all travel through Scorpio at some point. Mars, the ancient ruler of Scorpio, is dignified and comfortably in command of the sign. Venus, however, is debilitated; her basic nature clashes with the call of the battlefield and the ghastly realm of death and destruction. The Moon is in fall in Scorpio, for similar reasons. The Moon wants to nurture and protect her children, not kill them.

Compatibility

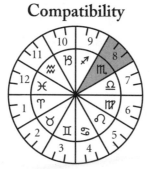

To assess Scorpio's compatibility with other signs, consider the elements. When water overcomes the earth, it can either wash away the soil or nourish the land. When Cancer combines with fire, it either quenches the flames or sizzles, steams, or evaporates. Water and air inevitably lead to clouds and rain; the mixture could even cause a hurricane. But when one body of water flows into another, a pool is formed.

You can also look at Scorpio's position on the zodiac wheel. Scorpio and Taurus are polar opposites. Scorpio wants power and control over the dark mysteries of life, but Taurus simply wants to ensure her comfort and security. Scorpio squares off against Aquarius and Leo. That's because all three are fixed signs, determined and set in their ways, and working at cross-purposes. Scorpio understands the other water signs, however. Scorpio, Cancer, and Pisces have an emotional bond, and they can commiserate with each other.

The Scorpio Writer

If you have the Sun, Moon, or Mercury in Scorpio, you're comfortable writing about the darker things in life. You know how to bring shadowy forces into the light, where you can study them at your leisure. You have the guts to write about sex, death, and resurrection. You might even enjoy writing about taboo subjects.

Twenty Questions

1. *How is your character like a scorpion?*
2. *Scorpio rules the reproductive organs. What does that mean for your character? Is she fertile or infertile? How have children—or their absence—changed her life?*
3. *Scorpio is deeply connected to sexuality—but it doesn't necessarily lead to promiscuity. In fact, a very, very Scorpionic character might avoid sex altogether. Does your character abstain from sex? Why or why not?*
4. *Scorpio is a deep and quiet water sign, fixated on emotional connections—and consequences. Some might even say it's the sign of obsession. What obsesses your character? How does she handle her obsessions?*
5. *Define your character's most pressing need—and then invent at least three ways to keep her from attaining it.*
6. *Scorpio is also the sign of death and regeneration. Write about an accidental death, a murder, or an easy passage into the afterlife. Then write about someone who's resurrected from the dead.*
7. *Scorpio is ruled by Pluto, the dark lord of the underworld. What dark mysteries has your character experienced?*

8. Write about the underworld, populated by spirits, ghosts, and shades of the past.

9. Describe the setting of the underworld as if it were a character in and of itself.

10. What ghosts from the past haunt your character's everyday life?

11. What ghosts and spirits haunt her dreams?

12. Write about gods in modern times—with or without their full power. Start with Pluto; pluck him from the underworld, and plant him firmly in an ordinary human existence. How will he adapt?

13. Outline short conversations between Pluto and the ordinary people he meets during the course of a day.

14. Give Pluto a catchphrase. How does it sum up your character's life and times?

15. Sprinkle your text with astrological omens as a form of foreshadowing.

16. Write about an unexpected inheritance.

17. Write about an inheritance that's been denied, delayed, or withheld. What was the result?

18. Write a poem about sex, death, and other people's money.

19. Have your character write a letter to someone who has died.

20. Use tarot or astrology cards to visualize your characters.

Sagittarius, the Archer

.

When you reach for the stars, you are reaching for the farthest thing out there. When you reach deep into yourself, it is the same thing, but in the opposite direction. If you reach in both directions, you will have spanned the universe.

—Vera Nazarian, *The Perpetual Calendar of Inspiration*

Characteristics

The archer of Sagittarius is a wily creature. Half-man, half-beast, he's a seamless blend of restless adventurer and ribald philosopher. He's a happy-go-lucky traveler who wanders the world in search of honest and visionary companions. He's enthusiastic, independent, footloose, and fancy-free—and he's got a wandering eye. Follow him, and you'll be off on the journey of a lifetime.

For Sagittarius—the sign of long-distance travel, higher education, and philosophy—getting there is half the fun. Sagittarius characters are always chasing the adventure and excitement that are waiting on the other side of the horizon. They're impulsive, restless, and on the move.

Fact Sheet

Ruling Planet: Sagittarius is ruled by Jupiter, the planet of luck and expansion. Jupiter imbues your Sagittarian characters with optimism, good humor, and old-fashioned good luck, even in the face of overwhelming odds.

Physical Associations: Sagittarius rules the hips and thighs—the "horsey" part of the legs that can bear weight and carry a rider across long distances of time and space.

Signature Animal: Sagittarius is represented by the archer, and in most renditions, that archer just happens to be a centaur—half-man, half-horse. He's tame, but he's wild at heart—and he typically has a wandering eye, always wondering what's over the horizon.

↗

Glyph: The glyph for Sagittarius looks like an arrow. With a single movement, the archer can unleash his weapon and send it soaring to a new land. Just as an arrow flies through time and space, physical and intellectual journeys broaden the mind and expand our horizons.

House Rulership: Sagittarius is the ninth sign. It rules the ninth house of the horoscope, where astrologers look for information about higher education, philosophy, and long-distance travel.

Mode: The Sun is usually in Sagittarius between November 21 and December 20. This sign marks the third and final month of fall. That makes it a mutable sign: it's changeable and varied, to ease the transition from one season to the next. Sagittarius will try anything once—and maybe twice, just for good measure.

Element: Sagittarius is a fire sign. In astrology, the element of fire symbolizes spiritual energy.

Career Counseling

Your Sagittarius characters are well suited to careers as philosophers, ministers, priests, rabbis, lawyers, politicians, professors—and, of course, explorers. Don't try to fence them in. They're restless and easily bored by routine. It's their nature to be adventurous and outgoing, meet new people, and test the boundaries of human imagination.

Costume Department

Any planets or personalities in Sagittarius will need plenty of pockets. A travel vest will do nicely: they can stuff it with books, brochures, train tickets, and passport—even if that passport happens to be a library card.

Sagittarian characters are physically appealing. They're tall and handsome, with cheerful faces and ready smiles. Most have a tendency to grin broadly—but it's endearing rather than ridiculous. Because they're half-horse, they gallop through life, chasing from one place to another and tripping over themselves in their enthusiasm to reach the finish line.

Because they're ruled by expansive Jupiter, Sagittarian characters always seem larger than life—and once they start trying the local cuisine, they actually do gain weight. You can also spot a Sagittarius by the stains on their shirts. They don't sit still or stop talking while they eat.

Comfort

Like the wandering stars they are, the planets all take turns passing through Sagittarius. Only one can call it home: Jupiter, the king of the gods, is in complete command when he returns to the sign he rules.

Mercury, on the other hand, functions at a loss. He rules short trips, not long journeys.

Compatibility

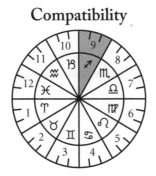

To determine how well your Sagittarius characters will relate to other signs, consider the elements. When fiery Sagittarius joins forces with other fire signs, the conflagration can only grow—or even explode. Fire is fueled by air signs. Water will either extinguish fire, or be evaporated by the encounter. And while fire can burn growth and structures to the ground, pure earth will extinguish flames.

You can also look at Sagittarius's position on the zodiac wheel. Sagittarius and Gemini are polar opposites—but they're both students. Gemini rules elementary education, and Sagittarius is in charge of higher learning. Sagittarius squares off at a 90-degree angle to Pisces and Virgo. While the three signs share the same easygoing mutability, they're all in different elements. Sagittarius is most like the other fire signs of the zodiac, Aries and Leo. He's not as egocentric, but when it comes to exploration and adventure, he'll give them a good run for their money.

The Sagittarius Writer

If you have the Sun, Moon, or Mercury in Sagittarius, you've been a reader and a writer all your life. Sagittarius rules publishing, in all its forms, so you'll probably be published at some point—even if you're not right now. You write to connect with other people, to exchange ideas, and to be recognized for your own authority. You might specialize in legal, religious, or academic subjects. While you can be deeply philosophical, you're also gentle, generous-minded, and good-humored in your work.

Twenty Questions

1. *How is your character like a horse?*
2. *How is he like an archer? What targets does he shoot for?*
3. *Describe your character's gait as he walks across a room or down the street.*
4. *Send your character on a trip, a foreign vacation.*
5. *Write about a character who is a blend of man and animal—a hybrid creature, like the centaur, half-man, half-horse, who often represents the archer of Sagittarius.*
6. *Write about an archer.*
7. *Write about a horseman.*
8. *Write a modern western.*

9. *Sagittarians are honest and outspoken—almost to a fault. Describe an incident during which your character seemed to suffer from hoof-in-mouth disease.*

10. *Force your character to lie to preserve and protect the truth.*

11. *Sagittarius rules the ninth house of higher education, long-distance travel, and philosophy. How far did your character get in his education?*

12. *Has he traveled? How far?*

13. *What languages does your character speak?*

14. *How does he feel about foreigners?*

15. *What are your character's political views? Is he liberal, conservative, or disinterested?*

16. *Is he religious, or is he a skeptic? What religion does he practice?*

17. *What's his relationship with God?*

18. *Is he scientific, or superstitious?*

19. *Start your character on a journey of a single step—and then force him to take two steps back as a result. In fact, try to develop a series of complications that will interfere with your hero's journey.*

20. *Rewrite the same scene from the perspective of two characters, or the same character in a different place and time.*

Capricorn, the Goat

Mr. Darling used to boast to Wendy that her mother not only loved him but respected him. He was one of those deep ones who know about stocks and shares. Of course no one really knows, but he quite seemed to know, and he often said stocks were up and shares were down in a way that would have made any woman respect him.

—J. M. Barrie, *Peter and Wendy*

Characteristics

Capricorn characters are all business—because Capricorn is a pragmatic sign. People who are born when the Sun is in Capricorn are usually hard workers, high achievers, and responsible partners both at work and at home. Characters with a strong Capricorn influence typically feel driven to prove themselves in business and society.

Fact Sheet

Ruling Planet: Capricorn is ruled by Saturn, the ringed planet of boundaries and limitations. Capricorn characters are practical creatures, firmly bound by gravity and rooted in the material world. They're closely acquainted with both the pleasures and pain of physical existence.

Physical Associations: Capricorn rules the knees, shins, and ankles—three components that are critical to anyone who wants to climb mountains and reach the pinnacle of career and social success. Capricorn also rules the skeleton and the skin, which provide structure to the human form.

Signature Animal: Like the sure-footed mountain goat, Capricorns are constantly climbing in search of greener pastures. They're ambitious, driven, disciplined, and industrious. They're also prudent, patient, stable, and enduring. Some artists depict Capricorn as a hybrid creature, half-goat and half-fish. The imagery dates back to myths about the Greek god Pan, who jumped into the Nile to escape the monster Typhon. When he was submerged from the waist down, his legs turned into a fish tail, but his upper body maintained its goat-like form.

♑

Glyph: The glyph for Capricorn looks a little like a goat, in profile. Its pointed face looks like a *V*, and its body is muscular and lean.

House Rulership: Capricorn is the tenth sign of the zodiac. It rules the tenth house of career and social status—both of which often come at great expense. No one understands that cost better than a Capricorn, who will pay almost any price for the privilege that power can bring.

Mode: The Sun is usually in Capricorn between December 21 and January 20. The sign marks the beginning of winter. It's a cardinal sign of leadership and initiation, which introduces a season of change and new beginnings.

Element: Not surprisingly, given its mountainous connections, Capricorn is an earth sign. In astrology, the element of earth symbolizes stability and security. It's the sign of tangible property, material resources, and physical existence.

Career Counseling

Capricorn is the sign of business and career—so if your Capricorn character can make money in a profession, he'll prove himself in it. Capricorn characters are ideally suited to careers in the corporate world, where they can become captains of industry. They like big business. They can also do well in careers where they have status and authority. They can be judges, police officers, headmasters, and high school teachers.

Costume Department

Even when they're wearing t-shirts and shorts, Capricorn characters look like they're dressed in three-piece suits. Like Saturn, the god of time, they always wear watches—and for the most part, they're dead serious about keeping track of time.

Any planet or personality in Capricorn seems serious and reserved. Capricorn children are especially so—but it's the one sign whose natives are said to grow younger with every passing year. So, at first glance, Capricorn characters might seem humorless, but look again, and you'll see a twinkle in their eyes. Rather than being joyless, they have a surprisingly dry and clever wit. They crack jokes at the most unexpected moments, and while they might catch their audience off-guard, they have an impeccable sense of comedic timing.

Capricorns speak with authority. They have strong, powerful voices, and they expect to be heard, seen, and obeyed. They're careful about where they walk and where they set their feet. They move slowly and deliberately, whether they're climbing toward the pinnacle of success or simply crossing the room. Since Capricorn rules the bones and skin, they have chiseled features and straight, white teeth.

Comfort

Around the world or around the universe, there's no place like home. Saturn, the ruler of Capricorn, is exceptionally well dignified in his domicile. The Moon, however, is debilitated; she'd rather be home than out and about in public. Mars is exalted in Capricorn, where it can put its executive skills to good use in business. Jupiter is in fall in Capricorn, the sign of business and industry, because there every reward must be earned.

Compatibility

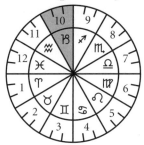

To gauge how well your Capricorn characters will relate to other signs, consider the elements. When earthy Capricorn combines with other earth signs, they literally build on each other's strengths. When earth mixes with air, the combination usually stirs up some dust—and could even lead to a windstorm. Earth and water can be a nurturing combination; rain nourishes natural growth. Earth and fire are generally a neutral combination, unless the earth is used to break a firestorm or quench the flames of desire.

You can also consider Capricorn's position on the zodiac wheel. Capricorn and Cancer are polar opposites, which means they see the world from opposing points of view. Capricorn is in a position of public visibility, while Cancer is safely ensconced at home. Because opposites attract, however, the two signs complement each other. Capricorn squares off against Aries and Libra; while they share the same cardinal signs of leadership and initiation, they tend to operate at cross-purposes. On the horoscope wheel, Capricorn, Taurus, and Virgo form an earthy pyramid of power. Their shared physical energy makes them especially well suited to work on building projects together.

The Capricorn Writer

If you have the Sun, Moon, or Mercury in Capricorn, you're all business when you put pen to paper. You write serious prose, for mature audiences. Don't let anyone tell you you're stodgy, though: your dry wit is always written between the lines. You probably like to write about business and finance, with a dash of politics and economics thrown in for good measure. You're a clear thinker with a definite message to share, and you always get right to the point.

Twenty Questions

1. *Capricorn is represented as a goat—and in some cases, a sea goat. How is your character like a goat? How is he like a fish?*

2. *Mountains symbolize obstacles to be overcome. What mountain is your character determined to climb?*

3. *What mountain of obstacles can you create to rise up in front of him?*

4. *Write about a social climber. What motivates his behavior?*

5. *It's often said that Capricorns are "born old." Describe your Capricorn character's childhood appearance. Did he look like a little old man?*

6. *Capricorn rules the bones and skin. Describe your character's complexion.*

7. *Capricorn is ruled by Saturn, the god of time. Write a scene in which time seems to come to a standstill.*

8. *Saturn could be compared to the Grim Reaper. How would your character react if he opened the door to find him standing there?*

9. *Can the Grim Reaper ever be an angel of mercy?*

10. *How would your character act if he were forced to play the role of the angel of death?*

11. *What does your character do for a living? Try to create a career path with an unexpected twist, like a doctor who's addicted to drugs, or a teacher who can't read.*

12. *Does your character like his job? Why or why not?*

13. *Describe your character's boss, co-workers, and underlings.*

14. *How has your character been rewarded for his work?*

15. *Capricorn rules the tenth house of the horoscope, where astrologers look for information about social status. Develop a storyline in which your character's reputation is destroyed by scandal.*

16. Base a character or a story on a prominent public figure.

17. Write about a character who has no class.

18. Go outside, look at the stars, and invent a constellation of your own, complete with modern mythology.

19. Use daily horoscopes to inspire story ideas.

20. Recast a favorite book, movie, or television show with characters based on the planets.

Aquarius,
the Water Bearer

Looking at these stars suddenly dwarfed my own troubles and all the gravities of terrestrial life. I thought of their unfathomable distance, and the slow inevitable drift of their movements out of the unknown past into the unknown future.

—H. G. Wells, *The Time Machine*

Characteristics

Aquarius is the sign of social consciousness and futuristic thinking—and the stars of its show are the visionaries who dream of a brighter tomorrow.

Fact Sheet

Ruling Planet: Aquarius is ruled by Uranus, the unconventional planet—which is one reason why Aquarians can be unpredictable characters. They're usually free thinkers. They're eccentric. And despite their love of humanity, they're not so fond of people on a one-to-one basis.

Physical Associations: Aquarius rules the shins, calves, and ankles. Most people are comfortable stepping into the river of time, but few characters dare to submerge themselves completely in the ever-changing future, as Aquarians do.

Signature Animal: Aquarius is usually pictured as young man with an amphora—a two-handled, oversized jar that held water or wine. According to myth and legend, he's Ganymede, the handsome young cupbearer of the gods. He lived with the gods on Mount

Olympus, where he kept their cups filled with ambrosia—the elixir of life, the nectar of the gods, and the drink of immortality. This imagery confuses a lot of people, who assume that Aquarius must be a water sign. Instead, it's an air sign. Aquarius is the sign of friends and social groups who gather to share their hopes, dreams, and ideas over a drink or two.

Glyph: The wavy glyph that represents this sign can symbolize waves of air, or wine sloshing around in a cup.

House Rulership: Aquarius is the eleventh sign of the zodiac. It rules the eleventh house of the horoscope, where astrologers look for information about social groups, social causes, and technology.

Mode: The Sun is usually in Aquarius between January 21 and February 20. This sign marks the third and final month of winter. That makes it a mutable sign: it's changeable and varied, to ease the transition from one season to the next.

Element: Aquarius is an air sign. The symbolism dovetails nicely with the fact that Aquarius, like Uranus, is comfortable broadcasting its technological vision over the airwaves.

Career Counseling

Aquarian characters are well suited to inventive and technological careers. They can be scientists, computer technicians, and software developers. They're masters of space-age technology, so they're comfortable in the cockpit of a jet or a space shuttle. They can also be mad scientists, alchemists, and inventors. They're visionaries, so they also make great novelists, photographers, and film makers.

Costume Department

Picture the most eccentric-looking person you can imagine, and you'll have found your Aquarius character.

Aquarians themselves aren't unattractive. In fact, just the opposite is true. They're usually just too preoccupied to pay attention to their looks. When they're busy pursuing their visions, their hygiene suffers. Their hair is messy and they could use a shower. Their clothes are wrinkled and mismatched. They might have forgotten to put on pants, or socks, or shoes. They look like they haven't slept for a while—because they haven't. They could use a little less coffee, and a little more food.

Comfort

Are you comfortable in a crowd? Are your characters? Saturn is—he's the traditional ruler of Aquarius, the sign of social groups and causes. As master of the domain, he can structure them in ways that boost their effectiveness and appeal.

The Sun, on the other hand, is debilitated in Aquarius—because he doesn't want to share the limelight.

Meanwhile, Mercury is exalted in Aquarius, the airy, intellectual sign that's associated with the technology of modern communication.

Compatibility

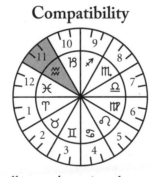

To determine how well your Aquarius character will relate to other signs, consider the elements. When airy Aquarius catches up with other air signs, they can join forces in a whirlwind of shared ideas and communication—or collide, like two massive cloud forms, in a thunderclap of energy. Aquarius's airy nature can feed and inspire fire—or blow it out. Aquarius also stirs up trouble with water; the air will either evaporates water, or whip it into a frenzy of crashing waves. When Aquarius brushes past the surface of the earth, it can either blow gently over the earth, raise clouds of dust, or twist and turn into a tornado.

You can also look at Aquarius's position on the zodiac wheel. Aquarius and Leo are polar opposites, which means they see the world from two different vantage points. Aquarius is high-minded and visionary; Leo sees himself as the center of the universe. Aquarius squares off against Taurus and Scorpio. The three signs share the same fixed mode, but they're typically too stubborn to work well together. Aquarius communicates best with the other air signs, Gemini and Libra; their shared element gives them plenty to talk about.

The Aquarius Writer

If you have the Sun, Moon, or Mercury in Aquarius, you write to change the world and create a brighter, better tomorrow. You have a utopian vision for the world that you want to share. You're an idealist, and your writing is one way you can effect real change. You're comfortable with the tools and technology of writing, too. In fact, you might not even rely on traditional publishing. You might self-publish your work, or broadcast your message through video or multimedia.

Twenty Questions

1. *Aquarius, the water bearer, is a glorified waiter—and you can tell a lot about people by the way they treat the waitstaff at a restaurant. How does your hero deal with those who serve him?*

2. *What gods—real or imagined—does your character serve?*

3. *Is your character an idealist? Why or why not?*

4. *Write about a character who loves humanity but hates all the people he knows.*

5. *Aquarius rules the eleventh house of the horoscope, where astrologers look for information about friends. Describe your character's social networks.*

6. *What brought them together? What keeps them connected?*

7. *How does your character behave at parties?*

8. *Is he good at small talk? What does he talk about?*

9. *Is your character outgoing or shy?*

10. *What is your character's favorite joke?*

11. *What are your character's dreams and visions for the future?*

12. *What social causes does your character support?*

13. *Aquarius is linked to eccentrics—and fools. How can you tell the difference?*

14. *Aquarius is ruled by Uranus, the planet of freedom, rebellion, and reform. What will your character rebel against, and why?*

15. *Will he succeed? How?*

16. *Both Uranus and Aquarius are linked to technology. Imagine a scientific discovery that could transform the world of your story.*

17. *Invent futuristic technology for your characters, or set your story in the future.*

18. *Aquarius is an air sign. Is your character intelligent, or simply an airhead?*

19. *Give your character an eccentricity. Consider, for example, an old-school hippie who's secretly a conservative at heart, or a university president who wears women's underwear under his three-piece suits.*

20. *Aquarians often break social norms. What boundaries will your characters cross? Will they be bigamists, nudists, or something even more unconventional?*

Pisces, the Fish

Seaward ho! Hang the treasure! It's the glory of the sea that has turned my head.

—Robert Louis Stevenson, *Treasure Island*

Characteristics

Pisces is the most mystical sign of the zodiac. While most people live entirely on the dry land of observable reality, Pisces characters are almost more comfortable swimming through the deep waters of intuition and spiritual transformation.

Pisces characters are sensitive and sympathetic. They're dreamy and idealistic. They're imaginative; sometimes it's hard for them to recognize the boundary between their visions and reality. More than anything, they're romantics who believe that beauty is truth and truth is beauty.

Fact Sheet

Ruling Planet: Pisces is ruled by Neptune, the planet of mystery and illusion. Neptune dissolves borders, just as a gently flowing river erodes its banks and waves wash away the shore.

Physical Association: Pisces rules the feet—the one part of the human form that's most in contact with the grounding qualities of the earth, but always ready to wade into the watery realm of emotion. On land, Pisces characters can be restless, changeable, and self-destructive. In water, their energy flows in more appropriate channels, and Pisces becomes adventurous, imaginative, creative, and artistic.

Signature Animal: Pisces is represented by a pair of fish. In Greek mythology, the two were Aphrodite and her son Eros. They turned themselves into fish to escape the monster Typhon, and they tied their tails together to make sure they didn't lose each other.

$$\mathcal{H}$$

Glyph: The Pisces glyph looks like two fish, tied with string.

House Rulership: Pisces is the twelfth sign of the zodiac. It rules the twelfth house of the horoscope, where astrologers look for information about our deepest, darkest secrets and desires—all submerged in the waters of memories, dreams, and reflections.

Mode: The Sun is usually in Pisces between February 19 and March 20. This sign marks the third and final month of winter. That makes it a mutable sign: it's changeable and varied, to ease the transition from one season to the next.

Element: Pisces is a water sign, which symbolizes Pisces' deep reserves of emotional energy.

Career Counseling

Because Pisces is so mystical, Pisces characters make great psychics, mediums, astrologers, and tarot readers. They can also be yoga masters and meditation guides. They can draw and paint their visions, too, or transform their ideas into stirring poetry and song.

Neptune's influence, however, often factors into the career path of some Pisces characters. They find themselves irresistibly drawn to drink—or drugs—where they can drown their sorrows and submerge themselves in an alternate reality. Send your character off to recovery, and then they can find work as bartenders and rehab counselors.

Pisces characters can also be excellent healers who feel at home as doctors, nurses, and therapists in hospitals and clinics.

Costume Department

When they're in their own element, Pisces fish are shimmering and mesmerizing. Don't fight it. Put your characters in swimsuits and scuba gear, and plunge them into the surf. If that's not possible, at least make sure they can dress in iridescent colors and scintillating jewels. They might even appreciate a few tattoos that look like scales.

Pisces characters are short, with soft skin and wavy hair. They move as if they're swimming, even on land. They're tranquil; they seem to float through life, with a dreamy expression and a tendency to drift off during conversation.

Comfort

Jupiter is the traditional ruler of Pisces, which makes the king of the gods feel as comfortable in water as on land. Mercury, however, is debilitated when he falls in this sign, because he's forced to wallow in the depths of Pisces' watery emotions. Venus is exalted in Pisces, a sign of emotional partnership and connection.

Compatibility

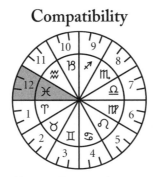

To determine how well your Pisces characters will relate to other signs, consider the elements. When watery Pisces nourishes earth, it nurtures the soil and promotes growth. When water combines with fire, however, it either quenches the flames or sizzles, steams, or evaporates. Water will dampen air; it could even lead to a downpour of torrential proportions. And when one body of water flows into another, it takes the shape of its container and rises to its own level.

You can also look at Pisces' position on the zodiac wheel. Pisces and Virgo are polar opposites. Virgo wants to pay precise attention to detail, but Pisces wants to float through an alternate reality. Pisces squares off against Sagittarius and Gemini. While they share the same easygoing mutability, their missions are elementally at odds. Pisces has the most in common with the other water signs, Cancer and Scorpio. Together, they can go with the flow.

The Pisces Writer

If you have the Sun, Moon, or Mercury in Pisces, you write to escape the harsh realities of everyday life and connect with kindred spirits. You're a born mystic—and when you write, you almost go into a trance. You're a natural empath and healer, and you might write about spirituality, meditation, or psychic ability. You should definitely keep a dream journal.

Twenty Questions

1. *The symbol for Pisces depicts two fish, tied together. What ties your character to other people? Is there one person in particular with whom she's inextricably linked?*

2. *How is your character like a fish?*

3. *Pisces rules the twelfth house of the horoscope, where astrologers look for information about buried secrets. What has your character submerged deep beneath the surface?*

4. *Snoop around in your character's medicine chest, cabinets, and drawers. What does she have hidden away from public view?*

5. *What skeletons are rattling in her closets?*

6. *Does your character have any repressed memories? Send your character to a hypnotist to find out.*

7. *Pisces is ruled by Neptune, the planet of glamour and illusion. What veil clouds your character's view of reality?*

8. *The twelfth house was traditionally linked to institutions like hospitals, asylums, and prisons. Has your character ever spent time in a secure facility? Why? Was she a client, or a care provider?*

9. *Set a story in the lockup of your choice.*

10. *Pisces is a mystical sign. Is your character psychic? How does that help or hinder her in her daily life?*

11. *Pisces is also a sign associated with vivid dreams. How could you use that in a story?*

12. *What thoughts bubble to the surface when your character is alone?*

13. *Pisces personalities tend to be highly addictive. You could write about a character who's hooked on alcohol or drugs—or you could devise an even more unusual addiction, like helium, or strong cheeses, or online crossword puzzles.*

14. *Pisceans are also escapists. Who—or what—does your character want to flee?*

15. *Where will she go?*

16. *Immerse your character in a realm completely different from her own. The naturally watery character associated with Pisces could be submerged in a fiery hell—perhaps of her own making.*

17. *Pisces is a mutable sign. Pisces characters can go with the flow. Is that one of your heroine's strengths, or is it her weakness?*

18. *Pisces rules the feet. How would you describe your character's feet?*

19. *What kind of shoes does she wear?*

20. *How does she stay grounded?*

Mix-and-Match Character Creator

Conflict and contradiction are hallmarks of the human experience, as well as the essence of good drama. With this mix-and-match character creator, you can develop characters that struggle against their own natures. You can invest them with unreasonable demands and unattainable desires. Simply give each character a role based on a planetary archetype in column A, combined with drives and desires from a zodiac sign in column B.

To heighten the drama even further, cast against type. Make a star a supporting character. Force a stand-in into a leading role. Turn your love interest into a hero. Surprise your readers with unexpected and unconventional combinations.

COLUMN A Central Casting		COLUMN B Character Types		
Planetary Roles		Zodiac Signs		
Planet/ Asteroid	Literary Archetypes	Sign	Motivation, Drives, and Desires	Typical Careers
Sun	Hero, Protagonist, King	Aries (Ruled by Mars)	Independence, Importance, Decisiveness, Leadership	Politician, Civic Leader, Business Executive, Soldier, Fighter, Athlete, Police Officer, Firefighter, Mechanic, Construction Worker, Surgeon, Dentist
Moon	Best Friend, Roommate, Wife, Mother, Grandmother, Queen, Girl Next Door			

COLUMN A Central Casting		COLUMN B Character Types		
Planetary Roles		Zodiac Signs		
Planet/ Asteroid	Literary Archetypes	Sign	Motivation, Drives, and Desires	Typical Careers
Mercury	Brother, Sister, Cousin, Sidekick, Gossip, Neighbor, Comic Relief	Taurus (Ruled by Venus)	Grace, Beauty, Comfort and Stability	Designer, Decorator, Singer, Musi- cian, Sculptor, Art Collector, Banker, Finan- cial Manager, Beautician
Venus	Lover, Love Interest, Object of Desire, Temptress, Seductress, Unfaithful Wife	Gemini (Ruled by Mercury)	Commu- nication, Information, Conversation, Clever Dis- course	Writer, Journal- ist, Broadcaster, Advertiser, Communicator, Grade School Teacher, Mes- senger, Mail Carrier, Taxi Driver, Courier
Mars	Antagonist, Adversary, Opponent, Warrior, Patriot, Compatriot, Comrade- in-Arms	Cancer (Ruled by the Moon)	Nurturing, Emotional Security, Family Connection	Homemaker, Caregiver, Chef, Restaurateur, Small Business Owner, Gar- dener, Farmer, Patriot
Jupiter	Benefac- tor, Kindly Uncle, Generous Grandfa- ther	Leo (Ruled by the Sun)	Dignity, Respect, Love, Honor, Admi- ration, Fame, Fortune	Actor, Enter- tainer, Model, Movie Star, Media Personal- ity, Politician

COLUMN A Central Casting		COLUMN B Character Types		
Planetary Roles		Zodiac Signs		
Planet/ Asteroid	Literary Archetypes	Sign	Motivation, Drives, and Desires	Typical Careers
Saturn	Father Figure, Authority Figure, Teacher, Commander, Disciplinarian	Virgo (Ruled by Venus)	Perfection, Discipline, Organization, Self-Control	Librarian, Researcher, Analyst, Nutritionist, Doctor, Nurse, Therapist, Medical Technician
Uranus	Rebel, Revolutionary, Instigator	Libra (Ruled by Venus)	Refinement, Grace, Charm and Popularity, Balance and Equanimity	Judge, Arbitrator, Negotiator, Mediator, Marriage Counselor, Ambassador, Artist, Musician, Dancer
Neptune	Free Spirit, Mystic, Celebrity, Addict	Scorpio (Ruled by Pluto)	Spiritual Depth, Psychological Understanding	Detective, Spy, Psychiatrist, Psychologist, Coroner, Mortician
Pluto	Grim Reaper, Mass Murderer, Serial Killer, Demon, Vampire, Monster	Sagittarius (Ruled by Jupiter)	Experience, Expertise, Knowledge, Authority, and Credentials	Traveler, Explorer, Philosopher, Minister, Priest, Rabbi, Lawyer, Publisher, Professor
Ceres	Earth Mother			
Pallas Athena	Activist, Amazon Warrior			

COLUMN A		COLUMN B		
Central Casting		Character Types		
Planetary Roles		Zodiac Signs		
Planet/ Asteroid	Literary Archetypes	Sign	Motivation, Drives, and Desires	Typical Careers
Juno	Faithful Partner, Jealous Wife	Capricorn (Ruled by Saturn)	Power, Recognition, Social Status, Financial Success	Big Business Owner, Entrepreneur, Captain of Industry, Philanthropist, High School Teacher, Police Officer, Judge
Vesta	Strong Single Woman			
Lilith	Woman Scorned			
Chiron	Wounded Healer			
		Aquarius (Ruled by Uranus)	Innovation, Social Change, Visionary Thinking	Pilot, Astronaut, Scientist, Inventor, Computer Technician, Software Developer, Novelist, Photographer, Filmmaker, Humanitarian
		Pisces (Ruled by Neptune)	Idealism, Mysticism, Compassion and Healing	Psychic, Medium, Astrologer, Tarot Reader, Yoga Master, Bartender, Rehab Counselor

Creative Guidance

It's important to note that astrology is a visual art. It's based on the observation of the stars and constellations. While there's a mathematical and scientific component to them, they're all illustrated with pictographic glyphs and symbols. If you'd like even more visual reminders about the imagery and associations of astrology, check out my books Tarot for Writers *and* Tarot and Astrology.

Behind the Scenes: The Twelve Labors of Hercules

Let's conclude our survey of the signs with a brief journey through one of the greatest astrology-based legends of all time: the twelve labors of Hercules. It demonstrates clearly how storytellers have tapped into the power of myth and legend for centuries.

Here's a brief overview.

Hercules was half-man, half-god. And even though Jupiter was his father, Hercules had the misfortune of having Hera for a step-mother. That's because Hercules was the result of Jupiter's affair with a woman named Alcmene.

Hera did everything in her power to keep Hercules from being born. When that failed, she sent snakes to kill the infant Hercules in his crib. Hercules strangled them before they could bite.

After years of torment, Hera eventually tricked Hercules into murdering his own wife and children. Grief-stricken, he fled to the Temple of Apollo to get advice from the Oracle of Delphi. There he was told that he could atone by serving the cruel King Eurystheus.

Eurystheus demanded that Hercules complete twelve impossible tasks—which just happen to correspond to the twelve signs of the zodiac.

1. *Aries and the Girdle of Hippolyta:* Hippolyta was the queen of the Amazons, and she owned a magical belt—or girdle—that had been given to her by the god Aries. King Eurystheus's daughter wanted it for herself. Hercules charmed Hippolyta, and she was willing to give him the belt—until Hera interfered. She posed as an ordinary

woman and planted seeds of distrust and dissent among the Amazons, who feared that Hercules was planning to carry away their queen. When they confronted him, Hercules overreacted and killed Hippolyta, and then left with the belt. How does the story connect to Aries? The constellation Andromeda sets in Aries. The constellation looks like Queen Hippolyta, right down to her three-starred belt. The Pleiades can be found there, too. The Greeks called the Pleiades the seven sisters, like a band of Amazons.

2. *Taurus and the Cretan Bull:* When a giant bull started wreaking havoc on the island of Crete, destroying crops and demolishing orchard walls, Eurystheus sent Hercules to capture the animal. Hercules simply strangled the bull with his bare hands. Eventually the bull was sacrificed to the gods, which is how it found its way into heaven as the constellation Taurus.

3. *Gemini and the Cows of Geryon:* Geryon was a three-headed giant who lived on the island of Erytheia. He had a herd of red cattle, guarded by a two-headed hound named Orthrus. Hercules killed the dog with a single blow from an olive branch, and then shot Geryon with an arrow that had been dipped in the venomous blood of the Lernaean Hydra. The stars helped ancient storytellers share the tale. They pointed out how Hercules crossed the deserted open space of Gemini to reach Geryon's dairy cows in the Milky Way. They also referred to Capella, the shepherd's star, the dog-shaped Canis Major, and the Dog Star Sirius.

4. *Cancer and the Hydra:* Hera had raised a nine-headed Hydra to kill Hercules. Instead, Hercules killed the monster—but only after realizing that simply cutting off its heads wouldn't work. For every head the hero cut off, two more heads grew in its place. Hercules called his nephew Iolaus to help; Iolaus used a torch to cauterize each stump before a new head could grow. When Hera saw that Hercules was winning his battle, she sent a crab to annoy and distract him. Hercules crushed it under his foot and kept fighting. Hera honored both the monster and the crab by turning them into the constellations Hydra and Cancer.

5. *Leo and the Nemean Lion:* The Nemean Lion was a shapeshifter who posed as a damsel in distress and devoured any warrior who came to her rescue. Hercules tried to shoot the lion with arrows, but its fur was impenetrable. Eventually, Hercules simply strangled the lion with his bare hands. For the rest of his labors, Hercules wore the lion's skin like armor. The lion, of course, is Leo's signature animal.

6. *Virgo and the Erymanthean Boar:* On his way to kill a wild boar, Hercules visited the centaurs—wild creatures that were half-men, half-horse. They started drinking wine; the centaurs got drunk and attacked Hercules. He defended himself with poisoned arrows, and in the process, he struck his friend and teacher Chiron. The wound was agonizing, but because Chiron was immortal, even death couldn't offer a release. Ultimately, Chiron agreed to trade places with Prometheus, who was chained to the top of a mountain where an eagle continually ravaged his liver. Unfortunately, Chiron still couldn't die, and the eagle attacked him until Hercules shot it from the sky. Relieved of his suffering, Chiron told Hercules that he could catch the boar by driving it into heavy snow. When the Sun is in Virgo, it's directly above the constellation Centaurus, which marks Chiron's place of honor in the heavens.

7. *Libra and the Apples of the Hesperides:* The Hesperides were three nymphs who guarded the golden apples of immortality. Hercules actually tricked Atlas into picking some of the apples for him, by offering to hold up the heavens in Atlas's place. When Atlas declared that he didn't want to resume his duties, Hercules tricked him again, saying he just needed a minute to adjust his cloak. Atlas shouldered his burden once more, and Hercules fled with the apples. The constellation Ursa Minor, directly above Libra, was once thought to be the Hesperides. It includes three bright stars.

8. *Scorpio and the Golden Hind:* The goddess Artemis owned a Golden Hind, a magical stag that was so fast it could outrun an arrow. Hercules tracked and hunted it for a year. Eventually he captured it. While King Eurystheus had hoped that Artemis would punish him for

capturing her sacred animal, Hercules begged for her indulgence and promised to return it after presenting it to the king. Hercules had to be clever to keep his promise: he pretended to hand the animal over to the king, but the minute he let it go, the Hind bounded back to Artemis. At one point, the constellation Hercules was considered to be a stag. It's next to the arrow-shaped constellation Sagitta, and it rises when the Sun is in Scorpio.

9. *Sagittarius and the Stymphalian Birds:* The Stymphalian birds were man-eating vultures with bronze beaks and metallic feathers. Hercules used a rattle to frighten them into the air, and then shot them down with his bow and arrow. When the Sun is in Sagittarius—the sign of the archer—three constellations associated with birds also happen to rise: Lyra, Aquila, and Cygnus.

10. *Capricorn and the Augean Stables:* King Eurystheus gave Hercules a task he knew was impossible: he gave him a single day to clean the Augean stables, where one thousand immortal cattle were housed. The stables hadn't been cleaned in decades, but Hercules simply rerouted two rivers to wash out the filth. The constellation of Capricorn was once known as Augeas, because the Sun seems to stable there during the winter.

11. *Aquarius and the Mares of Diomedes:* A man named Diomedes had stolen horses from an enemy king, and Eurystheus ordered Hercules to steal them back. Unfortunately, no one told Hercules that the horses were mad from eating human flesh. When Hercules asked his companion Abderus to guard the mares while he fought Diomedes, the horses ate the boy. Hercules retaliated by feeding Diomedes to the horses, too. The horses were contented with their feast, and Hercules simply bound their mouths shut and took them home. When the Sun is in Aquarius, the stars of the winged horse Pegasus rise in the heavens. In fact, Pegasus almost seems poised to eat the human form of Aquarius beneath him.

12. *Pisces and the Hound of Hell:* Cerberus was a three-headed dog who guarded the entrance to Hades' underground realm. Eurystheus wanted Hercules to capture Cerberus alive, without using weapons.

Athena, Hermes, and Hestia helped him in and out of the under-world, and Hades gave him permission to take his pet to Eurystheus. Hercules dragged the dog home. Eurystheus was so afraid of the animal that he agreed to release Hercules from his labors if he would simply return the hound to Hades. Astrologically, the constellation Pisces resembles two forms who are trapped and bound, just like some of the souls Hercules encountered in his travels through the underworld.

Creative Guidance

1. *Borrow the idea of Hercules' twelve labors, and give your character twelve zodiac-based challenges to overcome.*

2. *Use the twelve signs as the foundation of a travelogue, and write about the signs as if they were foreign places—either cities, states, or countries.*

3. *Describe opposing signs of the zodiac as two very different countries, opposite in every respect.*

4. *Develop a theme based on planetary archetypes and zodiac symbolism:*
   - *Aries—independence*
   - *Taurus—security*
   - *Gemini—curiosity*
   - *Cancer—emotional security*
   - *Leo—pride*
   - *Virgo—discipline*
   - *Libra—partnership*
   - *Scorpio—mystery*
   - *Sagittarius—exploration*
   - *Capricorn—success*
   - *Aquarius—vision*
   - *Pisces—connection*

The Hero's Journey

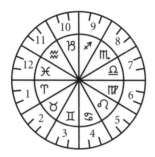

Many writers are familiar with the Hero's Journey—the mythical literary model that Joseph Campbell first outlined in his book *The Hero with a Thousand Faces*.[1] The Hero's Journey involves several rites of passage, all of which revolve around a basic storyline of separation, initiation, transformation, and return. The model dovetails with a number of popular epics, including *Star Wars* and the Harry Potter series. And even though the Hero's Journey dates back to the *Iliad* and the *Odyssey*, the storyline feels fresh and familiar to modern audiences, too.

The Hero's Journey corresponds perfectly with the archetypes of the zodiac. In fact, the Hero's Journey can even be mapped on the zodiac wheel.

Stages of the Hero's Journey

- *Aries: The Call to Adventure.* As a story begins, the hero is plunged into a new world—and a new reality. He's expected to leave his old world—and his old self—behind. While Aries is the sign of self-awareness, leadership, and initiation, personal growth always comes at a price. No one likes to leave the comfort of his old way of life behind.

---

1. Joseph Campbell, *The Hero with a Thousand Faces* (1949; reprint, Princeton, NJ: Princeton University Press, 1972).

- *Taurus: Refusal of the Call.* Unwilling to leave the life he's always known, the hero initially refuses to heed the call. Like Taurus, he fights to maintain the comfort and security of home. He might also recognize that he's not up to the task that's being asked of him—because he's not. Heroes aren't born: they're made.

- *Gemini: Allies, Mentors, and Helpers.* Gemini is the sign of intellect, thought, communication, and community. Forced to move out of his comfort zone, the hero learns that he doesn't have to rise to the challenge on his own. As he embarks on his journey, he meets a series of messengers, guides, and magical helpers. Some of his allies aren't obvious: they serve as guardians and gatekeepers, and it's their job to test the hero's commitment to his calling. He'll meet them coming and going, both as he embarks on his adventure and as he tries to make a return trip home.

- *Cancer: The Crossing of the Threshold.* The hero finds his footing in the new world and develops the foundation he needs to proceed with his quest. Cancer is the sign of home and family life, and at this point, the hero realizes that home is wherever he hangs his hat; it's an internal state. Likewise, he recognizes that family connections are emotional, and relationships can be chosen.

- *Leo: The Road of Trials.* Leo is the sign of courage and creativity. Like the king of beasts, the hero is forced to prove his courage and determination through a series of tests, tasks, or ordeals. Each challenge seems insurmountable, and they only increase in difficulty.

- *Virgo: The Belly of the Whale.* Virgo is the sign of intellect and discrimination. As the story reaches its climax, the hero finds himself in "the belly of the whale"—the final line between his old life and the new world that awaits him. Imprisoned and isolated by events and circumstances, the hero is forced into a period of self-examination. He finds the strength to overcome his fears. He faces his demons and slays his dragons. He realizes that true transformation occurs internally, through conscious analysis and choice.

- *Libra: Allies and Enemies.* Libra is the sign of intimate partnerships—and open enemies. As the story unfolds, the hero grows through his relationships with others. While he finds comfort and reassurance among those who swear allegiance to his cause, it's his sworn adversaries who force him to compete at a higher level.

- *Scorpio: The Ultimate Ordeal.* Scorpio is the sign of death, transformation, and unavoidable change. As the story moves toward its climax, the hero must fight for his very life—and come to terms with a devastating loss in the process. Once he's no longer afraid to die, he's free to live life to its fullest. A hard-fought victory at this stage will leave him feeling reborn, with a new awareness and a new appreciation for life.

- *Sagittarius: The Ultimate Boon.* Sagittarius is the sign of long-distance travel, philosophy, and higher education. A hero initially sets out in search of a mythical prize—a Holy Grail. After the ultimate ordeal, the hero discovers that his quest wasn't actually for a tangible reward, but for spiritual mastery. Each step of the journey along the way served to prepare him for that realization, and helped purify him to receive it. Once he passes through his ordeal and claims his reward, he realizes his ultimate truth and discovers the meaning of life.

- *Capricorn: Recognition and Reward.* Capricorn is the sign of career, social status, and public recognition. Once the hero has captured his prize, he's publicly recognized for his victory. That recognition, however, rings hollow, because he's still a stranger in a strange land. He needs to make his way back home.

- *Aquarius: The Return.* Aquarius is the visionary sign of friends, social groups, and personal causes. At this stage of the Hero's Journey, the hero's experience has broadened his vision and endowed him with a sense of vision and idealism. His new friends beg him not to leave. Circumstances demand, however, that he fight his way back to those he left behind.

- *Pisces: Return with Elixir, Master of Two Worlds.* Pisces is the mystical sign of spiritual growth. As the story concludes, the hero comes full circle. He returns to his starting point. He's not the same man, though. He's been transformed, both physically and spiritually. He's irrevocably changed, because he's conquered his primal drives and desires, and now he's the master of the inner and outer planes of existence. By the conclusion of the story, the hero has developed a sense of mastery over both of the worlds he's experienced. He can bridge the gap between ordinary life and magical ability, along with the extremes of physical and spiritual existence, inner and outer realities, and human and divine interactions. Ultimately, the hero will discover the best prize of all: wisdom.

Like a horoscope chart, the best stories come full circle, as characters move through phases of experience and understanding and then return to their starting point, older, sadder, wiser, forever changed, and richer for the experience.

Creative Guidance

1. *Send your character into a world completely different from his own. Perhaps his ordinary world is one of brightness and illumination. How does he deal with a shadowy reality? How does he find his way through darkness?*

2. *A hero's journey can be literal or metaphorical. Perhaps your character was born into the wealth and privilege of a New York penthouse, but he's compelled to travel to the slums and favelas of Rio de Janeiro. Maybe he's used to the bright lights of the big city, but then wakes up to find himself in the hills of Tennessee.*

3. *The concept works both ways: maybe he's a creature of darkness, like a vampire, who's cursed to rise with the Sun. Be creative. Simply take a character who's comfortable in one realm, and plunge him into a whole new world. The trip will be good for both of you.*

PART III

The Houses of the Horoscope

The twelve houses of the horoscope provide a backdrop and setting for the drama of human experience. If you're searching for the setting of your next story or scene, you don't need to look any further than a horoscope chart.

Setting:
A Cosmic Backdrop

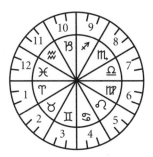

The planets and signs all come together in a horoscope chart—a visual snapshot of the sky at a given point in time. Like a map of the cosmos, it's a convenient way to pinpoint the positions of the planets as they move through the signs of the zodiac.

On paper, the zodiac is charted like a circle—which reflects our view of the solar system, looking out at space from our vantage point on Earth.

The chart is divided like a pie into twelve sections, or houses. That term comes from ancient astrologers who believed that each house of the horoscope was the dominion of a god.

In the next few pages, we'll learn how to read a horoscope chart. For now, however, we'll focus on the basic symbolism of the twelve houses.

Zodiac Houses

Each house of a horoscope naturally corresponds to one of the twelve signs of the zodiac—and from a symbolic standpoint, each house describes a specific focus on a separate area of life.

Here's a brief overview of the significance of each house, along with their ruling signs and planets. You'll probably notice some overlap between the symbolism of each house and its corresponding sign.

House	Rulership	Ruling Sign	Ruling Planet
First House	Physical appearance, first impressions, self-awareness	Aries, the ram; associated with leadership	Mars, planet of energy, self-assertion, and aggression
Second House	Money, possessions; values security, creature comforts, material resources	Taurus, the bull; associated with property	Venus, planet of love and attraction
Third House	Communication, thought process, learning style, siblings, neighborhoods	Gemini, the twins; associated with communication	Mercury, planet of speed and communication
Fourth House	Motherhood, home, family, emotional well-being, the ability to nurture and be nurtured, intuition	Cancer, the crab; associated with protection and nurturing	The Moon, orb of reflection and feminine cycles
Fifth House	Creation, procreation, recreation	Leo, the lion; associated with courage and showmanship	The Sun, source of energy and enlightenment
Sixth House	Work, duty, responsibility, service to others, health, attention to detail	Virgo, the virgin; associated with health and cleanliness	Mercury, planet of speed and communication
Seventh House	Marriage, partnerships, intimate relationships, balance, social skills, open enemies	Libra, the scales; associated with justice, equality, and balance	Venus, planet of love and attraction

House	Rulership	Ruling Sign	Ruling Planet
Eighth House	Sex, death, joint resources, other people's money	Scorpio, the scorpion; associated with the dark mysteries of life	Pluto, planet of death, resurrection, and unavoidable change
Ninth House	Philosophy, long-distance travel, higher education	Sagittarius, the archer; associated with honesty and exploration	Jupiter, planet of luck and expansion
Tenth House	Ambition, status, career, public image, fathers and authority figures	Capricorn, the goat; associated with work and rewards	Saturn, planet of structure, foundation, boundaries, and limitations
Eleventh House	Social groups; causes; futuristic, long-term thinking	Aquarius, the water bearer; associated with visions of a better world	Uranus, planet of independence, revolution, and rebellion
Twelfth House	Psychic ability, the occult, hidden places, subconscious mind, psychological health	Pisces, the fish; associated with intuition	Neptune, planet of mysticism and illusion

Creative Guidance

When you create characters, you'll need to know a lot about them. Filling in the wheel of a horoscope chart is a good starting point. You'll find a slot for every detail: physical appearance, possessions, childhood, family, hobbies, children, dietary habits, partners, philosophy, religion, higher education, career, social status, friends, dreams, and secrets. All have a place in the houses of the horoscope.

Behind the Scenes: Setting as Character

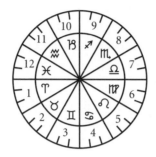

Cities, states, and countries all have birth charts—just like people do. The charts are based on the date and time of their founding, usually as documented by official records and articles of incorporation.

The United States, for example, was born on the Fourth of July, which gives it a Cancerian Sun. Cancerians are fiercely patriotic, nurturing, and emotional, but they're also driven to lead and take care of others. The United States also has a Sagittarius ascendant, which adds a dash of bravery, daring, optimism, and outspokenness to its people as a whole.

A well-developed setting can add character to any story—and even take on a life of its own. The environment your characters choose—or find themselves thrust into—offers challenges and benefits.

You can model your environment on planetary symbolism. Will your setting be harsh and unforgiving, like Saturn, or mystical and dreamy, like Neptune? Will your characters find themselves submerged in Pluto's underworld, or bounding across the low gravity of the Moon?

You could also choose to play with the imagery of the signs. Picture the possibilities that the elements present, as your characters find themselves in places that are earthy and grounded, watery and emotional, airy and intellectual, or fiery and spirited. Will they be engulfed in the fiery enthusiasm of Aries, Leo, and Sagittarius? Surrounded by the intellectual ideals of Gemini, Libra, or Aquarius, or submerged in the deep waters of Cancer, Scorpio, and Pisces? Maybe they'll focus on the earthy realities of Taurus, Virgo, and Capricorn.

The backdrop of your story can make or break your characters. Does it propel them or suffocate them? Does it provide drama and conflict? Is it a friend or a foe? Does it provide structure and guidance? Are there places where your characters can find sustenance and support? Does it offer obstacles that can be overcome, with room for growth? Will they stake their claim and live or die there?

How can your characters turn the setting to their advantage? The setting will become a part of them, for good or bad, where they discover their truest selves. Even scenes can be set in places that will reflect your characters' personalities, where they can blend into the crowd or set themselves apart.

Creative Guidance

The houses of the horoscope aren't merely symbolic. Each one can be linked to a clearly defined landscape. While you'll probably want to develop your own associations, here are some starting points.

- *Aries—a hot, dry desert*
- *Taurus—a cool green pasture*
- *Gemini—the clear blue sky*
- *Cancer—a shadowy, moonlit land*
- *Leo—a tropical jungle*
- *Virgo—a farmer's field*
- *Libra—a pleasant meadow*
- *Scorpio—graveyards and the underworld*
- *Sagittarius—a college campus*
- *Capricorn—a mountaintop*
- *Aquarius—outer space*
- *Pisces—an ocean*

The First House

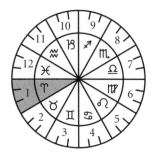

Image and Identity

Think of each house of the horoscope as a scenic backdrop, and you'll be able to evaluate the planets and signs that make every horoscope chart a unique place for a story to unfold.

The first house reveals the first thing you'll notice about anyone you meet—including your fictional characters. When the curtain rises on the first house of the horoscope, viewers see the stage for the first time. The first house establishes the time and place of a story, and anchors its characters in a fictional world. It's the house of physical appearances and first impressions, as well as the face we show the world. Occasionally, it is a façade. What you see isn't always what you get.

In literature, the first house is the main entry to the story. It's where readers can make a quick decision about the mood, tone, theme, and type of story. It's not fair to trick them with false starts or empty promises; make sure your establishing shot sets up the story you really want to tell.

In the natural zodiac, the first house is ruled by Aries, the sign of leadership and initiation. Aries is ruled, in turn, by Mars, the red planet of action, self-assertion, and aggression. Mars accentuates Aries' daring nature, and powers its drives and desires.

In real life, however, the earth is constantly revolving through the zodiac, so any of the twelve signs could mark the first house in a horoscope.

No matter what sign is on the cusp—or in the house—the first house will always be somewhat Arian in nature, and planets in the first house will always take on some of Mars's energy. And because the first house is so prominent, any planets here will be important indicators of personality, story, and setting.

Scenery and Setting

Most stories open with drama and action—which is just what you'd expect from Mars, the ruler of the first house. Mars is the ancient god of war, and when he steps into the spotlight, you can expect crisis and conflict. No one wants to read about an ordinary day in an ordinary life, and Mars delivers by offering us a wide range of tragic accidents, crimes against humanity, and physical and psychological attacks.

On a practical level, Mars's association with war links the first house to forts, armories, battlefields, and sports arenas. Mars's command of iron and weaponry connects the first house to factories, machine shops, tool sheds, junkyards, and hardware stores, as well as surgical centers, dental offices, and even barbershops.

Aries, the sign of leadership and initiation, also rules the first house. You can use its fiery elemental association to inspire scenes in dry, hot places, like bakeries, furnace rooms, boiler rooms, steel plants, and forges.

The Second House

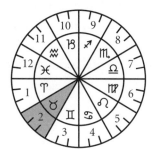

Treasured Possessions

How much money do your characters have? How do they earn it? How do they spend it? Take a peek into the second house, and you'll spot important clues about their financial situation, as well as their spiritual values. You'll even get a glimpse into their own self-worth.

The second house is the house of money, treasures, and possessions. It's ruled by Taurus—which is ruled, in turn, by Venus. Both the planet and the sign are naturally drawn to comfort—even opulence. They favor luxury and tradition, objects of beauty, fine art, and uplifting music.

More importantly, Venus and Taurus crave comfort and security. The signs and planets linked to the second house will show you how secure they truly are, as well as what kind of a roof your characters have over their heads.

Scenery and Setting

Planets and characters in the second house surround themselves with furnishings and belongings that make them comfortable. The second house is also where they can display sentimental treasures, as well as tokens of self-worth and self-esteem.

The scenery of the second house isn't necessarily designed to impress visitors; it's there for comfort and convenience. The planets and signs you'll find in the second house, however, can show you how your characters invest their hard-earned money, as well as how much money they can afford to spend.

When you use the second house to suggest scenery and settings, picture the earthy Taurus bull. He can usually be found in a bucolic countryside, in a meadow or grassy pasture. You can expand that association to imagine more civilized settings of wealth and luxury, like banks, stock brokers, jewelry stores, and high-end gift shops.

Venus, the cultured goddess of beauty and attraction, might also inspire thoughts of museums, art galleries, concert halls, orchestras, opera houses, movie theaters, ballet companies, and Broadway shows.

The Third House

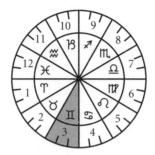

Community and Communication

The third house of a horoscope describes your characters' neighborhoods—the communities of family and friends they were born into, as well as those they build for themselves.

The small world of the third house is ruled by Mercury, the messenger of the gods. When he was at his peak, his work took him all over Mount Olympus, ferrying communiqués to and from the pantheon of gods—most of whom were related to one another.

The third house is home to the Gemini twins, which links it to sibling relationships. The third house also covers interactions with aunts, uncles, and cousins.

What sort of neighborhood will you choose for your story? Will it be urban and crowded, packed with planetary influences, or wide like the open prairie? Check the sign on the cusp, as well as any intercepted or changed signs within the house. A fire sign might suggest a busy neighborhood, while an earth sign could hint at a bucolic country life. An air sign might be an upscale city skyscraper or a mountaintop community. A water sign could be a beachfront neighborhood—or an island oasis, in or out of civilization. Use your imagination. Let the planets and the signs lead you to your own conclusions.

Scenery and Setting

Gemini, the sign of thought and communication, rules the third house. The sign's connection to primary education often suggests grade-school settings, including classrooms, playgrounds, lunch rooms, gymnasiums, and auditoriums.

Mercury's presence will make itself felt in the adult world, too. The god of communication is comfortable in libraries, newsrooms, radio stations, libraries, and bookstores. You'll find him wherever there's a computer, a phone, or a stack of mail. He might even lead you to a post office, a telegraph bureau, or a dispatch station.

If you're looking for an outdoor setting, consider the airy elemental association, and look up, where the air is thin and rarified, or anywhere the wind blows.

The Fourth House

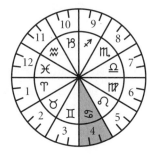

Home and Family

The fourth house is the foundation of the chart, so it describes the emotional foundations of home and family, as well as childhood nurturing and memories. It's the home base. It's the place we leave to work and see the world, and it's the place that beckons us back at the end of the day or the end of our lives.

In the natural zodiac, the fourth house is ruled by Cancer, the sign of motherhood. The sign represents emotional and physical well-being, along with fierce protectiveness. After all, Cancer's crab carries its home on its back, and fights fiercely to defend it.

Cancer is ruled, in turn, by the Moon, the celestial sphere of reflection and cyclical change. It's the landscape of memories, dreams, and reflections. The Moon also casts a soft, silvery light on the feminine realm of marriage and children.

Scenery and Setting

The signs and planets in your character's fourth house reflect their upbringing, as well as the home and family life they'll try to create for themselves.

A fourth-house setting will probably lead straight to a kitchen— the heart of the home, and the place where both body and soul can find sustenance. Cancer's love of food also links the fourth house to gardens, fields, pastures, vineyards, and orchards, as well as grocery stores, bakeries, restaurants, cafeterias, and dining rooms. Cancer's more generalized link to homemaking could also suggest places where we conduct the mundane tasks of family life, like pantries and laundry rooms. Cancer's association with nurturing could suggest a setting in a nursery school or day care center.

The sign's connection to family foundations might also suggest a setting in an ancient city, an ancestral homeland, a castle, or a family farm.

The sign's signature animal, the crab, carries its home on its back. It's a mobile home. Your characters might be living in a trailer park, or simply camping in a national park.

If you'd like to take your characters outside, lead them to water, and let them spend time at the beach, or near fountains, lakes, rivers, streams, waterfalls, and oceans.

The Fifth House

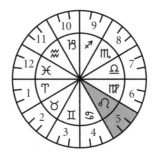

Creation, Recreation, and Procreation

Leo, the king of beasts, rules the fifth house of the horoscope. It's a lion's den of amusement and enjoyment, where your characters will find room for creation, recreation, and procreation.

Leo is ruled, in turn, by the Sun, the showman of the zodiac. He uses the fifth house as a stage, where he can perform for the pleasure of his company.

No matter what sign or planet is linked to the fifth house of a chart, planets that land in the rec room will automatically assume a playful, creative energy.

Scenery and Setting

The fifth house is a place for fun and frolic. It's also a center for arts, crafts, and entertainment. You can think of it as a rec room, a craft room, or a man cave. When your characters want to prove themselves in games of skill and chance, they'll head for the den. You can also find them there when it's time to watch the big game on TV.

Leo rules gambling and games of chance, so you might be inspired to set part of your story in a casino, a betting parlor, or a pool hall. Your characters might want a seat at a poker table, or spend time at a golf course or a race track. Leo also likes to play and compete physically, so your characters might need to spend time in a gym, at a fitness center, or on a playing field.

Leo, the dramatic showman of the zodiac, also likes to spend time in places where he can see and be seen, like restaurants, bars, taverns, and nightclubs.

Since the fifth house describes procreation and children, the fifth house of the horoscope could also represent a child's room.

Don't forget that the king of the jungle might also find himself back in his natural environs. In captivity, you'll find him in a zoo or a circus.

The Sixth House

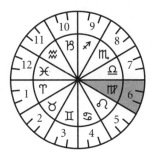

Work and Service

The sixth house is the house of work and service—but in the hands of a skilled writer, it can be transformed into a location that's anything but routine.

In real life, the sixth house of the horoscope describes the primary work you perform in service to others, as well as the work you employ others to do for you. In literature, there's more room for creativity. The signs and planets connected to the sixth house will reveal the tasks and burdens of your characters, as they manage the responsibilities of daily life. If they're lucky enough to have staff and servants, you'll find them here. And if your characters live to serve others, this is where you'll discover their attitudes and approach, as well as the opinions they keep about their employers.

The sixth house is ruled by Virgo, a sign that specializes in detail. Virgo is ruled, in turn, by Mercury, the planet of thought and communication. Mercury is a dual ruler, who's also responsible for overseeing Gemini. When he reaches Virgo, the god of communication shifts gears. Instead of merely collecting and conveying information, he focuses on critical thinking and analysis. Characters with a strong Virgo influence are questioning and methodical, and they can drive others to distraction with their attention to detail. Happily, they usually have an office or a study where they can retreat to read and write in quiet.

Scenery and Setting

The most obvious setting for the house of service might be literal: try setting part of your story in the servant's quarters, a butler's pantry, or a kitchen galley.

The Virgo virgin, who's usually pictured holding a sheaf of wheat, is often linked to healthy eating, too. That connection could suggest a garden, farm, orchard, or health-food store. You can also send your characters to a clinic, doctor's office, hospital, or health spa. If their best efforts fail, send your characters to their sickbeds.

Because pets are a daily responsibility, the sixth house is where you'll find small animals. As a result, your characters might find themselves in a dog house—literally or figuratively. They might also be found near an aviary, animal pen, petting zoo, barnyard, or pasture.

The Seventh House

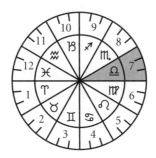

Marriage and Partnership

The seventh house of the horoscope describes marriages, partnerships, and open enemies. Does that sound contradictory? Just spend some time in divorce court.

The seventh house is the place where you can look for information about commitments and lifelong attachments, as well as the closely guarded secrets that bond characters for life. An intimate partner isn't necessarily a romantic soul mate; many people also place their confidence and trust in doctors, lawyers, clergymen, and accountants.

The seventh house is ruled by Libra, the sign of balance and partnership. The scales of Libra are a reminder that marriage is both a social and a legal institution.

Libra is ruled, in turn, by Venus, the goddess of love and attraction.

Scenery and Setting

With the sign's and the planet's focus on romance, the seventh house signifies a place where couples meet—or prepare for an encounter. When you choose seventh-house settings, think of beauty shops, manicure salons, shoe stores, and fashion boutiques, as well as dressmakers, tailor shops, and fitting rooms.

Once your characters are ready for an evening of romance, put them in a taxi and send them off to date-night destinations like five-star restaurants and nightclubs. Let them dance in the Stardust Ballroom, or give them tickets to a concert. As the night winds down, they might even want to check into a motel.

When Venus sets her sights on marriage, you might be inspired to write about wedding chapels, churches, and cathedrals. Will your characters elope to Las Vegas, or say their vows at Westminster Abbey? And after the wedding, where will they honeymoon? If love is blind, it won't matter whether you send them to the Wisconsin Dells or a private island in the Bahamas.

You can also write about a love nest, an empty nest, or a broken home.

The Eighth House

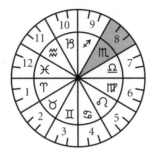

Sex, Death, and Other People's Money

If a zodiac chart represented a real home, the eighth house would be the bedroom. That's the place we usually go to sleep, have sex, and die—but not necessarily in that order.

The eighth house is ruled by Scorpio, the master of transformation. After all, we retreat to the darkness for rest and recuperation. We climb into bed at night so we can be reborn in the morning. And when we fall sick at the end of our days, we lie in our deathbed and wait for Pluto's sweet release.

Pluto, of course, is Scorpio's ruler. Pluto was the lord of the underworld, which makes Pluto the planet of death, destruction, and deliverance. It's a chilling fact that planets in the eighth house will often describe how your characters will die—either literally or metaphorically. They might find themselves falling into bed simply to experience the little death of sexual release.

Because sex is traditionally bound to marriage, the eighth house describes joint resources and inherited wealth. Planets and signs in the eighth house can reveal what your characters are willing to pay for intimacy, or what they're willing to trade in exchange for security.

Scenery and Setting

The eighth-house focus on sex will determine how far your characters will go—and whether the storyline leads them to the bedroom or the back seat of a car.

Since the sign rules unpleasant subjects like death and elimination, Scorpio might prompt you to write about mortuaries—or bathrooms. You might find your characters in a dump ground, recycling facility, underground sewer system, cesspool, or swamp. Death's bony hand could be literal—and visceral—in a setting like a butcher shop or a meat-processing plant.

Scorpio is fascinated by dark mysteries and secrets. The sign's connection to the underworld might lead you to think of mob dens, secret rooms, shady massage parlors, speakeasies, and police interrogation quarters.

If you put Pluto in power, you might find your characters whisked into a subway system—or across the River Styx, into the afterlife, or dropped into a living Hell of their own making.

The Ninth House

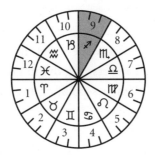

The Higher Mind

While the Library of Alexandria burned centuries ago, its spirit lives on, in the symbolism of the ninth house of the horoscope. It's where you'll find every manuscript and every book ever written, in every language. When you reach this point on a chart, you might want to leave your characters to their own devices, and spend some time browsing the shelves yourself.

The ninth house is ruled by Sagittarius, the mythical archer who shoots an arrow across the vast horizon of time and space so he can experience the wonders of a far-flung world.

Sagittarius, in turn, is ruled by Jupiter—the largest planet in the solar system, named for the king of the gods. Jupiter rules the highest realms of philosophy, religious traditions, law, and politics. All told, Jupiter is interested in the moral, ethical, and philosophical reaches of civilization.

Scenery and Setting

Sagittarius is known for a sense of wanderlust and adventure—which could inspire you to write about distant lands and foreign places. The traveling associations of the sign might also take your characters along heavily traveled routes, through airports, train stations, and bus terminals, or down winding roads and highways.

Jupiter's rule over legal principles could prompt you to set your story in a courtroom or lawyer's office. Its connection to academics might prompt you to write about the ivory tower of academia, a university campus, or a college classroom. Jupiter's connection to religious tradition might inspire you to write about churches and temples. Its associated reach into print publishing could push you to set your story in a library, bookstore, magazine stand, or newsroom. Similarly, modern forays into broadcasting—the equivalent of publishing—might suggest a radio or television station.

If you're going to invoke Jupiter, you could even go all the way and set your story where the king of the gods will recognize himself, like a palace, the Parthenon, or Mount Olympus.

The Tenth House

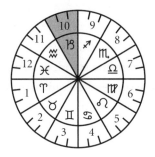

Career and Social Status

The tenth house is the house of career and social status. There, at the top of the chart, you'll often find characters who have reached the pinnacle of success.

But that's where the twists and turns begin. Fame and fortune can be cruel, and success always comes at a cost. Characters who seem to be at the top of the world often feel like failures; they might live up to the demands of others, but they can't live up to the expectations they set for themselves.

The tenth house is ruled by Capricorn, the sign of ambition, status, career, and public image.

Capricorn is ruled, in turn, by Saturn, the ringed planet of limitations, restrictions, boundaries, and structure.

Scenery and Setting

The concept of career and social status might tempt you to set your story in the corner office of a city skyscraper, where your characters can make a name for themselves. Like a tireless mountain goat, they can climb ever higher up the ladder of success.

Traditionally, however, Saturn suggests a darker setting for your stories. Saturn, the ancient god of time and harvest, is a foreboding figure. His long shadow casts a pall—literally—over our lives. His influence could suggest a funeral parlor, cemetery, or church yard.

Historically, Saturn has always symbolized a dry and barren land-scape—which means your characters might find themselves cast out of civilization, where they'll wander across a rocky field, a thorny out-cropping, or a barren mountainside. You might want to set them down in a place that has outlived its usefulness, like an abandoned building, a vacant lot, or an overgrown yard.

On a less austere note, Saturn might also inspire a monumental setting, like a courthouse, clock tower, or city hall.

The Eleventh House

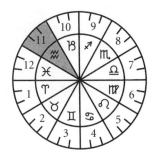

Friends and Fellow Travelers

To move your story forward, your characters need to get out in the world, rub elbows, and find like-minded fellows. You can help them connect with kindred spirits based on the eleventh house—the community center of a horoscope chart.

The eleventh house is ruled by Aquarius, the futuristic sign with long-range, utopian vision.

Aquarius is ruled, in turn, by Uranus, the planet of revolution and reform.

Planets and signs in the eleventh house will reveal the types of friends and social groups your characters attract—or are attracted to. Fire signs are charismatic. Earth signs are practical. Air signs are intellectual, and water signs are emotional and empathic.

Scenery and Setting

In myth and legend, Aquarius is often compared to Ganymede, the cupbearer to the gods. He kept their goblets full of ambrosia, the elixir of life—and ultimately, his service was rewarded and he was given a place of honor in the skies.

In astrology, the traditional imagery associated with the sign features a woman carrying a huge amphora of wine.

What could that mean for your story? You might as well go with the flow and send your characters to a bar, where they can bare their souls to a bartender and drown their sorrows in the bottom of a glass.

Many people think, understandably, that Aquarius is a water sign—but, in truth, it's an air sign. The wavy lines that constitute the glyph for Aquarius are actually meant to represent waves of water and air. The symbolism suggests that your characters simply need to be wherever people congregate for conversation and debate. You could send them to a coffee shop or a café. The social aspect of the eleventh house might also suggest a country club or a civic center.

You can even tap into the technological association of both Uranus and Aquarius, and arrange for your characters to meet in a computer room, a science lab, or a science-fiction setting, like a spaceship, a satellite station, or a distant planet.

The Twelfth House

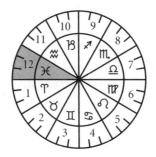

Secrets, Dreams, and Illusions

The twelfth house of the horoscope is a gold mine for writers.

In ordinary astrology, the twelfth house is a storehouse of secrets and repressed memories. It's the place where we hide our darkest fears, both from other people and ourselves.

As a writer, though, you're not only unafraid to open forbidden doors and look in locked closets—you're expected to pry. The twelfth house is where you can find information about your characters' distant past, hidden enemies, and unspoken, unrealized dreams.

The twelfth house is ruled by Pisces, the sign where mysteries and secrets can be submerged in the watery world of the subconscious.

Pisces, in turn, is ruled by Neptune, the glamorous, mystical visionary immersed in an alternate reality.

Scenery and Setting

In some cases, the twelfth house describes the solitude and confinement of institutions, prisons, asylums, and hospitals. The twelfth house could suggest a sanitarium, convalescent home, convent, or retirement community. Your characters might find themselves there for rest and recuperation—or to work.

Pisces is often associated with drugs and alcohol, so a Piscean reliance on mood-altering substances could drive your characters to drink—or to a wine cellar or a bottle shop. You might choose to plunge them into an opium den or crack house, or send them wandering down a dark alley in search of a fix. You might see them whisked away in a paddy wagon, or sprawled in the back seat of a police cruiser. You could also find them drying out in detox or recovering in rehab. If your characters choose a more natural means to experience altered states, you might find them in a yoga studio or meditation room or at a mountain retreat.

Pisces' influence also compels some people to spend time near water. Your characters might be drawn to fish tanks and aquariums, or they could don scuba gear and dive beneath the waves to commune with their finned friends. Then again, you might also find them fishing from the comfort of shore, paddling a rowboat or canoe, or perched at the end of a pier.

Creative Guidance

What sort of stories fall naturally into each house of the horoscope? Here are some examples.

- *Aries—stories of war, conquest, and exploration*
- *Taurus—rags-to-riches accounts*
- *Gemini—stories for children and young adults, as well as journalistic expositions*
- *Cancer—memoirs and stories about mothers, children, and families*
- *Leo—stories of action and adventure, sports, and the call of the wild*
- *Virgo—stories of duty and responsibility; moral tales and fables*
- *Libra—love stories, romances, and artistic and cultural accounts*
- *Scorpio—ghost stories and erotic fiction*
- *Sagittarius—travel and adventure stories, as well as philosophical tomes*
- *Capricorn—business books and historical accounts*
- *Aquarius—science fiction and futuristic tales*
- *Pisces—surreal stories and psychological dramas*

How to Read a Horoscope Chart

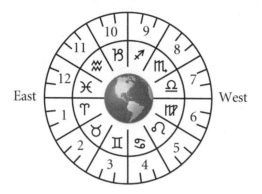

A horoscope chart might look like a mystic cryptographer's puzzle, but it's surprisingly easy to read—once you know how it's constructed.

A Panoramic View

The word horoscope comes from the Greek word *hora*, or "hour," and *skopos*, "watching." It's a sketch of the solar system, and it depicts what you'd see if you were standing in a particular place on Earth at a specific time.

Wherever you are right now, look around. You'll notice that you have a 360-degree view of the world around you. Ancient astronomers could see that, too—but they extended that worldview to include the entire sphere of heaven, like a cosmic bubble surrounding the globe.

The exact center of a horoscope chart represents a specific latitude and longitude on Earth. In theory, if you were to stand on that spot, you could look east and west along the horizontal line that separates the top half of the chart from the bottom. That's because the horizontal line actually does represent the horizon.

From that position, if you were to look straight up, you'd be looking at open sky above your head. And if you were to look straight down, you'd see the earth beneath your feet. In real life, you could only see the top half of the chart from where you were standing. The sky above the horizon would be visible, but the rest of the cosmos would be hidden from view on the other side of the world.

House Positions

The first house of a horoscope chart is always on the left, at the nine o'clock position, and the houses run counterclockwise.

In theory, each house is a 30-degree section. In practice, however, the size of the houses can vary. The earth is tilted on its axis, so from some latitudes, the view of the twelve signs and houses is skewed. Don't worry about the mathematics that go into chart calculation, because they don't affect how you read a horoscope.

House Coordinates

As the planets make their journey through the sky, they move through the signs of the zodiac. While the signs of the zodiac offer a fixed backdrop, our view of them changes from moment to moment. That's because the earth is moving, too, spinning through all twelve signs during the course of a twenty-four-hour day.

Here's a simple way to picture the difference between the signs and the houses. Pretend you're in a revolving restaurant at the top of a tall building. As you look out the window, you'll notice certain landmarks—a park, for example, or a church. Like the constellations and signs of the zodiac, those landmarks are fixed. Your view of them, however, will change as you, and the restaurant—like the earth itself—revolve through space. You could map those landmarks at any one moment, but their relative positions would steadily shift with time.

And the planets? They're like the cars and trucks you can see down below. They travel down streets and highways, at their own speed, and along their own course. You could map them, too, relative to the land-mark signs and houses, just as astrologers plot their positions on an astrological chart.

Planets and Signs

On a horoscope chart, every planet is depicted as a pictograph, or glyph, and listed by the degree and minute of its position in a sign.

The houses are also labeled with glyphs for the signs. The houses run counterclockwise, and the signs of the zodiac always appear in the same order, from Aries through Pisces.

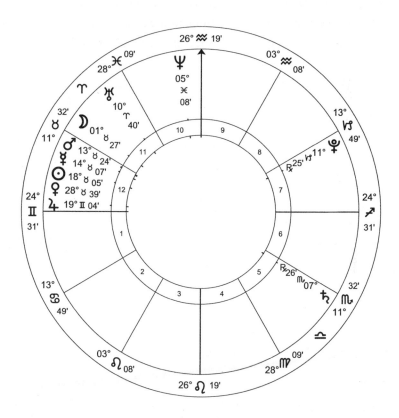

House Cusps

The cusps—the dividing lines between the houses—mark the transition from one astrological sign to another. Even though planets often land close to the cusps, the divisions are firm: a planet can be in only one house at a time. Even so, their energy might be felt in the adjoining house, just as a noisy neighbor can be heard through a wall.

Empty Houses

All ten planets and all twelve signs appear in every horoscope chart. Because the planets are constantly cycling through space at different speeds, however, most charts usually have at least one or two empty houses. You'll frequently see more than two empty houses, because planets are constantly on the move, and they're often grouped together.

That doesn't mean that empty houses are bereft of energy or activity. They're still ruled by a sign, which means they offer one avenue of expression for the planet that rules the sign. They'll also be visited, over time, by transiting planets.

The Moon, for example, visits every sign during the course of a month. The Sun travels through all twelve signs every year.

An empty house could even be a good thing: it could indicate that the energy of the sign and house is peaceful and easy, and mastery of its realm comes naturally to the subject.

The Secret History of the Horoscope

For centuries, ancient astrologers watched the Moon rise and set against the backdrop of the zodiac. Night after night, they also watched constellations rise and fall, like clockwork.

In fact, if you were to stand outside every night and watch your favorite stars rise and set on the horizon, you would see the same thing for yourself. You might even notice that the starry backdrop of the zodiac seems to shift about 1 degree every day, so that every 30 days, the Sun rises and sets against the backdrop of a new sign. By the time we go through a full calendar year, we return to the same place we started.

Ancient astronomers used their observations to devise the calendar system we use to this day. The math is simple—but ingenious.

There are 360 degrees in a circle, which roughly corresponds to the 365 days in a year. The zodiac divides perfectly into twelve equal sections of 30 degrees, which led to our division of months. The fact that the system wasn't exact doesn't mean it wasn't easy to adjust; even now, we add a leap day every four years to keep our calendar in sync with the Sun.

You might be aware of the fact that the constellations we see today no longer correspond to the signs of the zodiac. Even though it makes headlines every few years, it's not news to astrologers. In fact, even ancient astrologers could see that our view of the constellations was constantly shifting and changing. From a symbolic standpoint, it doesn't matter. Modern astrologers still use the ancient zodiac, because it's easy to measure, and it's a fun way to describe the qualities of each sign.

The Oddities of a Horoscope Chart

Reading a horoscope would be a lot easier if it weren't for the quirks of history and time.

For one thing, the compass points aren't what you'd expect. On a horoscope chart, the eastern horizon is on the left, and the western horizon is on the right. North is at the bottom, and south is at the top. That's because charts are constructed from the perspective of the northern hemisphere—which is just where ancient astronomers stood at their posts in Greece and Egypt and Mesopotamia, looking south toward the ecliptical path of the Sun. For that reason, when you read a chart, picture yourself standing on top of the globe, looking toward the equator. East will be on your left, and west will be on your right.

Imagine you're an ancient astrologer, too, when you consider the signs of the zodiac. Thousands of years ago, when astrologers were first developing the principles of their art, they saw the Sun rise and set against the backdrop of a different constellation each month.

The wheel of the zodiac used to match the constellations—but it doesn't anymore, because Earth's rotation isn't perfectly aligned with the stars. Instead of maintaining a steady orbit, Earth wobbles on its axis, caught in a cosmic tug-of-war between the gravitational pull of the Sun and the Moon. Even so, rather than abandoning or adapting the ancient zodiac, we simply use the signs as a symbolic way to divide space into measurable coordinates.

If our calendar year were 360 days long, it would align perfectly with the 360 degrees in the zodiac wheel. Instead, there are 365¼ days in a solar year. While we can make some adjustments to compensate—by inserting a leap day every four years, for example—we still need a computer, an astrological calendar, an almanac, or an ephemeris to determine just when the Sun will move from sign to sign during the course of any given year.

Creative Guidance

To create a fully rounded character, think like an astrologer.

Astrologers start their assessment of character and personality by assessing the two brightest lights in the sky—the Sun and the Moon, which symbolize the head and the heart, respectively. From there, they move on to the other planets and points in a horoscope chart. Mercury symbolizes the intellect. Venus represents love and attraction. Mars describes primal drives and desire. Jupiter represents growth and expansion, while Saturn symbolizes limitations and restrictions. Uranus adds a touch of the unusual and unexpected. Neptune is the planet of glamour and illusion—the veil that divides dreams from reality—while Pluto brings that curtain of reality crashing down in the end.

Working with Fictional Horoscopes

A horoscope chart is more than just dots on paper. It's a symbolic master plan that can offer an overview of life's journey, and outline a drama like a script.

Reading a chart for a fictional horoscope is no different than reading a chart for a real person. While you can analyze every planet in a chart, most astrologers focus on three key points.

The Sun. The Sun is the central focus of any horoscope chart. In a natal chart, it describes the essence of the self—the burning passions and desire that drive a character. Start your chart assessment by noting the Sun's sign and house placement, as well as its element (fire, earth, air, or water) and mode (cardinal, mutable, or fixed).

The Moon. The Moon's position describes emotional makeup—the psychological needs and desires, based on inborn characteristics and early upbringing. It symbolizes emotion, memory, and mood. Just as you did with the Sun, consider the Moon's sign, house, element, and mode.

The Ascendant. In a natal chart, the ascendant, or rising sign, is the face you show the world. It's based on the sign that was rising on the eastern horizon at the moment of birth, and it symbolizes first impressions, physical appearance, and disposition. The ascendant is also the cusp of the first house. You can find it at the nine o'clock position on the chart. In actual use, it embodies a lot of the same associations you'll find in the first house.

Creative Guidance

You don't need to be a master astrologer to be inspired by a horoscope. In fact, it's good practice to create a completely fictional horoscope for your character. Simply invent a birth date, a birth place, and a birth time. Plug the data into any chart calculation software, online or on your computer, and print it out.

Just remember that a horoscope is merely a map. The planets are pictured as glyphs, and they're positioned by house and sign. The little numbers next to each planet are simply their mathematical coordinates—the degrees and minutes of each sign.

You'll see an entire universe of personality traits unfold. Use the descriptions of the planets and signs in this guide as a starting point for your character's story.

Practice Chart

Here's a practice chart you can try right now, for a fictional character we'll call Miss M.

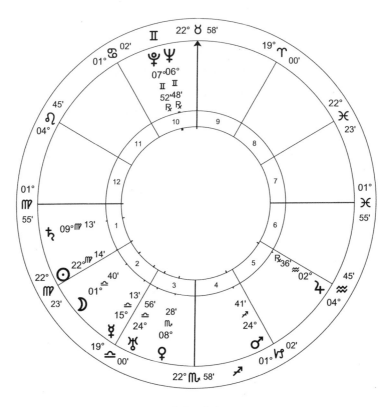

Miss M

September 15, 1890 / 4:00 am UT / Torquay, United Kingdom
Placidus Houses

- *The Ascendant.* Let's start with first impressions. Look at the rising sign—the glyph that marks the first house, on the far left of the chart. (You can see the house numbers on the inner wheel, and the zodiac signs on the outer wheel.) So what does Miss M look like? Virgo is on the ascendant, and it takes up the entire first house. That suggests that Miss M looks prim and proper, and she pays keen attention to detail.

- *The Sun.* How does she think and see the world? Look for the Sun, the marker of one's focus and worldview. In this case, the Sun is in the first house; it's also in Virgo, the sign of conscientious duty and service to others.
- *The Moon.* Finally, find the Moon, the luminous orb of memories, dreams, and reflections. In astrology, the Moon describes a character's emotional makeup—and in Miss M's chart, you'll see it in the second house, not far from the Sun. Miss M's Moon happens to be in Libra, the sign of partnership and balance.

That was easy, right? Already you can start to see a character take shape. If you were to study every planet in the chart, by sign and by house, you could quickly work up a complete personality profile.

In fact, this chart actually belongs to a real person—mystery writer Agatha Christie, the creator of an amateur detective named Miss Marple.

Don't let the facts get in the way of your imagination, though. Keep playing with the planets, signs, and houses, as you develop characters, stories, and scenes of your own.

Twenty Questions

1. *Think about a story you'd like to write. Where would your characters live? Which house of the horoscope would each of them call home?*
2. *What would each character see from his or her home?*
3. *How would that environment shape or change them?*
4. *How would they feel about their homes?*
5. *Try moving your hero's home base from house to house. Experiment with combinations that will add drama and conflict to your story. If your hero is naturally fiery, for example, try moving him into a watery, airy, or earthy house. How will he cope? What changes will he be forced to make?*
6. *Send your hero on a trip through all twelve houses. What landmarks could he expect to see at each stage of the journey?*

7. *Start two characters on journeys at different points of the zodiac wheel. Write their stories in parallel, as seen from their two separate vantage points.*

8. *What sort of story could you write based on the symbolism of each of the twelve houses?*

9. *Describe the vastly different landscape of each house of the horoscope, as you might use them in a story.*

10. *Calculate a horoscope chart, either based on a specific date, a key moment for your story, or a time and place chosen completely at random. (You can use astrology software or a free online service like astro.com to do the calculations.) Study the sign that marks the first house. What could that tell you about the setting of your story?*

11. *What could it tell you about the hero of your story?*

12. *Look for the Sun in a horoscope chart, and use its position to inspire the setting for a crucial scene in a story. Start by examining the symbolism of the house itself. Is it a public place, or is it private? Describe it.*

13. *Next, consider the sign. Is the Sun in an active fiery or airy sign, or a quiet earth or water sign? What sort of information can that add to your scene?*

14. *Now think of the Sun in terms of character development. What can you know about a character's focus based on the Sun sign? What can you tell about his or her surroundings based on the Sun's house position?*

15. *Find the Moon in a chart, and use it to discern a few telling details about your hero's partner or companion. Does it seem as though a character based on the Moon's sign will be sympathetic and understanding, or will she prod your hero to make changes and take action? There's no right or wrong answer; simply use the symbolism associated with the Moon's sign and position to trigger your imagination.*

16. *The Moon's position might also inspire you to develop detailed associations about your hero's childhood memories or his relationship with his mother. How would you interpret it in that light?*

17. *Look at the ascendant, or rising sign, that marks the first house of a horoscope. If the chart was calculated for a story, what would the ascendant say about the general setting?*

18. *If the chart belongs to a character, what can the ascendant tell you about his appearance? What sort of first impression would he make?*

19. *Are the planets grouped together in any of the houses or signs? What can that tell you about the focus of your story or its characters?*

20. *If you have some time to experiment, evaluate all of the planets in the chart, by sign and by house. Feel free to use the quick reference guides in the back of this book to compare and contrast the symbolic significance of the planets, signs, and houses.*

Conclusion

Physicists say we are made of stardust. Intergalactic debris and far-flung atoms, shards of carbon nanomatter rounded up by gravity to circle the sun. As atoms pass through an eternal revolving door of possible form, energy and mass dance in fluid relationship. We are stardust, we are man, we are thought. We are story.

—Glenda Burgess, *The Geography of Love: A Memoir*

Our travels through the planets, signs, and houses have drawn to a close. Happily, that doesn't mean the journey's over. In fact, the adventure has just begun.

Astrology is everywhere. Look closely, and you'll find it behind the scenes of your favorite stories, shows, and scripts.

Now it's yours, too, whenever you need creative inspiration. Whether you're working on a poem, screenplay, or the next Great American Novel, astrology's tools are at your disposal.

You can move on, of course, to a more formal study of astrology—or you can simply reach for the stars whenever you need a boost.

But from this point forward, I hope you'll always have stars in your eyes.

—Corrine Kenner

PART IV

Quick Reference Guides

Use this section to clarify concepts as you incorporate astrology into your creative writing practice.

Quick Reference Guides

The Planets

Glyph	Planet or Sign	Significance
☉	Sun	Illumination, the self, the ego; the glyph looks like the Sun at the center of the solar system.
☽	Moon	Cycles, reflection; the glyph looks like a crescent Moon.
☿	Mercury	Speed, communication; the glyph looks like Mercury, messenger of the gods, in his winged helmet.
♀	Venus	Love, attraction, spiritual treasure, fertility; the glyph looks like a woman's hand mirror.
♂	Mars	Energy, aggression, self-defense, action; the glyph looks like a sword and spear.
♃	Jupiter	Luck, growth, expansion, enthusiasm; the glyph looks like the number 4, which sounds like "fortune."
♄	Saturn	Discipline, limits, boundaries, tradition; the glyph looks like a church and steeple.
♅	Uranus	Independence, rebellion, freedom; the glyph looks like a satellite and antenna.
♆	Neptune	Glamour, illusions, sensitivity; the glyph looks like Neptune's trident.
♇	Pluto	Death, regeneration, unavoidable change; the glyph looks like a holy chalice and a host, or a resurrected body rising from a grave.

The Asteroids

Glyph	Planet or Sign	Significance
⚳	Ceres	The earth mother; goddess of the harvest
⚴	Pallas Athena	Goddess of wisdom and justice
⚵	Juno	The loyal partner and jealous wife
⚶	Vesta	The temple virgin; goddess of hearth and home
⚸	Lilith	The dark mother; the woman scorned
⚷	Chiron	The master teacher; the wounded healer

The Signs

Glyph	Sign	Description	Mode	Element	Motivation
♈	Aries, the Ram	(March 21– April 20) The initiator; ruled by Mars; the glyph looks like the horns of a ram.	Cardinal (Initiation)	Fire	Leadership
♉	Taurus, the Bull	(April 21– May 20) The maintainer; ruled by Venus; the glyph looks like a bull's head.	Fixed (Maintenance)	Earth	Stability, Physical Safety

Glyph	Sign	Description	Mode	Element	Motivation
♊	Gemini, the Twins	(May 21–June 20) The questioner; ruled by Mercury; the glyph looks like two people side by side.	Mutable (Transition)	Air	Intellectual Stimulation
♋	Cancer, the Crab	(June 21–July 20) The nurturer; ruled by the Moon; the glyph looks like the claws of a crab or a woman's breasts.	Cardinal (Initiation)	Water	Emotional Security
♌	Leo, the Lion	(July 21–August 20) The loyalist; ruled by the Sun; the glyph looks like a lion's mane or tail.	Fixed (Maintenance)	Fire	Power, Acclaim
♍	Virgo, the Virgin	(August 21–September 20) The modifier; ruled by Mercury; the glyph looks like a *V* and an *M*, the initials of the Virgin Mary.	Mutable (Transition)	Earth	Order, Perfection

Glyph	Sign	Description	Mode	Element	Motivation
♎	Libra, the Scales	(Sept. 21–October 20) The judge; ruled by Venus; the glyph looks like a balanced scale.	Cardinal (Initiation)	Air	Balance
♏	Scorpio, the Scorpion	(October 21–November 20) The catalyst; ruled by Pluto; the glyph features the stinger of a scorpion's tail.	Fixed (Maintenance)	Water	Emotional Intensity
♐	Sagittarius, the Archer	(November 21–December 20) The adventurer; ruled by Jupiter; the glyph looks like an arrow.	Mutable (Transition)	Fire	Adventure
♑	Capricorn, the Goat	(December 21-January 20) The pragmatist; ruled by Saturn; the glyph looks like the head and body of a goat.	Cardinal (Initiation)	Earth	Control

Glyph	Sign	Description	Mode	Element	Motiva-tion
♒	Aquarius, the Water Bearer	(January 21– February 20) The reformer; ruled by Uranus; the glyph looks like rolling waves of water or air.	Fixed (Maintenance)	Air	Idealism
♓	Pisces, the Fish	(February 21– March 20) The visionary; ruled by Neptune; the glyph looks like two fish kissing.	Mutable (Transition)	Water	Connection

The Houses

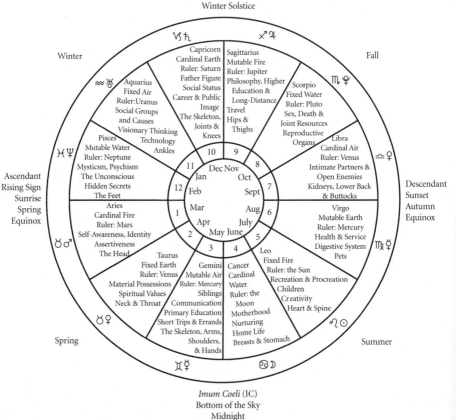

Midheaven
Medium Coeli (MC)
"Middle of the Heavens"
Noon
Winter Solstice

Winter

Fall

Capricorn
Cardinal Earth
Ruler: Saturn
Father Figure
Social Status
Career & Public
Image
The Skeleton,
Joints &
Knees

Sagittarius
Mutable Fire
Ruler: Jupiter
Philosophy, Higher
Education &
Long-Distance
Travel
Hips &
Thighs

Scorpio
Fixed Water
Ruler: Pluto
Sex, Death &
Joint Resources
Reproductive
Organs

Aquarius
Fixed Air
Ruler: Uranus
Social Groups
and Causes
Visionary Thinking
Technology
Ankles

Pisces
Mutable Water
Ruler: Neptune
Mysticsm, Psychism
The Unconscious
Hidden Secrets
The Feet

Libra
Cardinal Air
Ruler: Venus
Intimate Partners &
Open Enemies
Kidneys, Lower Back
& Buttocks

**Ascendant
Rising Sign
Sunrise
Spring
Equinox**

**Descendant
Sunset
Autumn
Equinox**

Aries
Cardinal Fire
Ruler: Mars
Self-Awareness, Identity
Assertiveness
The Head

Virgo
Mutable Earth
Ruler: Mercury
Health & Service
Digestive System
Pets

Taurus
Fixed Earth
Ruler: Venus
Material Possessions
Spiritual Values
Neck & Throat

Gemini
Mutable Air
Ruler: Mercury
Siblings
Communication
Primary Education
Short Trips & Errands
The Skeleton, Arms,
Shoulders,
& Hands

Cancer
Cardinal
Water
Ruler: the
Moon
Motherhood
Nurturing
Home Life
Breasts & Stomach

Leo
Fixed Fire
Ruler: the Sun
Recreation & Procreation
Children
Creativity
Heart & Spine

10 9 8 7 6 5 4 3 2 1 11 12

Dec Nov Oct Sept Aug July May June Apr Mar Feb Jan

Spring

Summer

Imum Coeli (IC)
Bottom of the Sky
Midnight
Summer Solstice

Glossary of
Astrological Terms

Air: One of the four elements. Considered active, masculine, mental, intellectual, and communicative.

Air Signs: The "thinkers" of the zodiac: Gemini, Libra, and Aquarius.

Angles: The cusps of the angular houses of a horoscope chart: Ascendant (ASC), Descendant (DSC), Midheaven (MC), and *Imum Coeli* (IC).

Angular Houses: The powerful first, seventh, tenth, and fourth houses of a horoscope chart.

Aquarius, the Water Bearer: Fixed air. Humanitarian, progressive, futuristic, visionary, utopian, nonconforming, independent, unconventional, impersonal, detached, aloof. Ruled by Uranus. Rules the eleventh house of social groups and causes.

Arabic Parts: These are sensitive points in a chart, and are calculated using specific formulas whereby two planets or points are added together, and a third planet or point is subtracted from that result.

Aries, the Ram: Cardinal fire. Energetic, assertive, impulsive, commanding, courageous. Ruled by Mars. Rules the first house of the self.

Ascendant: Also known as the rising sign. The sign on the cusp of the first house, the point at which planets and signs rise like the Sun on the eastern horizon. The ascendant reflects the face you show the world; the persona, personality, and self-perception.

Aspect: An angular, geometric relationship with another planet. Commonly used aspects include the conjunction (0°), opposition (180°), trine (120°), square (90°), sextile (60°), and quincunx (150°).

Benefic: In classical astrology, Jupiter and Venus are benefic; they are fortunate planets that grace everything they touch. Saturn and Mars are malefic. Other planets are neutral.

Cadent Houses: The third, sixth, ninth, and twelfth houses of a chart; the last house in each quadrant of a horoscope. Classical astrologers believed planets in cadent houses were weakened.

Cancer, the Crab: Cardinal water. Emotional, nurturing, protective, sensitive, sentimental, sympathetic, intuitive, instinctual. Ruled by the Moon. Rules the fourth house of home and family.

Capricorn, the Goat: Cardinal earth. Pragmatic, responsible, disciplined, dutiful, methodical, organized, patient, persistent, cautious, ambitious, reserved, somber. Ruled by Saturn. Rules the tenth house of career and social status.

Cardinal Signs: Aries, Cancer, Libra, and Capricorn mark the start of each new season, and symbolize leadership and initiative.

Celestial Equator: An extension of the earth's equator out into space.

Chart Ruler: The planet that rules the sign on the ascendant also rules the chart.

Chiron: An asteroid between Saturn and Uranus, named for the wounded healer of Greek mythology.

Classical Planets: The seven planets that can be seen with the naked eye: Sun, Moon, Mercury, Venus, Mars, Jupiter, and Saturn.

Conjunction: An aspect that conjoins, unifies, and intensifies the energy of two planets that share the same sign and degree in a chart.

Cusp: The dividing line between signs or houses in a chart, and the degree where one sign ends and the next begins.

Decan: A 10-degree division of a sign. Also known as a decanate.

Declination: The distance of a celestial body north or south of the celestial equator.

Degree: One of the 360 degrees of a circle.

Descendant: The cusp of the seventh house; the point at which planets and signs descend like the setting Sun on the western horizon.

Detriment: A planet's weakness, found in the sign opposite its own rulership.

Dignities: Classifications of a planet's power: rulership, exaltation, detriment, and fall.

Direct: A planet that seems to be moving forward through the zodiac, as seen from our perspective on Earth.

Dispositor: The planet that rules a sign also holds some power over any planet that happens to be in that sign; technically speaking, a dispositor may dispose of (rule over) the visiting planet as it sees fit.

Diurnal Chart: A chart cast for the daytime hours when the Sun is above the horizon.

Diurnal Planets: The Sun, Jupiter, and Saturn are day planets, which are strongest in diurnal charts. Mercury is diurnal if it rises before the Sun. See also *Nocturnal Planets.*

Domicile: A planet's natural home; its place in the sign or house that it rules.

Earth: One of four ancient elements. Symbolizes the physical world, materialism, practicality, and reality.

Earth Signs: The "maintainers" of the zodiac: Taurus, Virgo, and Capricorn.

Easy Aspects: Aspects that are considered to be beneficial and helpful (sextile, trine).

Eclipse: A solar eclipse occurs when the Moon passes between the earth and the Sun; lunar eclipses occur at the full Moon, when the earth is between the Sun and the Moon. In astrology, eclipses represent sudden and dramatic change.

Ecliptic: The great circle of the Sun's apparent path through the sky, as seen from Earth.

Electional Astrology: A branch of astrology used to choose favorable dates and times for an event.

Elements: The four ancient elements are fire, water, air, and earth. The zodiac is divided into elements, and signs of the same element share the qualities of that element.

Ephemeris: A list of planetary positions by date and degree.

Equinox: A time when days and nights are of equal length; the vernal equinox occurs when the Sun enters Aries, and the autumnal equinox occurs when the Sun enters Libra.

Exaltation: A planet is exalted in the sign of its greatest power and influence, like a visiting dignitary in a foreign court. Exaltation is a planet's second-strongest placement; rulership is its first.

Fall: A planet's weakest placement, found in the sign opposite its exaltation.

Feminine Signs: Earth and water signs are considered feminine: Taurus, Cancer, Virgo, Scorpio, Capricorn, and Pisces. Feminine signs are also called receptive, reactive, negative, magnetic, and passive.

Fire: One of four ancient elements. Represents spirit, will, inspiration, enthusiasm, desire, zeal, warmth, idealism, and creativity.

Fire Signs: The "initiators" of the zodiac: Aries, Leo, and Sagittarius.

Fixed Signs: Taurus, Leo, Scorpio, and Aquarius mark the middle month of each season. They are stable, consistent, constant, patient, and reliable.

Geocentric: A model of the universe that puts the earth at the center of the solar system.

Glyphs: Symbols for the signs, planets, and aspects.

Grand Cross: A stressful configuration that involves four or more planets, in two sets of oppositions that combine to form four squares. The planets are usually related by mode: cardinal, fixed, or mutable.

Grand Sextile: A rare configuration that involves six planets in sextile to each other in six different signs.

Grand Trine: A beneficial configuration that involves three planets 120 degrees apart; they form an equilateral triangle. The planets in a grand trine are usually in the same element.

Hard Aspects: Aspects that create tension and friction (opposition, square).

Horary Astrology: The art of answering a question by analyzing a horoscope chart drawn for the precise moment the question was asked.

Horoscope: An astrological chart. The word *horoscope* comes from the Greek word *hora*, or "hour," and *skopos*, "watching."

House Ruler: The planet that rules a house in a horoscope.

Houses: The twelve divisions of a horoscope chart that correspond to the twelve zodiac signs.

Imum Coeli (IC): The cusp of the fourth house; the lowest point in a horoscope chart; it relates to foundations, home, and family life. *Imum Coeli* is Latin for "bottom of the sky," and is directly opposite the *Medium Coeli* (MC), or Midheaven.

Inner Planets: The Sun, Moon, Mercury, Venus, and Mars. See also *Personal Planets.*

Interception: A sign that is completely contained within a house.

Jupiter: The expansive planet of luck and generosity. Symbolizes good fortune, prosperity, extravagance, higher thought, religion, law, and long journeys. Rules Sagittarius and the ninth house of philosophy, long-distance travel, and higher education.

Leo, the Lion: Fixed fire. Regal, warm-hearted, loyal, generous, dramatic, proud, creative, domineering. Ruled by the Sun. Rules the fifth house of creativity, procreation, and recreation.

Libra, the Scales: Mutable air. Gracious, charming, social, cooperative, fair, balanced, refined, harmonious, indecisive, indolent. Ruled by Venus. Rules the seventh house of marriage and partnership.

Luminaries: The Sun and the Moon.

Lunation: In astrology, the exact moment the new Moon is conjunct the Sun.

Malefic: In classical astrology, Saturn and Mars are malefic; they bring misfortune. Jupiter and Venus are benefic. Other planets are neutral. See also *Benefic.*

Mars: The fiery red planet of energy, action, assertiveness, aggression, courage, desire, passion, drive, will, and initiative. Rules Aries and the first house of self.

Masculine Signs: Fire and air signs are considered masculine: Aries, Gemini, Leo, Libra, Sagittarius, and Aquarius. Masculine signs are also referred to as active or positive.

Medium Coeli (MC): See *Midheaven.*

Mercury: The fast-moving planet of speed and communication. Represents logic, reason, wit, writing, and speech. Rules Gemini and Virgo, and the third and sixth houses.

Midheaven: The cusp of the tenth house; the highest, most elevated point in a horoscope chart; it signifies career, public image, status, and recognition. It's also known as the *Medium Coeli* (MC), which is Latin for "middle of the heavens."

Midpoint: An equidistant point between two planets, angles, or cusps, used for additional chart interpretation.

Mode: The three categories of the signs—cardinal, fixed, and mutable—that correspond to the three months of each season.

Moon Phases: New, waxing, full, waning.

Moon: The luminous orb of reflection, inner life, and the cycles of life. Symbolizes emotion, memory, mood, and motherhood. Rules Cancer and the fourth house of home and family.

Mundane Astrology: The study of countries, cities, provinces, and states. Weather forecasting is also a form of mundane astrology.

Mutable Signs: Gemini, Virgo, Sagittarius, and Pisces mark the third and final month of each season. They are transitional, adaptable, and flexible.

Mutual Reception: Planets placed in each other's signs of dignity enhance each other's strength.

Natal Chart: A horoscope chart based upon the date, time, and place of birth.

Native: The person for whom a natal chart is erected.

Neptune: The planet of imagination, dreams, illusion, spirituality, idealism, escapism, sacrifice, confusion, and deception. Rules Pisces and the twelfth house of mysteries and secrets.

New Moon: A new or dark Moon is the beginning phase of a lunar month, when the Moon and Sun are conjunct. See also *Lunation.*

Nocturnal Chart: A chart cast for the nighttime hours when the Sun is below the horizon.

Nocturnal Planets: The Moon, Venus, and Mars are night planets, which are strongest in nocturnal charts. Mercury is nocturnal if it sets after the Sun. See also *Diurnal Planets.*

Nodes: The mathematical points where the Moon's orbit around the earth crosses the ecliptic, the apparent path of the Sun around the earth. The South Node symbolizes gifts and talents that are inborn; the North Node represents lessons that must be learned.

Opposition: An aspect between two planets that are 180 degrees (or six signs) apart. Energy can be confrontational.

Orb: The degree within which an aspect is considered to have an effect. The luminaries generally have a greater orb than the planets.

Outer Planets: Uranus, Neptune, and Pluto. See also *Transpersonal Planets.*

Part of Fortune: A point in the chart that shows natural talent and suggests where joy and fortune can be found. One of the Arabic Parts.

Personal (Inner) Planets: The Sun, Moon, Mercury, Venus, and Mars have a personal and direct effect on personality. See also *Transpersonal Planets.*

Pisces, the Fish: Mutable water. Imaginative, compassionate, self-sacrificing, impressionable, empathetic, illusionary, secretive, victimizing or victimized. Ruled by Neptune. Rules the twelfth house of the unknown, mysteries, and secrets.

Planetary Rulers: Each sign is ruled by a planet that shares its qualities.

Planetary Sect: The division of day planets from night planets. See also *Diurnal Planets* and *Nocturnal Planets.*

Planets: Sun, Moon, Mercury, Venus, Mars, Jupiter, Saturn, Uranus, Neptune, and Pluto.

Pluto: The planet of transformation, regeneration, unavoidable change, endings, death, destruction, elimination, power, compulsion, and analysis. Rules Scorpio and the eighth house of sex, death, and other people's money.

Polarities: Active signs are masculine; receptive signs are feminine. Polarities may also refer to signs that are 180 degrees apart.

Prime Meridian: The line of longitude that runs through Greenwich, England, and divides the eastern and western hemispheres.

Predictive Astrology: A branch of astrology used to forecast trends and events in an individual's life, typically through the analysis of transits and progressions.

Progression: An astrological technique that advances the planets' positions in a chart forward through time. The usual formula is a day for a year.

Quadrants: Four divisions of a chart. The quadrants start at the cusps of the first, fourth, seventh, and tenth houses.

Qualities: Polarities, modes (quadruplicities), and elements.

Quincunx: The angular relationship between planets that are 150 degrees (or five signs) apart. A stressful aspect.

Rectification: The process of determining an unknown birth time based on life experiences and events.

Retrograde: From our viewpoint on Earth, the planets (with the exception of the Sun and Moon) periodically seem to move backward through the zodiac. The phenomenon is an optical illusion with symbolic significance. The qualities of retrograde planets in a natal chart are internalized, reversed, or slower to develop.

Rising Sign: See *Ascendant.*

Sagittarius, the Archer: Mutable fire. Adventurous, philosophical, optimistic, enthusiastic, candid, tactless. Ruled by Jupiter. Rules the ninth house of philosophy, higher education, and long-distance travel.

Saturn: The ringed planet of boundaries and limitations. Symbolizes responsibility, restriction, structure, discipline, caution, control, ambition, inhibition, delay, father figures, authority, and old age. Rules Capricorn and the tenth house of career and social status.

Scorpio, the Scorpion: Fixed water. Intense, penetrating, secretive, jealous, introspective, passionate, strong-willed, possessive, intimate, psychic, fascinated with the dark mysteries of life. Ruled by Pluto. Rules the eighth house of sex, death, and other people's money.

Sextile: The angular relationship between planets that are 60 degrees (or two signs) apart; this aspect can be cooperative and offer opportunity.

Sign Ruler: The planet that rules a sign. Planets are strongest in the signs they rule.

Signs: Aries, Taurus, Gemini, Cancer, Leo, Virgo, Libra, Scorpio, Sagittarius, Capricorn, Aquarius, and Pisces.

Solar Return: A birthday horoscope, calculated for the moment when the Sun returns to the exact degree, minute, and second of celestial longitude it occupied at birth.

Solstices: The longest and shortest days of the year, when the Sun reaches its maximum distance north or south of the equator.

Square: The angular relationship between two planets that are 90 degrees (three signs) apart; it can be a challenging and stressful aspect.

Stellium: Three or more planets in the same sign or house; a stellium adds emphasis.

Succedent Houses: The second, fifth, eighth, and eleventh houses of a chart, which succeed (follow) the cadent houses. According to classical astrology, they derive their power from the cadent houses.

Sun: The center of our solar system, it symbolizes self, ego, will, purpose, vitality, individuality, pride, authority, and fatherhood. Rules Leo and the fifth house of creativity, recreation, and procreation.

Synastry: The practice of comparing the natal charts of two or more people to assess their compatibility.

Taurus, the Bull: Fixed earth. Determined, stubborn, materialistic, possessive, security-oriented, sensual, patient, stable, practical. Ruled by Venus. Rules the second house of values and possessions.

Transit: A planet's movement through signs and houses.

Transpersonal (Outer) Planets: Uranus, Neptune, and Pluto are slow-moving, so their effect is as much generational as it is personal. See also *Personal Planets.*

Trine: The angular relationship between two planets that are 120 degrees (or four signs) apart; this aspect is usually friendly and flowing, because the planets share an element.

Triplicities: Zodiac signs that share an element. The fire triplicity is Aries, Leo, and Sagittarius. Earth: Taurus, Virgo, and Capricorn. Air: Gemini, Libra, and Aquarius. Water: Cancer, Scorpio, and Pisces.

Tropical Zodiac: A system that defines the signs in relation to the position of the vernal (spring) equinox, commonly used in Western astrology.

T-square: A stressful combination in which two planets square each other, and a third focal planet squares both of them.

Uranus: The planet of sudden change, disruption, and revolution. Symbolizes technology, originality, and futuristic thinking. Rules Aquarius and the eleventh house of social groups and causes.

Venus: The planet of love, beauty, and attraction. Represents affection, artistry, harmony, and values. Rules the second house of Taurus (values and possessions) and the seventh house of Libra (relationships and partnerships).

Virgo, the Virgin: Mutable earth. Analytical, practical, detail-minded, organized, discriminating, productive, health-conscious, critical. Ruled by Mercury. Rules the sixth house of sign of work, health, and service to others.

Void-of-Course Moon: A designation that describes the Moon at the end of one sign, about to enter the next. When the Moon is void-of-course, it has completed all its major aspects to other planets, and symbolically, it's disconnected from the rest of the universe until it enters the next sign.

Waning Moon: The gradually diminishing Moon, following the full Moon and before the new Moon. Symbolizes endings and completion.

Water Signs: The "feelers" of the zodiac: Cancer, Scorpio, and Pisces.

Water: One of four ancient elements. Symbolizes emotions, intuition, compassion, relationships, and femininity.

Waxing Moon: The gradually increasing Moon, following the new Moon and before the full Moon. Symbolizes beginnings and growth.

Western Astrology: Founded by Ptolemy in the second century CE; a continuation of Hellenistic and Babylonian astrology.

Yod (Finger of God): A configuration that suggests a radical point of view; it consists of two planets in sextile to each other, and quincunx a third.

Zodiac: The elliptical belt of space surrounding the earth, divided into twelve signs; the planets travel from west to east, transiting through one sign after another in their order from Aries to Pisces. In Greek, zodiac means "circle of animals."

Recommended Reading

Burk, Kevin. *Astrology: Understanding the Birth Chart.* Saint Paul, MN: Llewellyn Publications, 2001.

Frawley, John. *The Real Astrology.* London: Apprentice Books, 2001.

Gerwick-Brodeur, Madeline, and Lisa Lenard. *The Complete Idiot's Guide to Astrology.* New York: Alpha Books, 1997.

Guttman, Ariel, and Kenneth Johnson. *Mythic Astrology: Archetypal Powers in the Horoscope.* Saint Paul, MN: Llewellyn Publications, 1993.

Hampar, Joann. *Astrology for Beginners: A Simple Way to Read Your Chart.* Woodbury, MN: Llewellyn Publications, 2007.

Herring, Amy. *Astrology of the Moon: An Illuminating Journey Through the Signs and Houses.* Woodbury, MN: Llewellyn Publications, 2010.

MacGregor, Trish. *The Everything Astrology Book.* Holbrook, MA: Adams Media Corporation, 1998.

Riske, Kris Brandt. *Llewellyn's Complete Book of Astrology: The Easy Way to Learn Astrology.* Woodbury, MN: Llewellyn Publications, 2007.

Rogers-Gallagher, Kim. *Astrology for the Light Side of the Brain.* San Diego, CA: ACS Publications, 1995.

Tierney, Bil. *All Around the Zodiac: Exploring Astrology's Twelve Signs.* Saint Paul, MN: Llewellyn Publications, 2001.

To Write to the Author

If you wish to contact the author or would like more information about this book, please write to the author in care of Llewellyn Worldwide Ltd. and we will forward your request. Both the author and publisher appreciate hearing from you and learning of your enjoyment of this book and how it has helped you. Llewellyn Worldwide Ltd. cannot guarantee that every letter written to the author can be answered, but all will be forwarded. Please write to:

Corrine Kenner
℅ Llewellyn Worldwide
2143 Wooddale Drive
Woodbury, MN 55125-2989

Please enclose a self-addressed stamped envelope for reply,
or $1.00 to cover costs. If outside the U.S.A., enclose
an international postal reply coupon.

Many of Llewellyn's authors have websites with additional information and resources. For more information, please visit our website at http://www.llewellyn.com.

Tarot and Astrology
Enhance Your Readings with the Wisdom of the Zodiac
Corrine Kenner

Enrich and expand your tarot practice with age-old wisdom from the stars.

Entwined for six centuries, the link between tarot and astrology is undeniably significant. This unique and user-friendly guide makes it easy to explore and learn from this fascinating intersection—and you don't even need to know astrology to get started. Discover how each major arcana corresponds to an astrological sign or planet, where each minor arcana sits on the Zodiac wheel, how the court cards and tarot suits are connected to the four elements—and what all this means. Also included are astrological spreads and reading techniques to help you apply these new cosmic insights.

978-0-7387-2964-0, 312 pp., 7⅕ x 9⅛   **$17.95**

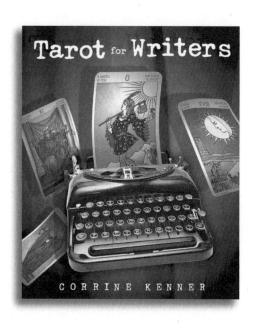

Tarot for Writers

CORRINE KENNER

Tarot for Writers
CORRINE KENNER

Once reserved for mystics and seers, the tarot is one of the best tools for boosting your creativity and shifting your imagination into high gear. Famous authors such as John Steinbeck and Stephen King have used the tarot deck to tap into deep wells of inspiration, and you can enliven your own writing the same way—whether you craft short stories, novels, poetry, nonfiction, or even business proposals.

This book on reading tarot cards and applying them to your writing will guide you through each stage of the creative process, from fleshing out a premise to promoting a finished work. Enhance your storytelling technique through over 500 enjoyable writing prompts, exploratory games for groups and individuals, tarot journaling, and other idea-stimulating activities that call upon the archetypal imagery and multi-layered symbolism in the tarot. Infuse flair and originality into your work as you learn to:

- Interpret symbols, myths, and learn to read all seventy-eight cards in the tarot card deck
- Use classic tarot layouts and spreads to structure your story
- Brainstorm story ideas and develop dialogue and plot
- Create detailed settings, powerful scenes, and dynamic characters
- Overcome writer's block and breathe new life into existing projects

As a writer, you hold the power of creation in your hands. By exploring the tarot and incorporating it into your writing practice, you will set your creative potential soaring to new heights.

978-0-7387-1457-8, 384 pp., 7⅕ x 9⅛   **$19.95**
